Modernity and the Problem of Evil

- evil within not orig. Sin

- The Memo - New Yorker

- "They are our slaves"

- principles from both

EDITED BY ALAN D. SCHRIFT

Modernity and the Problem of Evil

INDIANA UNIVERSITY PRESS
Bloomington and Indianapolis

This book is a publication of

Indiana University Press
601 North Morton Street
Bloomington, IN 47404-3797 USA

http://iupress.indiana.edu

Telephone orders   800-842-6796
Fax orders   812-855-7931
Orders by e-mail   iuporder@indiana.edu

© 2005 by Indiana University Press

The paper used in this publication meets the minimum requirements of American National Standard for Information Sciences—Permanence of Paper for Printed Library Materials, ANSI Z39.48-1984.

Manufactured in the United States of America

Library of Congress Cataloging-in-Publication Data

Modernity and the problem of evil / edited by Alan D. Schrift.
p. cm.
Includes bibliographical references and index.
ISBN 0-253-34550-2 (cloth : alk. paper) — ISBN 0-253-21758-X (pbk. : alk. paper) 1. Postmodernism. 2. Good and evil. I. Schrift, Alan D., 1955–
B831.2.M633 2005
170—dc22

                                                    2004020285

1 2 3 4 5   10 09 08 07 06 05

When I came to men I found them sitting on an old conceit: the conceit that they have long known what is good and evil for man. . . . and whoever wanted to sleep well talked of good and evil before going to sleep.

—Nietzsche, *Thus Spoke Zarathustra*

To say briefly now what good and evil are in themselves, we begin as follows:

Some things are in our intellect and not in Nature; so these are only our own work, and they help us to understand things distinctly. Among these we include all relations, which have reference to different things. These we call *beings of reason*.

So the question now is whether good and evil should be regarded as *beings of reason*. For one never says that something is good except in respect to something else that is not so good, or not so useful to us as something else. So one says that a man is bad only in respect to one who is better, or that an apple is bad only in respect to another that is good, or better. None of this could possibly be said if there were not something better, or good, in respect to which [the bad] is so called.

Therefore, if one says that something is good, that is nothing but saying that it agrees well with the universal Idea which we have of such things. But . . . things must agree with their particular Ideas, whose being must be a perfect essence, and not with universal ones, because then they would not exist.

As for confirming what we have just said, the thing is clear to us, but to conclude what we have said we shall add the following proofs.

All things which exist in Nature are either things or actions. Now good and evil are neither things nor actions. Therefore, good and evil do not exist in Nature.

—Spinoza, *Short Treatise on God, Man, and his Well-Being*

Contents

Preface

This collection owes its beginnings to the first year of operation of the Grinnell College Center for the Humanities in the 2001–2002 academic year. That fall, the Center invited as its inaugural Distinguished Visiting Professor, Peter Dews, who directed a faculty seminar on the topic "Modernity and the Problem of Evil." As fate would have it, Peter arrived on Grinnell's campus on September 10, 2001, and the seminar's first meeting was scheduled for September 11th. Neither Peter nor I could have possibly anticipated how our planning for the semester's exploration into the question of whether or not the concept of evil had a role to play in a secular society would be affected by the events of September 11th and the days and weeks that followed. For myself, as the events of that year unfolded, this question became both more relevant and more urgent as the dominant rhetoric from the leaders of both sides in this newly declared "war" were equally comfortable framing the situation as a battle between the forces of good and the forces of evil. While neither George W. Bush nor Osama bin Laden had the least doubt that they spoke for the forces of good when they branded their enemy "evil," many people, including myself, were forced to question just how secular our society really was. This question remains in play to this day, and while none of the essays collected here will definitively answer this question, all contribute important suggestions as to how we might think about the role the concept of evil should and does play in a secular society.

Many people have contributed to the coming together of this collection. First and foremost, I would like to thank the contributors to this collection, all but one of whom accepted my invitation to write a new essay in response to the questions that this collection sought to explore and who all completed their contributions on schedule. The sole essay that has appeared previously, Henry Staten's "'Radical Evil' Revived: Hitler, Kant, Luther, Neo-Lacanians," so perfectly fit the intentions behind my putting this collection together that I felt no need to ask him to write something new, and I wish to thank Henry and the editorial board of *Radical Philosophy* for allowing me to reprint his essay with only minor alterations from its original appearance in *Radical Philosophy* 93 (November–December 1999).

I would also like to acknowledge the support of my editor at Indiana University Press, Dee Mortensen, whose enthusiasm for the project matched my own and who did everything possible to facilitate the volume's prompt publication. The volume was shepherded through the production process by managing editor Jane Lyle, whose work is also gratefully acknowledged. I particularly want to thank the copy editor, Elizabeth Yoder, who, in addition to careful attention to the editing details, offered many insightful comments and intelligent suggestions that were very much appreciated by the authors and myself. This collection is much improved by her suggestions, both stylistic and substantive.

Many of my colleagues at Grinnell College have helped me to focus my thinking on the questions confronted in this collection. In particular, I would like to acknowledge the participants in that inaugural faculty seminar with Peter Dews, along with the colleagues that serve with me on the advisory board of the Center for the Humanities at Grinnell. The Center would not exist were it not for the institutional and financial support offered by the president of Grinnell College, Russell K. Osgood, the dean of the college, James Swartz, and the Board of Trustees of Grinnell College. This support is here gratefully acknowledged.

I have benefited from the able assistance of two of my students at Grinnell, Sara Eilert and Sarah Hansen, who read all of the contributions and made numerous stylistic and substantive suggestions. Ben Johannsen and Ariel Wolter also assisted in proofreading the text and Adam Schwartz helped with the compilation of the index. I would also like to thank Angela Winburn, who prepared the manuscript for submission to the publisher at a very busy time of the academic year and whose patience and attention to details is very much appreciated.

The final note of acknowledgment must go to Jill, who daily shows me what it means to be good, and to whom this collection is dedicated.

Modernity and the Problem of Evil

1 Introduction

Alan D. Schrift

> Hitherto, the subject reflected on least adequately has been good and evil: it was too dangerous a subject. Conscience, reputation, Hell, sometimes even the police have permitted and continue to permit no impartiality; in the presence of morality, as in the face of any authority, one is not allowed to think, far less to express an opinion: here one has to—*obey!*
>
> —Nietzsche, *Daybreak*, Preface 3

Nietzsche is well known for being the philosopher who sought to go "beyond good and evil." But what he meant by this has often been crudely misunderstood as precisely the opposite of what he wrote; that is to say, to go "beyond good and evil" is misunderstood as meaning to go beyond judgment as to right and wrong—indeed, to go beyond any normative judgment at all. Even a casual reader of Nietzsche cannot fail to note, however, that Nietzsche is continually making judgments, even "moral" judgments about cultures and cultural practices, so surely going "beyond good and evil" did not entail the nihilistic and empty relativism of unconditional acceptance or an "anything goes" attitude that precludes judgment altogether. In fact, Nietzsche is fairly explicit in indicating that the intention behind "that dangerous slogan" that he placed as the title of his book *Beyond Good and Evil* was not to go beyond judgment when he wrote, at the close of the First Essay of *On the Genealogy of Morals*, "At least this does *not* mean 'Beyond Good and Bad.'"

The difference between "Good and Evil" and "Good and Bad" is the ostensible topic of the *Genealogy's* First Essay, and reflecting on whether this difference *makes a difference* is one of the motivations behind bringing together the essays in this collection. To simplify Nietzsche's point in the extreme, while the distinction between "Good and Bad" remains in some sense grounded in the natural, the "Good and Evil" distinction is grounded in the divine. While the originators of judgments of "Good and Bad" had sufficient confidence in their own natural instincts to establish these moral categories on their own, the originators of judgments of "Good and Evil" lacked this confidence (in Nietzsche's language, they lacked the strength) and sought a transcendent justification for their judgments in the will of God. For many thinkers after Nietzsche, the concept of evil is simply a residue of an outdated theological perspective on the world. But for others, it remains an indispensable part of our ethical vocabulary that can and must be rescued from its theological trappings, especially when we confront atrocities of the past century like the Holocaust, the Rwandan genocide, or, more recently, the many events associated with 9/11.

Nietzsche's thoughts concerning the influence of religion on the rhetoric of evil are not the only ones that frame these essays. At the beginning of the continental philosophical tradition, Kant's *Religion within the Limits of Reason Alone* raised three crucial questions that continue to inform debates about evil:

1. Can the use of this concept be justified in purely philosophical terms, or does it require a rethinking of the relation between religious and philosophical discourse?
2. Can human beings be motivated by the sheer perverse desire to do harm or wrong, or, as Kant claimed, must there always be some underlying motive of self-interest?
3. Can evil be "explained" or at least made intelligible (for example, psychoanalytically or sociologically)? Or is our notion of evil essentially intertwined with a sense of ultimate resistance to comprehension?[1]

While Kant is often positioned as the leading proponent of Enlightenment belief in the powers of reason and the perfectibility of humanity, we see in his late text on religion an account of "*radical* evil" as the original debt which human beings incur and that "whatever a man may have done in adopting a good disposition, and, indeed, however steadfastly he may have persevered in conduct conformable to such a disposition, *he nevertheless started from evil,* and this debt [*Verschuldung*] he can by no possibility wipe out."[2] In an earlier time, the paradigmatic example of an evil was the Lisbon earthquake, an instance of "natural evil" that raised the question of why God might have allowed it to occur.[3] Now it appears to Kant that the paradigm of evil is not an act of nature but a feature of human nature, namely, that "radical evil" which is a propensity of a "will which is free" and which "is *radical,* because it corrupts the ground of all maxims; it is, moreover, as a natural propensity *inextirpable* by human powers, since extirpation could occur only through good maxims, and cannot take place when the ultimate subjective ground of all maxims is postulated as corrupt."[4]

For both Kant and Nietzsche, the concept of evil is caught in a tension between the natural and the theological, and it has remained there through much of the twentieth century, as "Auschwitz" and the "Holocaust" served as names for an "evil" that raised questions both as to what a human will was capable of and what a God might allow to occur. This tension can be seen in Adorno's famous remark that "to write poetry after Auschwitz is barbaric,"[5] and in his "Meditations on Metaphysics: After Auschwitz" at the conclusion of *Negative Dialectics.*[6] It is seen as well in Lyotard's reflections on Adorno and discussion after Auschwitz.[7]

Where both Kant and Nietzsche see the concept of evil caught in a tension between the natural and the theological, the most recent re-emergence of the rhetoric of evil raises disturbing questions as to whether this tension has been resolved in favor of the theological. President George W. Bush, in his first public comments following the September 11 attacks, concluded his brief remarks this way: "This will be a monumental struggle of good versus evil, but good will prevail."[8] One month later, in the first formal White House press conference of his administration and the first after the September 11 attacks, the president mentioned "evil" or "evildoers" twelve times.[9] What is most disturbing about these remarks is the relative absence of the adjectival form, as "Evil" takes its place as a proper noun—indeed, a proper name. We are reminded about "the evil that was done to us"; we're urged to "condemn hate and evil and murder and prejudice"; we're told "we must defeat the evildoers where they hide"; we're told (remember, this was only five weeks after the attacks) in one of the few adjectival forms that "There's no question that the leader of Iraq is an evil man" and that "on our TV screens the other day, we saw the evil one threatening." (The reference would appear to be to Osama bin Laden, but it might refer to Satan as well—about which more in a moment.) Perhaps most distressing, we are told that "we learned a good lesson on September the 11th, that there is evil in this world," and that "it's essential that all moms and dads and citizens tell their children we love them and there is love in the world, but also remind them there are evil people." And, the president said explicitly, "We're fighting evil."

Were these comments citations from Tolkien's *Lord of the Rings,* one might be comfortable with the ease with which the personification of evil has been effected. We are not talking about Sauron, however, but about US foreign policy. And the problem gets worse. Consider the case of Lt. General William "Jerry" Boykin, promoted in 2003 to Deputy Undersecretary of State of Defense for Intelligence.[10] Boykin has said that President Bush was chosen by God to lead the global fight against Satan. He told one gathering: "Why is this man in the White House? The majority of Americans did not vote for him. He's in the White House because God put him there for a time such as this." To a group of Baptists in Florida he spoke about a victory over a Muslim warlord in Somalia, who had boasted that Allah would protect him from American capture: "I knew my God was bigger than his. I knew that my God was a real god and his was an idol." In June 2003, General Boykin told an Oklahoma congregation that Osama bin Laden and Saddam Hussein were not the enemy: "Our enemy is a spiritual enemy because we are a nation of believers . . . His name is Satan." As to what kind of nation of believers we are, Boykin leaves no doubt: appearing in dress uniform before a religious group in Oregon in June, Boykin said Islamic extremists hate the United States "because we're a Christian nation, because our foundation and our roots are Judeo-Christian . . . And the enemy is a guy named Satan."

That an army general with a significant position in the intelligence community would say such things and think them appropriate is frightening enough; that Defense Secretary Donald H. Rumsfeld does not seem particularly bothered by them is terrifying. "My references to Judeo-Christian roots in America or our nation as a Christian nation are historically undeniable," Boykin is reported to have said, to which Rumsfeld responded only, "It is not our statement, it is his statement." "We're a free people. And that's the wonderful thing about our country," Rumsfeld said. "I think that for anyone to run around and think that that can be managed and controlled is probably wrong. Saddam Hussein could do it pretty well, because he'd go around killing people if they said things he didn't like." Perhaps Rumsfeld should talk to John Ashcroft about this. Does anyone imagine that if these remarks were not in support of our being a "Christian country," this general would still be in his current position?

I mention these comments from Lt. General Boykin, Secretary of Defense Rumsfeld, and President Bush not simply to be alarmist—although some alarm at this point seems warranted—but to focus the issue to which this collection of essays responds, namely, Is the rhetoric of "evil" inherently tied to a religious or theological framework such that we can and should move seamlessly between Boykin's remarks and those of George Bush, or can the concept of evil function within a secular but normative discourse that strives to understand the modern world? Is "evil" just "bad + God," or do we need a concept of "evil" that is distinct and different from "bad" or "wrong"? To put the question most bluntly: What is it that we add to the statement "What the hijackers did when they flew those planes into the Twin Towers on 9/11/2001 was *wrong*, or *bad*" when we say, instead, "What the hijackers did when they flew those planes into the Twin Towers on 9/11/2001 was *evil*"?

The essays collected in this volume, all but one of which are published here for the first time, respond to these questions as they explore modern uses of the concept of "evil" and some of the problems raised by the use of this concept. Several address explicitly the Kantian formulation of the problem of (radical) evil and challenge, explicitly or implicitly, the hegemonic position that Kant's moral theory occupies in contemporary moral discourse. In "'Radical Evil' Revived: Hitler, Kant, Luther, Neo-Lacanians," Henry Staten offers a Nietzschean critique of the neo-Lacanian redefinition of free will as an expression of "radical evil." Synthesizing Freud's concept of the primordial patricide with Kant's doctrine of the Moral Law, the neo-Lacanians argue that the Law should be conceived as purely transcendent, unknowable, enjoining only "our respectful listening" and "abandonment of self." We know the Law only in and through the feeling of guilt that it arouses in us, our feeling of insufficiency to its purely formal demand. The choice of evil is therefore not something that can be explained naturalistically, in terms of cause and effect, but is instead an originary choice made freely by the human will. Staten's critique of this neo-Lacanian argument proceeds through a careful rereading of Freud as supporting the Nietzschean position against Lacan. Nietzsche's naturalization of ethics does not imply the destruction of the notion of ethical responsibility, and Freud's myth of the primordial patricide is an incoherence in his otherwise thoroughly Nietzschean account (in *Civilization and Its Discontents*) of the origin of the sense of guilt through the internalization of aggression. Staten concludes that the neo-Lacanian revival of the idea of radical evil is in fact a crypto-Christian continuation of the problematic of transcendence, and he recommends the Nietzsche-influenced ethical theory of Bernard Williams as an alternative.

In "Liquidating the 'Nearly Just Society': Radical Evil's Triumphant Return," William L. McBride revisits the question of classical Manichaean-type thinking, of which Kant's Enlightenment conception of "radical evil" is a faint shadow. McBride focuses on the transformation, in the work of John Rawls, from his assumption that ours is a "nearly just society" in his early classic, *A Theory of Justice*, to his recent *The Law of Peoples*, where among other things, he refuses to seriously consider global needs for resource redistribution, accepts the demonizing terminology of "rogue states," and assumes that underdeveloped societies have mostly themselves to blame. McBride treats this "liquidation" of the "nearly just society" as at once both a real-world process and an ideological one. That is to say, for McBride, the transformation in Rawls's thinking mirrors both a political and ideological transformation in Western liberal democracy, as recent political and military actions by the United States reflect just the sort of hubris that Rawls exemplified in his later work, where the illusion of justice gives way to practices by which powerful nations exert domination over others, practices that he concludes we can only call "unjust."

In "Violence and Secularization, Evil and Redemption," Martin Beck Matuštík uses Kierkegaard's distinction between the aesthetic and the ethical to expose several problems he locates in Kant's *Religion within the Limits of Reason Alone*. For Matuštík, Kant's assumption that evil must be attributed to the weakness of human will attests at the same time to the dignity of human freedom and to the rational will's innate orientation to do good. Yet by translating the religious mode of sin into the moral language of radical evil, Matuštík asks whether Kant does not muddle the issue. Relying on Kierkegaard's religious grasp of evil, Matuštík shows that there is nothing wholly secular about violence, nor is there anything redemptive or holy in war on evil. His essay ends with an appeal to a redemptive critical theory that envisions a postsecular hope coming to terms with human finitude and death without either inflicting pain and violence on others in the process or positing an ultimate purification of the world from the possibility of radical evil.

In Peter Dews's "Disenchantment and the Persistence of Evil: Habermas, Jonas, Badiou," he explores the difficulties of addressing the question of moral evil within a purely secular vocabulary. Following a discussion of Kant's account of "radical evil," he examines how the modern Kantianism of a thinker like Habermas, working in the discourse-ethics tradition, tries to ignore this dimension of Kant's thinking, arguing that, in Habermas's case, the question of evil returns to disrupt the "primal anthropological trust" on which he bases his notion of a communicative ethics. Dews goes on to look at Hans Jonas's celebrated essay, "The Concept of God After Auschwitz," arguing that attempts to "secularize" the content of this essay into a vision of "radical finitude" and the inevitability of evil as a contrast to the good, fail to capture what is most powerful in Jonas's position as a response to evil. When he examines the explicitly atheistic conception of ethics put forward by Alain Badiou, Dews finds that even as Badiou challenges the religious overtones of Levinas's ethical position, Badiou's own thought is shot through with religious motifs. Through his examination of both religiously and nonreligiously oriented thinkers, Dews concludes that while modern secular culture may try to avoid the concept of evil, this concept is not only difficult to avoid when we wish to address certain extreme moral phenomena but is also deeply resistant to detachment from its original religious context.

Not all the essays respond to the question of evil as posed by Kant. Some choose to respond in the context of a particular historical event. For example, Debra B. Bergoffen, in "How Rape Became a Crime against Humanity: History of an Error," uses a famous passage from Nietzsche's *Twilight of the Idols* to raise the question: What does the death of God mean for the life of patriarchy? Bergoffen defines monotheistic patriarchy as a sociality where the sexual difference is rendered as the difference between man—the one who embodies truth, subjectivity, and justice—and woman, the inessential other, who partakes of truth, subjectivity, and justice only insofar as she reflects man's standard of truth, subjectivity, and justice back to him. Bergoffen finds that with the death of God, the structure of monotheistic patriarchy also collapses insofar as the monotheistic God's death is also and necessarily the death of the idea of the one—one truth, one law, one standard of justice. A consequence of patriarchy's collapse is the necessary change in the meaning and criteria of what counts as a crime against humanity, and Bergoffen analyzes the recent rape convictions of Bosnian-Serb soldiers by the UN Yugoslavia war tribunal as suggesting that the implications of the death of God for the end of patriarchy are being felt. Drawing on Simone de Beauvoir's distinction between an other and an inessential other, Bergoffen suggests that the decision to classify wartime rape no longer as a necessary, albeit regrettable evil of war, but as a crime against humanity, holds the promise of changing the status of women from man's inessential other to his other. This changed status of women carries profound implications for a postpatriarchal notion of justice: once rape is understood as a crime against humanity, that is, once it is understood as a crime that violates the dignity and integrity of the lived woman's sexed body, women's vulnerability becomes the mark of the human. Violating her body becomes a violation of the trust that makes just human communities possible.

Like Bergoffen, Robert Meister's essay, "Ways of Winning: The Costs of Moral Victory in Transitional Regimes," responds to a particular historical-legal event—South Africa's Truth and Reconciliation Commission (TRC)—and asks the question "What is the appropriate moral attitude toward an evil that is past?" He analyzes and criticizes the conception of moral victory offered by the TRC as it is distinguished from two other forms of political victimhood—the unreconciled victim who is the subject of revolutionary struggle, and the morally damaged victim who is the object of counterrevolutionary fears. Meister argues that the TRC allows the victims of past injustice a moral victory on the understanding that some of the beneficiaries of that past injustice will get to keep their gains without being seen to perpetuate the unjust and disgraced regime, and by doing this it avoids the revolutionary idea of a continuing struggle by unreconciled victims who should never regard an evil as truly past until its aftereffects are gone. But, Meister asks, is something more required in order for the politics of reconciliation to be a way of winning for victims of oppression who once hoped for revolutionary change? In other words, should former victims accept *moral* victory as victory enough? He argues that the TRC's approach to transitional justice focuses too heavily on persuading nonvictims (both beneficiaries and bystanders) that the old regime was evil while allaying their fears of empowering the victims, and that this approach has the effect of reducing the broad spectrum of collective injury to individual acts of cruelty. From this perspective, political evil itself (the evil that is past) is redefined as cruelty—an insensitivity to the pain of others—and insofar as pain is an adversity that can be put in the past, the moral victory over pain is insufficient as a foundation for forward-looking justice, to the extent that it rules out militancy of all kinds and blocks the demand for large-scale (structural) change.

In "Abjection and Film: Displacing the Fetishistic, Racist Rhetoric of Political Projection," Tina Chanter takes Kristeva's notion of abjection beyond the Oedipal narrative to which Kristeva's account adheres and explores the social and political ramifications of abjection. While not necessarily conscious, voluntary, or deliberate, abjection, she argues, sets in motion a dynamic by which an individual or a group—whether political, religious, or ethnic, whether in terms of race, gender, class, or sexual preference—establishes itself as pure and good by requiring others to occupy a place of impurity, a place of evil. Examining this dynamic through an analysis of several films, Chanter suggests that the dynamic that, at the individual level, makes abject the racial or sexual other, sheds light on the disturbing dynamic underlying recent political events that justify themselves in terms of a rhetoric that sanctifies as innocent the actions of Western governments at the expense of dehumanizing and demonizing others as evil and impure. Moving between the cinematic and the political, Chanter argues that a pervasive fetishistic discourse permeates not only academic discourse but also the political rhetoric underlying recent political events, and that such discourse is in need of demystification. To that end, she concludes that the notion of abjection provides a more adequate framework for thinking about both the evil of political projection and the evils that such projection then is taken to authorize and legitimate.

In "Faith, Territory, and Evil," William E. Connolly uses the event of 9/11 as a point of departure to explore the lived experience of evil within the frame of two classic stories: the Augustinian portrayal of human responsibility for evil, which has become hegemonic in the West, and the Spinozistic portrayal, which represents a counter story of attempting to forestall evil without necessarily blaming or holding others responsible for it. Connolly is drawn to both stories and seeks to develop an account of existential faith that allows these two stories to compete actively within it. For Connolly, existential faith of some sort is ineliminable from human life; at the same time, existential faith has within it the tendency toward evil insofar as it tends to anathematize those who do not share one's faith. This leads Connolly to raise two political questions: first, how can a pluralistic society come to terms with the experience of evil in a world where different faiths enter into its definition? And second, how can we both appreciate the ubiquity of faith and come to terms with a problem of evil inhabiting faith itself? His answer, framed by the complex relations between political territory and existential faith, challenges the monistic identification of political territory with a single faith by encouraging what he calls a "double-entry orientation to faith" that allows one to "honor the terms of [one's own] faith, while acknowledging its contestability in the eyes of others and by cultivating a sensibility of presumptive generosity toward them." This, he suggests, is the best response to the potential to evil within faith that stands as a challenge to the multicultural and deeply pluralistic world we now inhabit.

A third approach taken in some of the essays is to address the problem of evil in terms of the thinking of a major figure in twentieth-century philosophy. In "Hannah Arendt on the Bourgeois Origins of Totalitarian Evil," Robert B. Pippin examines Arendt's claim, in *The Origins of Totalitarianism*, that twentieth-century totalitarianism is unique, absolutely unprecedented in history, and completely unanticipated in any political philosophy. Her most evocative and poetic descriptions of this new human condition portray it as burdened with an intolerable loneliness, as having lost something like the "love of the world," the artificial human world of civilization. In trying to account for this phenomenon, Arendt, in her most radical and controversial claim, ties the unique phenomenon of totalitarian evil ("terror") to the utilitarian, pragmatic world of modern bourgeois culture itself, suggesting that the intensity and insanity of totalitarianism is some measure of the intolerable anomie and loneliness characteristic of the bourgeois world of atomistic and isolated subjects. While broadly sympathetic to Arendt's account of totalitarianism and impressed by the scope of her argument, Pippin finds both problematic and paradigmatic her introduction of what he regards as a somewhat arbitrary theological dimension into what had been an admirably secular narrative concerning the origins of totalitarianism. Pippin argues that when she appeals to the authority of "the absolute and transcendent measurements of religion or the law of nature," or to Plato's comment that "not man, but a god must be the measure of all things," or by recalling that there is a creator of the world and we are not its masters, or again, in the words of her teacher, that "only a god can save us now," this runs counter to the whole trajectory of her account. Instead, Pippin argues that she should have drawn the conclusion that she proposed later in her account of Eichmann, namely, that the "problem of evil" is not "the continuing obsession with the idea that such evil deeds create some deep problem, as if it signals some rebellion against cosmic order which we fear and are fascinated by"; but rather, the "problem of evil" resides in its being "human, all too human."

In "Evil, Evils, and the Question of Ethics," Adi Ophir adopts a Heideggerian approach that explores the "question of Evil" as an aspect of the "question of Being" and focuses on what might be called the forgetting of the ontologico-ethical difference between "evils" and "Evil." Contrary to Heidegger's own position, for Ophir ethics does not "enframe Being," it enframes Evil, understood as being in excess, which is always also an excess of Being. "Originary ethics" is thus a concern, not with the truth of Being, but with its excess, which appears as a plurality of evils. To this, Ophir suggests, we must draw a distinction, one that Heidegger failed to make, between "ethics"—in the modern sense of the word that covers a certain form of moral discourse and a specific branch of philosophy—and "the ethical" on the basis of the distinction between the plurality of expressible evils and a residue of Evil that ethics still, and always, conceals. For Ophir, an ethics, as a particular formation of the ethical, enframes Evil but does not allow it to appear as such. Instead, an ethics lets Evil appear as a series of evils that are reified as objects to be rejected, prevented, and, when unavoidable, justly distributed and compensated. At the same time, no ethics can exhaust Evil; at any particular moment an ethics enframes *only some* of the existing evils and lets *only some* of its victims come into presence and assume a voice of their own. The ethical, on the other hand, is an attitude that subsists on the margin of a particular ethics, nurtured from its sources, but that aspires to transcend its limits and always maintains a residual openness to that Evil which escapes articulation within that particular ethics. The ethical, Ophir concludes, is attentive to that Evil which ethics has made one forget; it lets Evil appear or—it comes to the same thing—lets a certain excess of Being appear as that which should not have been.

In "Incursions of Evil: The Double Bind of Alterity," Edith Wyschogrod begins with Emmanuel Levinas's view that ethics originates in alterity, in the otherness of the other person, but argues that the idea of evil that one draws from Levinas's account requires expansion insofar as some manifestations of evil take the form of harm one does to oneself. She draws upon Bateson's model of the double bind—a model that suggests that no matter what one does, one cannot win—to show both that double binds arise not only in individual but in sociohistorical contexts, and that as such, the double bind is intrinsic to the emergence of the moral life. She explores this notion through examining a series of examples: George Ainslie's discussion of temporal distance as affecting our preference for present satisfactions over remote gains; evils that are inherent in the very modes of rationality that govern contemporary collective life; and Dominique Janicaud's analysis of techno-discourse, a mode of rationality underlying the radical evils of a global society and a totalizing discourse. These disparate modes of evil, Wyschogrod concludes, can only be understood in terms of the double binds that come into play in the self's relation to itself and within a sociocultural whole.

In their own ways, each of these essays responds to the questions raised by Kant as they reflect on the problem of evil. Together, they offer various ways to think about how a philosophical concept of evil might avoid falling into a theologically motivated discourse. While most of the authors are unwilling to follow Nietzsche's call to move "beyond good and evil," they all mindful of the dangers that can follow the rhetorical proliferation of evil. Commenting on Christianity's determination of the passions to be evil, Nietzsche asked over a century ago: "Must everything that one has to combat, that one has to keep within bounds or on occasion banish totally from one's mind, always have to be called *evil!* Is it not the way of *common* souls always to think an enemy must be *evil!*"[11] And, in a comment that rings distressingly prescient, Nietzsche wrote:

> Picture "the enemy" as the man of *ressentiment* conceives him—and here precisely is his deed, his creation: he has conceived "the evil enemy," "*the Evil One,*" and this in fact is his basic concept, from which he then evolves, as an afterthought and pendant, a "good one"—himself![12]

Whether or not we can or should eliminate "evil" from our conceptual vocabulary, let us hope that we might be able to eliminate this overheated Manichaeanism that too often passes today for moral high-mindedness.

Notes

1. These questions were suggested by Peter Dews as the underlying questions for a faculty seminar he directed in Fall 2001 at the Grinnell College Center for the Humanities, a seminar that served as the initial impetus for this collection.

2. Immanuel Kant, *Religion within the Limits of Reason Alone,* trans. Theodore M. Greene and Hoyt H. Hudson (New York: Harper and Row, 1960), p. 66.

3. Susan Neiman cites T. D. Kendrick's *The Lisbon Earthquake* (Philadelphia: Lippincott, 1957) and comments that "the Lisbon earthquake was said to shock Western civilization more than any event since the fall of Rome" (*Evil in Modern Thought: An Alternative History of Philosophy* [Princeton, N.J.: Princeton University Press, 2002], p. 240).

4. Kant, *Religion within the Limits of Reason Alone,* p. 32.

5. Theodor W. Adorno, "Cultural Criticism and Society," in *Prisms,* trans. Samuel and Shierry Weber (Cambridge, Mass.: MIT Press, 1967), p. 34.

6. See the final chapter of Theodor W. Adorno, *Negative Dialectics,* trans E. B. Ashton (New York: Seabury, 1973).

7. Jean-François Lyotard, "Discussions, or Phrasing 'after Auschwitz,'" trans. Georges Van Den Abbeele in *The Lyotard Reader,* ed. Andrew Benjamin (London: Blackwell, 1989), pp. 360–92; and *The Differend: Phrases in Dispute,* trans. Georges Van Den Abbeele (Minneapolis: University of Minnesota Press, 1988), sections 152–60.

8. The president's complete, three-minute comments from September 12, 2001, can be found at www.whitehouse.gov/news/releases/2001/09/20010912-4.html.

9. See the White House transcript of the Press Conference of October 11, 2001 distributed by the Office of International Information Programs, US Department of State at http://usinfo.state.gov/topical/pol/conflict/bprc1011.htm.

10. The following remarks from General Boykin and Secretary Rumsfeld are taken from David Rennie, "God put Bush in charge, says the general hunt-

ing bin Laden" (Filed: 17/10/2003): www.telegraph.co.uk/news/main.
jhtml?xml=/news/2003/10/17/wboyk17.xml.

11. Friedrich Nietzsche, *Daybreak,* trans. R. J. Hollingdale (Cambridge: Cambridge University Press, 1982), Section 76.

12. Friedrich Nietzsche, *On the Genealogy of Morals,* trans. Walter Kaufmann and R. J. Hollingdale (New York: Random House, 1967), Essay One, Section 10.

2 "Radical Evil" Revived: Hitler, Kant, Luther, Neo-Lacanians

Henry Staten

In the aftermath of 9/11, the notion of evil was freely brandished by public figures and the media in a way that was transparently ethnocentric—the evil one as the alien, and specifically in the form of the conscienceless heathen. But what about a case in which the killers belong, not to "them," but to "us"—for instance, the mass murderers at Columbine High School in Littleton, Colorado, a few years ago? Here we cannot contain the disturbance by treating it as an externally caused trauma, neatly ejecting the dark body of the cause out of the closed circle of our own socius. Columbine, therefore, might have called forth reflection on a more profound sense of evil than that aroused by 9/11. Yet the Columbine murders were not characterized in the public forum in terms of evil. From all sides came the anguished questions: "How could such a thing happen?" "What sort of people could do it?" And in response, the experts pointed to the alienation of the young shooters and the failure of their parents or school authorities to recognize the "warning signs." A commentator on television opined that "anyone who would do such a thing has to be in a lot of pain." Thus, despite the monstrosity of the event, despite the shock and horror with which it struck the culture, the prevalent worldview held steady. Columbine was explained as a failure of society—possibly a very deep failure, betokening a chronic and accelerating fraying of the social bond, but still one that could be addressed at the level of sociological cause and effect, without recourse to any notion of metaphysical evil or of a radical flaw in the human will. Even spokesmen for the "religious right"—at least those like Jerry Falwell who reach a mainstream audience—did not speak of the ineradicable evil of human nature; they recommended palliatives like putting prayer back in schools.

I cannot disagree with the secular experts at least; I am committed to the Nietzschean project of "reinscribing man back into nature," and therefore in some way to the naturalistic perspective that guided the assessments of these "experts." And yet I feel uneasy about the intellectual complacency underlying the culturewide, but transient, emotional shock. Nietzsche's naturalism was intended to disturb the pieties of his culture: to deny the existence of anything *higher* than this world, whether transcendent or transcendental, that could give the rule to human existence, and through this denial to open a more vigorous, even heroic attitude toward life than the one he saw around him. He did not foresee a time in which the naturalistic perspective would be transformed into a pacifying murmur by a vast bureaucracy of counselors and psychologists. In particular, he did not foresee that to conceive human motivation completely in terms of natural causality would turn the subject into an *ethical cipher,* the very opposite of the spontaneous creator of new, higher values that Nietzsche envisioned.

In the context of this unease, I turn with interest to the recent efforts by a group of thinkers influenced by Lacan, including Slavoj Žižek, Juliet Flower MacCannell, and the two on whom I will focus because they offer the most polemical theses—Joan Copjec and Jacob Rogozinski—to revive the notion of metaphysical or, in a term derived from Kant, "radical" evil as the only plausible explanation for the horrors of human history, including that most horrifying horror of all, the Holocaust.[1] Copjec and Rogozinski stress that we need to conceive radical evil as the principle of an originary choice made *freely* by human will, which is therefore responsible for its crimes in a way no naturalism can revoke. While I am not predisposed to favor the resuscitation of the notions of free will and radical evil, Copjec and Rogozinski make a powerful point when they suggest that the reigning ethical discourses are not pitched at a depth adequate to the horrors of history, and especially modern history with its totalitarianisms and genocides.

In a persuasive reading of Hannah Arendt's work, Rogozinski argues that her notion of the banality of evil, because it ascribes Eichmann's evil to "an absence of will, . . . a freedom which has renounced itself," supports the contemporary retreat from ascription of responsibility. In her earlier work on the Holocaust, however, Arendt invoked Kant's notion of radical evil in a way that in Rogozinski's view comes much closer to the mark. In fact, Arendt's reflections on Nazism that Rogozinski cites from various of her books strikingly parallel the essentially Lacanian account Rogozinski favors, which claims to explain the specifically modern shape of evil under totalitarianism. On this account, the dark side of the modern movement toward democracy and egalitarianism is the decay of the "symbolic order," such that, with the effacement of "longstanding differences of condition and status" that used to confer identity on individuals, the seemingly natural distinction of race becomes the last boundary against narcissistic panic in the face of "a chaos in which all identity dissolves." In this chaos of indistinction, the anti-Semite models his own quest for mastery after his fantasmatic image of the Jew as secret master of the world. Hence, Hitler's fascination with the *Protocols of the Elders of Zion,* which Arendt suggested was used by the Nazis as "a model for the future organization of the German masses for purposes of global domination." But the Jew, as antagonistic double of the German, must be exterminated because, as Hitler is said to have declared, "there cannot be two chosen peoples."[2]

The crucial point for Rogozinski is that this play of identifications occurs in a context in which the moral law has ceased to be considered as transcendent and has been assigned a worldly locus (a process Copjec dubs "subreption"[3]), as the law of racial superiority. "The Nazi borrows an objectified law from the discourse of science, which is converted into a law of nature, and whose docile servant he wishes to be, the agent of its historical fulfilment"; but precisely because this law is understood as immanent, it can be understood by Hitler at the same time as "the law of the Subject, of a conscious will that aspires to domination." As such, Hitler made a "free decision" in which Nazi totalitarianism originated:

> By contrast, what characterizes the position of the law in Judaism, and its reworking in Kant's ethics, is the fact that the subject is . . . determined as obliged or held hostage by a prescription whose source remains forever indeterminate, A law without author or master, which is uttered in an empty place, inaccessible to a finite subject. The pure practical imperative, which "gives us nothing to see," assures us of no theoretical knowledge, no power, no enjoyment, which demands nothing but our respectful listening, the obedience of a being who is obliged, his abandonment of self.[4]

This rich and thought-provoking account, which has Heidegger as well as Kant and Arendt behind it, participates in a widespread movement of recent French thought (including, for example, though in quite different modalities, Levinas, Derrida, Lyotard, and Alain Badiou) in conceiving the principle of ethical being as something infinitely mysterious, abyssal, and indeterminable, yet absolutely exigent.[5] And Rogozinski is on solid ground when he points to modern biology as an essential component in Nazi race ideology, for recent work has made clearer than ever the rootedness of twentieth-century racism in its peculiar appropriation of science—an appropriation to which such a major scientific figure as Ernst Haeckel made a significant contribution.[6] We must have the Law, Rogozinski argues, but the specter of fascism warns us against any naturalistic immanentizing of law; hence, this difficult thought of "a prescription whose source remains forever indeterminate" but which forbids us to do evil.

But now comes an intriguing twist in the direction of Freud and Lacan. Rogozinski goes on to gloss the "law without author" as follows: "This empty place of the Other is that of the dead father, whose withdrawal is marked by the Law. Freud taught us to recognize, in the murder of the father, the primordial event which inaugurates the symbolic debt binding each subject to the Law."[7] Here Rogozinski follows Lacan's account in Seminar 7 of Freud's myth of the primordial killing of the father, "the myth of a time for which God is dead."[8] "But if for us God is dead," Lacan continues in Seminar 7, "it is because he has always been dead, and that's what Freud says." Whereas Nietzsche saw in the death of God the crisis of nihilism, Freud, on Lacan's telling, saw in it the deepest essence of the spiritual or ethical truth of Judaism and Christianity: that ethical humanity is constituted by a relation of infinite guilt toward a hidden or vanished figure that can only be conceived as Father, such that the destructive aggressivity of the subject is channeled back against himself through the circuit of love and guilt that the crime against the father activates. God is dead, yet the place of his disappearance marks the locus of the debt and the obligation to which the law holds us hostage.

Now if this seems a far-fetched supplement to Kant, we should remember the deeply irrational impulses of *Massenpsychologie* that animate fascism, in particular the cathexis of a Leader who incarnates the Law for the masses and sends them off on their rampage; as Arendt reminds us, Eichmann began as a strict Kantian but eventually learned to set Hitler's command in place of the categorical imperative. There is, the neo-Lacanians argue, an obscene *jouissance*, arising from unconscious sources, in the identification with the immanent fascist law and in the violence that this law authorizes, and any ethical discourse that seeks to counter the tendencies toward such *jouissance* must recognize them for what they are, in all their irrational depth. The Law must be set out of the reach of appropriation for the ends of those whose real wish is to be lawless or to pervert the command of the law so as to authorize their obscene enjoyment; the myth of the primordial murder is the adequate representation of the noumenal character of the Law, "causing us," as Copjec says, "to respect a father with whom we are unable to identify and a law to which we are unable to conform."[9]

I cannot pretend to do justice to the richness and subtlety of the arguments of these writers, who, moreover, disagree on key points; but the above sketch captures what I take to be the central outline of their position.[10] While I find this position fascinating and provocative, it is one against which Nietzsche sets me on my guard, as an attempt to refurbish the Christian anthropology and ethic in contemporary terms that do without the reference to God. Kant, with his attempt to make the transcendent "thou shalt not" self-uttering, is the key figure in the historical movement toward the philosophical sanitizing of Christianity; but the neo-Lacanians put Kant through a Heideggerian refurbishing to yield Lacanian transcendentalism or hyper-transcendentalism (it is hard to know what name to give to post-Heideggerian metaphysics with its transcendence-that-vanishes). Copjec and Rogozinski claim to be liberating from the text of Kant (especially *Religion within the Limits of Reason Alone*) a conception of evil that makes a radical break with the entire Western intellectual tradition. In order to show the crypto-Christian nature of this conception, I want to re-situate the question of evil within the intellectual context that is its proper home: Christian theology.

Kant, Christianity, and Free Will

Copjec and Rogozinski claim that Kant's idea of radical evil was totally new because prior to him the entire Western tradition denied the possibility of a will that freely and consciously chooses evil. As Rogozinski puts it, "The Western tradition has continually affirmed that 'no one is wicked voluntarily,' that Being and the Good are the same, and that evil comes from nothingness, that it is nothing but impotence and privation of being." This account is an oddly confused mixture of Plato and Augustine. The Platonic texts did, of course, advance an optimistic doctrine of the will, and Augustine developed the doctrine, fundamentally influential in the later development of Christianity, that evil is a privation of being rather than a substance. But Augustine did not hold the Platonic doctrine that the will only wills good, and he most emphatically did not hold the doctrine that Copjec claims to be orthodox in the Western tradition, the doctrine that an "external incentive" or "pure animal interest" could, "in the absence of will . . . govern the actions of men." Quite the contrary: as Augustine declared around the end of the fourth century in his treatise *On the Free Choice of the Will,* "nothing can make the mind a companion of desire except its own will (*voluntas*) and free choice (*liberum arbitrium*)." This doctrine, which became orthodox in Catholic Christianity (and was never renounced by Augustine himself, who obscurely reconciled it with his later predestinarianism), holds that human beings are not only capable of being wicked voluntarily but that it is only voluntarily that they *can* be wicked. That is why God can justly condemn them to hell for their sins. Indeed, to hold that one sins by the compulsion of the flesh was held by the church to be the kind of heresy of which Manichaeanism is the prototype; the Cathars or Albigensians of southern France were massacred in the thirteenth century, probably in part for holding such a doctrine. Free will is no mere privation but is, in the technical sense of the term, a "positive" force by which the human soul *turns* toward nullity; indeed, in the *Confessions* Augustine suggests that to will evil is to attempt to be like God—to produce "a darkened image of omnipotence." The notion that evil is "privation of being" coexists, in orthodox Christianity, with this "positivity" of free will.[11]

Copjec and Rogozinski cannot be unaware of these elementary facts about Christian doctrine; they presumably do not think these details affect the essentials of their argument. On my view of the matter, however, these details are essential because they bear on the major point I want to emphasize: that Kant's doctrines of radical evil and free will cannot be understood abstractly as philosophical but must be referred to their discursive context, a longstanding intramural debate within Christian theology over the limits of the human will.[12]

Kant himself made no secret of the fact that his project was to preserve the structure of the Christian system of belief by translating it into philosophically respectable terms. He gives the impression of an advance beyond Christianity by invoking the "freedom" and "autonomy" of human beings as rational beings; as he famously assures us in the second *Critique,* the only constraint the human will endures in its submission to the moral law is that which is exercised "through the legislation of one's own reason." This sounds very progressive and enlightened, and has proved highly successful in snaring the interest of a philosophical tradition that has little interest in theology, yet this law that purportedly belongs to the legislation of our very own reason is, in Kant's conception, separated by an uncrossable ontological abyss from human beings as worldly, embodied selves; it is only our noumenal selves that are free, and our noumenal selves are as infinitely removed from our worldly "phenomenal" selves as is the kingdom of God from this world. (In fact, the notion of the noumenon is a philosophical transliteration of what Christianity calls "spirit"; this is more obvious in an explicitly theological tract like the religion and reason essay than it is in Kant's more strictly philosophical treatises.)

Yet despite the distance between phenomenon and noumenon, Kant believes, in orthodox Christian fashion, that it is possible for the evil will to be born again, to undergo a total transformation of heart such that we become capable of willing the moral law in its purity as the sole ground of all our maxims.[13] In *Religion within the Limits of Reason Alone*, Kant rejects the Lutheran and Calvinist notion that only divine grace can bring the human will to will the good in favor of a position that, at least with regard to the question of free will, is practically identical to the Catholic view that Erasmus had championed in 1524 in his treatise berating Luther for his denial of free will. This view, common to Erasmus and Kant, is that in some way that we cannot understand, grace is the ultimate fount of regeneration, but that it is damaging to the morale of believers to think their own initiative has nothing to do with salvation; consequently, we must frame our moral deliberations *as though* we really could do something toward making ourselves suitable recipients of God's grace.[14]

Copjec and Rogozinski are both concerned, though in different ways, with saving Kant from his optimistic turn in order to liberate from his text what they consider his crucial insight: the ineradicable evil of human nature. But if this is what they are looking for, why not look to Luther and Calvin, who do truly assert just such a doctrine? No doubt Luther and Calvin lack the philosophical authority of Kant, but that is not the only reason they will not serve Copjec's and Rogozinski's purpose; they also deny the freedom of the will, which Copjec and Rogozinski want to save. Copjec and Rogozinski are, however, equally intent on rejecting the optimistic voluntarism of the Enlightenment, the belief in the freedom of the human will to perfect itself (secular equivalent of what is known theologically as the "Pelagian heresy"), because they see in this belief the roots of the immanentizing or "subreption" of transcendence that eventually produces totalitarianism. Thus the free will they propose to hold responsible for evil must be one that, although free, nevertheless inveterately fails to will the Law and is therefore perpetually "guilty."

This feeling of guilt, recall, is the way in which the Law announces itself and is therefore essential and ineradicable—hence the ineradicability of the will to evil. But then where is the freedom that is supposed to render me responsible for my wrongs? The free will proclaimed by Copjec and Rogozinski is a will that cannot choose good but only evil, and in choosing evil discovers its guilt under the Law—and by virtue of this guilt, its "transcendence" of nature. This transcendence is what they are really interested in, and it is what they call freedom— not freedom to choose good or evil but *freedom of something about the subject from the embrace of nature*. Since the free will they propose is ineradicably skewed toward evil, however, it is practically indistinguishable from the "will in bondage to evil" of Luther and Calvin.

Was Freud a Lutheran?

Lacan's account of transcendent Law is more thoroughly secularized than is Kant's. But if we turn to Lacan's major published discussion of the evil will in Seminar 7, we find that, even as he translates the Christian concepts into his own language, he insists on their Christian provenance. He is fond of quoting Augustine's famous remark about the babe in arms who is already consumed with envy and hatred of another baby; and in Seminar 7 St. Paul and Luther come in for special notice as authorities on the evil of the human will, on the same side as Freud against the classical tradition of ethical philosophy (including the Catholic tradition after Aquinas)—a tradition that Lacan labels "hedonist." By "hedonist" Lacan means that this tradition is oriented toward the notion of the good as the natural telos and resting place of the human will. Aiming at the good is generally conceived as the opposite of a hedonistic motive, but Lacan has a valid point because both Plato and Christianity make a distinction between the "lower" pleasures of the hedonist and the "higher" pleasures of the moral or spiritual person, which are the *real,* dependable pleasures. As opposed to this higher hedonism, according to Lacan, "Freud is telling us the same thing as St. Paul, namely, that what governs us on the path of our pleasure is no sovereign good." For Plato and Aquinas, when human beings are dominated by impulses that do not aim at the good, it is because they stray from the goal that is proper to the essential nature of the soul; but for St. Paul and Freud, according to Lacan, the soul *in its ultimate nature* is governed by the aim at evil.[15]

The intermediate figure between Paul and Freud is Luther, who (Lacan argues) in his debate with Erasmus pulled Christianity back onto the true Pauline-Augustinian path from which it had strayed:

> Luther writes of the following—God's eternal hatred of men, not simply of their failures and the works of their free will, but a hatred that existed even before the world was created. . . .
> Not to recognize the filiation or cultural paternity that exists between Freud and [this] new direction of thought . . . constitutes a fundamental misunderstanding of the kind of problems Freud's intellectual project addresses.[16]

Whether or not this is an accurate account of the "cultural paternity" of Freud's thought—and I vigorously deny that it is—it is an unimpeachable statement of the paternity of Lacan's. He places himself squarely in the line of descent that comes from Luther's condemnation of the human will as—apart from the inexplicable gift of God's grace—completely, inescapably corrupt. It is to Lacan's credit that he, at least, makes no secret of the genealogy of his own stance; he announces that he follows Paul, Augustine, and Luther. But is he correct in claiming this as Freud's genealogy too, or is Lacan rather presumptuously attributing a Christian genealogy to the Jewish Freud?

Here we return to the fascinating synthesis of Kant, Luther, and Freud that Lacan posits as the matrix of his own thesis and to the prominence he gives to Freud's myth of the primordial murder of the father. This myth has acquired a good deal of currency in poststructuralist writing, in part for the very reasons that it used to be held in disrepute—namely, that it never happened and, even if it had happened, the species-memory of the crime was posited by Freud on discredited Lamarckian principles (Freud never having quite caught up with Darwin). This empirical implausibility becomes a virtue of Freud's thesis for Lacan and his followers because the primordial murder of the father, as mythical, can be assigned to that noplace and notime that is the transcendent locus of the Law.

It cannot be denied that Freud did in fact posit the prehistoric murder of the father ("a crime that must have been repeated many times") and that he continued to hold to it as the ultimate source of the feeling of guilt right to the end of his career. However, it is also true that this speculative or mythical account coexists in Freud's text with another, properly psychoanalytic account of the ontogenesis of conscience in childhood relations with one's parents—an account that belongs to that predominant stratum of Freud's thought that has made him one of the main sources of the modern tendency deplored by Copjec as "the historicist error," the tendency to explain evil as a result of bad parenting rather than in terms of the loss of a transcendent dimension in the symbolic order. Does this mean that there are two Freuds—a transcendentalist Freud and a naturalistic Freud—and that one can take one's pick? Or is one of these the "true" Freud—and if so, how would we decide which one is which? Won't the decision be determined by our presuppositions concerning the type of explanation—transcendental or naturalistic—that we consider valid?

Let's go back to Freud's text and see what he actually says. Instead of just plucking the convenient bits from Freud's discussion, as is commonly done, I want to follow the trajectory of his argument to see what questions he is trying to answer with the theses he introduces and where he comes out with regard to these theses at the end of his investigation. In fact, what we will see is that there is a fundamental flaw in the architecture of Freud's argument that seriously vitiates the thesis of the primordial patricide on grounds internal to Freud's own text.

Freud posited a phylogenetic origin of the sense of guilt based on the prehistoric killing of the father, but this was before he had fully worked out his theory of the instincts or drives, work he accomplished beginning with the metapsychological papers of the mid-1910s. He never did give up the earlier speculative hypothesis concerning the origin of the sense of guilt, reasserting it at the end of his life in *Moses and Monotheism;* but he tried in 1930, in chapter 7 of *Civilization and Its Discontents,* to synthesize the earlier phylogenetic thesis with the new account, based on his new theory of drives, of the ontogenesis of the superego. According to the new theory, there are two fundamental drives, Eros and aggression; and the sense of guilt arises out of the internalization or turning against the self of aggression that is originally aroused in each child against an "unattackable authority"—the parent—who prohibits the child from attaining some desired instinctual satisfaction. Since a child feels helplessly dependent on its parents, and the loss of their love would leave the child exposed to the dangers from which it is shielded by the parents' love—especially the danger that they will turn their own punishing aggression against him—the child's greatest fear is this loss. This fear motivates the turning-inward of aggression in the form of that psychic self-punishment that we call guilt. From a philosophical standpoint, the radical significance of Freud's ontogenetic theory of guilt is that it is thoroughly naturalistic in its account of the origin of the moral sense: guilt in its origin is simply fear of loss of love, and the function of conscience develops out of the habitual practice of internalization of aggression under the goad of this fear. "At the beginning . . . what is bad is whatever causes one to be threatened with loss of love."[17]

This theory—which repeats Nietzsche's fundamental notion that morality is born out of the internalization of aggression, while transposing this genesis from culture and history on to individual development—seems complete as stated.[18] Why, then, does it need to be supplemented by the theory of the primordial patricide?

The suture between the two accounts is quite flimsy. Freud introduces the phylogenetic account purely and simply in order to explain what he declares to be the *excessiveness* of children's reaction to their "first great instinctual frustrations"; a reaction whose aggressivity exceeds what, according to Freud, is "currently justified." This rage, disproportionate as it is, on Freud's telling, to the aggression perpetrated against the child by the nineteenth-century father, is commensurate with the aggression of the prehistoric father, who was "undoubtedly terrible" in his aggressiveness toward his children. Hence the terrible aggression of the prehistoric father called forth an equally terrible aggression from the prehistoric sons; and this patricidal aggression, repeated many times in prehistory, established the phylogenetic fund of aggressivity on which modern children draw when they make the first, *excessive*, "installment" on the aggressivity of their own superegos by overreacting to parental prohibition and then turning the energy of this overreaction against themselves.[19]

We might pause to wonder what measure Freud uses to calculate the "excessiveness" of the child's response. What amount of aggressivity is "justified" in a small child's reaction to parental curbs? Is it even meaningful to speak of justification here? Is there anything more behind Freud's judgment than a nineteenth-century bourgeois male adult's insulation from the affective life of infants? There would be no need, and indeed no room, in Freud's account for the mythical phylogenetic account if it were not for this undefended assumption about the unjustified, excessive character of the child's emotions. Even more important, however, and more damaging to contemporary attempts to make hay with the mythical account, is the fact that the intensity of the child's aggressivity is the *only* thing that Freud even pretends to explain with this account. What it will not explain, he confesses, is the main point at issue, the original source of guilt. The historical myth merely pushes Freud's problem concerning how guilt got started back into the past without resolving it. For if the prehistoric brothers felt guilt for killing their father, Freud reasons, this guilt *presupposes* the existence of conscience:

Remorse of this sort, therefore, never can help us to discover the origin of conscience and of the sense of guilt in general. . . . But if the human sense of guilt goes back to the killing of the primal father, that was after all a case of "remorse." Are we to assume that . . . a conscience and a sense of guilt were not . . . in existence before the deed? If not, where, in this case, did the remorse come from?[20]

Freud's aporia here has great appeal for contemporary commentators, who draw from it the conclusion that indeed the origin of conscience is logically un-accountable in terms of any empirical genesis and that we must therefore go transcendental. Freud himself, however, emerges from his aporia by renounc-ing the assumption that had led up to it, the assumption that the feeling of guilt presupposes the existence of conscience. He now concludes, to the con-trary, that conscience or the superego did not yet exist when the primordial re-morse emerged, but *guilt,* on the other hand, *did already* exist. We have to wait until chapter 8 of *Civilization and Its Discontents* for this conclusion to be ex-plicitly stated: "As to the sense of guilt, we must admit that it is in existence before the super-ego, and therefore before conscience too."[21]

Rereading chapters 7 and 8 with this conclusion in mind, one is struck by the fact that, in the remarks cited, Freud restates more boldly the position that he had somewhat timidly articulated at the beginning of his discussion of guilt. In small children, he had said, the sense of guilt is "clearly only a fear of loss of love, 'social' anxiety." At that point, apparently under the influence of philoso-phical orthodoxy, Freud minimized the moral significance of this form of guilt. He initially calls it guilt, but then hedges. He cannot yet bring himself to call this guilt in the full sense because he still clings to the notion that guilt, properly speaking, only enters in with the internalization of the accusing agency. Yet this dependence of guilt on the function of conscience is precisely what he rejects in chapter 8, because it leads him into the aporia that there is no need for him to be stuck with: all he needs to do is reassert his own theory of the psychic dynamics out of which guilt is born.[22]

According to orthodox philosophical ideology, the sense of guilt is supposed to be the crown jewel in the superiority of Christian civilization and its heirs to "primitive culture"; it is, by definition, a product of that internalized agency of ethical judgment that we call conscience, and it involves the emergence of the human spirit from the plane of mere nature to the plane of transcendence. Be-fore the development of the sense of guilt, one is properly capable only of that more rudimentary moral feeling, rooted in the heteronomy of social life, called *shame;* even the Greeks of the classical period are suspected of not having tran-scended such a primitive morality. But Freud's final position on the origin of the sense of guilt in *Civilization and its Discontents* is radically naturalistic. Con-science originates out of guilt, and guilt is "at bottom nothing else but a topo-graphical variety of anxiety," "the *immediate expression* of fear of the external authority . . . the *direct derivative* of the conflict between the need for the au-thority's love and the urge towards instinctual satisfaction."[23]

What, then, does Freud achieve toward filling out his ontogenetic account of the origin of conscience with the detour through phylogenesis? The phylogenetic account was supposed to fill in something that was missing from the ontogenetic account, but in its final form, once we throw out the ungrounded and unexplained notion of excessiveness, it turns out to be nothing but a *repetition of the ontogenetic account,* and a repetition that creates incoherence. In throwing the account of the origin of guilt back into prehistory, Freud merely imagines the primal brotherhood as young adults going through precisely the same process of anxiety-producing conflict with the father that we moderns go through as children. But how could the prehistoric brothers have failed to develop a superego as children by this very same process? And if the phylogeny of the superego is identical with its ontogeny, then what is gained by positing a phylogeny at all?

It's true that Freud finds it impossible to relinquish the idea of the prehistoric murder of the father. But while that tells us something about the nature of Freud's own obsessions, it lends no structural significance to this idea within the architecture of his overall theory of guilt. Once the economic account of the origin of guilt out of anxiety has solved the paradox of the origin of conscience, the only distinctive mark (and one whose significance he depreciates) that Freud assigns to the primordial murder in chapter 8 is that it is an aggression actually committed, as opposed to aggressions that are repressed and internalized. At this point Freud implies what seems very dubious—that modern humans from the very beginning of their lives feed their superegos with repressed aggression without ever having expressed any (but in that case, whatever led him to think their aggressivity is *excessive*?)—a fact, if it were a fact, that the phylogenetic account would explain. But if guilt originates in the anxiety of conflict with the loved-hated authority, there is no need to postulate anything so drastic as the *murder* of this authority; anything the subject does that provokes the law-enforcing aggression of the authority, and therefore the urge in the child to strike back, would set off this anxiety. There would thus be in the life of any child plenty of occasion for guilt to arise, especially in relation to those erotic impulses that Freud himself stresses.

The myth of the primordial murder of the father, far from pointing to the essence of Freud's insight into the nature of the superego, is thus an idiosyncratic excrescence in Freud's otherwise Nietzschean account. Freud can be no more validly invoked as an intellectual antecedent of the theory of radical evil than Kant, although for different reasons—Kant, because he is an optimistic neo-Christian humanist who believes that the perverse human heart can be born again; and Freud because, insofar as his account is coherent and intelligible, his fundamental concern is with the empirical conditions under which human beings develop a sense of guilt, and thus one of those who, in Copjec's terms, commit the historicist error.

Nietzsche contra Lacan

The real target that Copjec and Rogozinski are attacking is the notion fundamental to modern thought in the tradition of Nietzsche, Freud, and Marx that human beings are mortal, finite beings and nothing more. As Copjec puts it, if the subject becomes "totally assimilated to its mortality," it follows that the transcendent dimension of the subject, "the fact [sic] that the subject is free" must reassert itself in the assertion of totalitarian power by which human beings deny death and the existence of any "checks on the power of the human will."[24] Reduced to its bare bones, there is nothing new about this claim: it is the idea that when human beings stop believing in God, they start to think they *are* God. In the aftermath of Kant, Heidegger, and Lacan, this claim is restated in a way that preserves the structure of the old claim while volatilizing or hyper-sublating the God-concept into notions like "the empty place of the Law" and "the invisible horizon of transcendence."

Yet the basic point that, on my reading, the radical evil theorists assert is plausible: it may be (as I, from my inveterately naturalistic standpoint would want to put it) that human evolution has produced an animal who cannot live in society without setting up a symbolic order oriented toward a transcendent source of authority of some sort. I am loathe to believe this, and I think it far from proven; but I concede that it might be so, and this claim alone makes the whole radical evil thesis worth debating.

My counter thesis is that human beings come to feel the need for transcendence because they are socialized to feel this need, in the manner that ideologies of all sorts institute in subjects the psychological structures corresponding to their ideological forms. Since all Western societies to this day exist in the shadow of Christian transcendentalism, it's no surprise that the notion of the need for transcendence still commands widespread credence. Nietzsche's analysis of the advent of nihilism is still the best account we have of this situation, and in my view gives us a more accurate sense of the state of European society at the birth of Nazism than does the account of the radical evil theorists. What was wrong with European civilization in Nietzsche's view was chiefly its mendacity, its irresistible inclination to clothe human motivation in the pious garb of submission to what is more and higher than human. European civilization by the nineteenth century had put all its ethical eggs in the basket of transcendence, but the same instinct for truth that had created the system of transcendence had now called it into question, and with the collapse of this system, the specter of meaninglessness loomed.

The Lacanians would no doubt argue that what is needed in such a situation is precisely the new form of transcendence or hyper-transcendence that they supply: one that does not rely on any positive belief or belief in a transcendent being but instead on the very disappearance of all positivity in the realm of the transcendent. For the historicizing Nietzschean, by contrast, if Nazism is to be understood as a subreption of the transcendent, which is plausible, this is just one case more of the old habit of mendacity—a problem, not of too little transcendence, but of still not enough immanence. Germany in the first part of the twentieth century was still under the influence of a Christian or Christian-derived ideology of transcendence. If there was a decidedly pagan impulse in Nazism, this did not stop the orthodox churches, both Protestant and Catholic, from lending their wholehearted support to Hitler; and as Bishop Martin Sasse of Thuringia gleefully pointed out in 1938, it was peculiarly fitting that the burning of the synagogues on *Kristallnacht* took place on Luther's birthday, that very Luther whom Sasse celebrated as "the greatest antisemite of his time."[25] What motivated the immanentizing of transcendence in Nazism could thus well be, not a transhistorical or transcendent need for transcendence, but a need generated by a preexistent ideology of transcendence. How easily the old transcendence and the new immanence can dovetail is evident from the declaration by the German Catholic episcopate in 1936 that "race, soil, blood and people are precious natural values which God the Lord has created and the care of which he has entrusted to us Germans."[26] And from this point of view, Lacan's and Copjec's and Rogozinski's hyper-sublation of the ideology of transcendence into the disappearance of the law or the withdrawal of Absolute Spirit is interpretable, not as the solution, but as the continuation of the problem it pretends to solve, insofar as it enables the ideology of transcendence to continue its crypto-Christian afterlife in the guise of a super-sophisticated, post-poststructuralist demystification of the demystifying discourse of modernity.[27]

However, it is one thing to advocate the creation of Nietzschean "life-affirming" values, as so many Nietzsche-inspired thinkers do, and another to actually create them. Certainly one must, as liberationist movements of various sorts have done from the beginning of the century, sift Nietzsche's doctrines to separate those that contribute to such a task from those that helped the Nazis conceive of themselves as agents of a natural law of race.[28] In addition, the problem remains of how to counter the prevailing tendency toward the reduction of ethical responsibility to an effect of ineluctable natural causes; I wholly agree with Copjec and Rogozinski's diagnosis of this tendency as an ethical ill that afflicts our civilization.

The reduction they deplore can, however, be analyzed as a result, not of the "historicist error," but of an erroneous historicism—indeed, an inept and sentimental ideological simulacrum of historicism. As Bernard Williams has shown, investigation of real societies, including our own, in their real historical functioning, reveals, not the bare fact that human action always follows on causal antecedents and paralysis in the face of this fact, but functioning concepts of responsibility and customs of *holding-responsible* for which the notion of the "voluntary" is only one factor, and one for which a metaphysical ground is neither possible nor necessary.[29] As Williams says, adverting to the story of Oedipus, "in the story of one's life there is an authority exercised by what one has done, and not merely by what one has intentionally done."[30] Banal or not, metaphysically free or not, Eichmann was hanged for his crimes, and hardly anyone doubts that he deserved it. There is "a necessary gap between deliberation and result,"[31] and this gap opens up a variety of possibilities for ascription of responsibility, possibilities that are variously actualized in different cultures—and variously actualized in our own culture, in different types of situations governed by different kinds of law.[32]

In the end, both Zarathustrian values and post-Heideggerian vanishing law are such intellectually sophisticated notions that they are unlikely to have any significant effect at the level of communities and nations. The best way to use Nietzsche is probably Williams's way: not as a guide to a new, *übermenschlich* morality, but as a reminder of the human-all-too-human nature of all values. The rhetoric of hyper-transcendence creates the mirage of a transphenomenal boundary majestic enough to stem the tide of history. The naturalistic perspective has at least the virtue of not encouraging this delusion.

Notes

An earlier version of this essay was published in *Radical Philosophy* 93 (November–December 1999): 6–15. I wish to thank the editors of *Radical Philosophy* for their permission to republish this essay, slightly altered, here.

1. The sourcebook for this debate is the collection edited by Joan Copjec, *Radical Evil* (London: Verso, 1996), which includes essays by the four writers mentioned. This collection provided much of the impetus behind the international conference on evil held at the University of Southampton under the sponsorship of the John Hansard Gallery in May 1998, for which the original version of the present article was written. I am grateful to Joan Copjec and Slavoj Žižek for their critical responses to my paper at that time. My summary of the Lacanian position will draw heavily on Rogozinski's account of radical evil in an earlier article, "Hell on Earth: Hannah Arendt in the Face of Hitler," trans. Peter Dews, *Philosophy Today* (Fall 1993): 257–74.
2. Rogozinski, "Hell on Earth": 260, 269, 270, 262, 265.
3. Joan Copjec, "Introduction: Evil in the Time of the Finite World," in *Radical Evil*, p. xx.
4. Rogozinski, "Hell on Earth": 266, 262, 261, quote from p. 266.
5. Badiou has recently been referred to by Jean-Jacques Lecercle ("Cantor, Lacan, Mao, Beckett, *même combat*," *Radical Philosophy* 93 [January-February 1999]: 6–13) as a thinker of immanence (7), but I fail to see how this can be said when Badiou's thinking is radically universalistic, based on a feature, the "event," which is, as Lecercle himself notes, "outside of time" (12).
6. On Haeckel's role, first as champion in Germany of Darwinism, and subsequently in the development of Nazi race ideology, see Pat Shipman, *The Evolution of Racism: Human Differences and the Use and Abuse of Science* (New York: Simon and Schuster, 1994), pp. 73–103.
7. Rogozinski, "Hell on Earth": 266.
8. Jacques Lacan, *The Seminar of Jacques Lacan: Book VII, The Ethics of Psychoanalysis,* ed. Jacques-Alain Miller, trans. Dennis Porter (New York: W. W. Norton, 1992), p. 177.
9. Copjec, "Introduction: Evil in the Time of the Finite World," p. xxii.
10. Žižek debates the positions of Copjec and Rogozinski in *The Plague of Fantasies* (London: Verso, 1997), pp. 225–39.
11. Rogozinski, "Hell on Earth": 260; Copjec, "Introduction: Evil in the Time of the Finite World," pp. x–xi; Augustine, *Free Choice of the Will*, trans. Anna S.

Benjamin and L. H. Hackstaff (Indianapolis: Bobbs-Merrill, 1964), 1, xi; *Confessions,* trans. Rex Warner (New York: Mentor, 1963), 11, vi.

12. A major new contribution to our understanding of the evolution of Kant's ethical thinking has been made by J. B. Schneewind in *The Invention of Autonomy: A History of Modern Moral Philosophy* (Cambridge: Cambridge University Press, 1998). I find nothing in Schneewind's account that would contradict the very schematic remarks about Kant that I make here.

13. Immanuel Kant, *Religion within the Limits of Reason Alone,* trans. Theodore M. Green and Hoyt H. Hudson (New York: Harper and Row, 1960), p. 43.

14. Ibid., pp. 40–47.

15. Lacan, *Seminar 7,* pp. 221, 95.

16. Ibid., p. 97.

17. Sigmund Freud, *Civilization and Its Discontents,* Vol. 21 of *The Standard Edition of the Complete Psychological Works of Sigmund Freud,* trans. James Strachey (London: Hogarth Press, 1961), p. 124.

18. Freud seems to have cribbed most of his argument in *Civilization and Its Discontents* from *On the Genealogy of Morals.* See Lorin Anderson, "Freud, Nietzsche," *Salmagundi* 47–48 (Winter-Spring 1980): 3–39.

19. Freud, *Civilization and Its Discontents,* p. 131. In the paragraphs I am discussing, Freud also makes his famous remark, much beloved and cited by theorists in recent years, that "the severity of the super-ego which a child develops in no way corresponds to the severity of the treatment which he has himself met with" (p. 130). It is almost never noted that Freud immediately qualifies this categorical pronouncement, adding that "it would be wrong to exaggerate" the "independence" of the two factors; for what we really have is another instance of "a universal aetiological condition for all such processes," the convergence of "innate constitutional factors and influences from the real environment" (p. 130).

20. Freud, *Civilization and Its Discontents,* pp. 131–32.

21. Ibid., pp. 132, 136.

22. Ibid., p. 80.

23. Ibid., pp. 82, 136; emphasis added.

24. Copjec, "Introduction: Evil in the Time of the Finite World," p. xx.

25. Julius H. Schoeps, *Leiden in Deutschland: Vom antisemitischen Wahn und der Last der Erinnerung* (Munich: Piper, 1990), p. 60; cited in Daniel Jonah Goldhagen, *Hitler's Willing Executioners: Ordinary Germans and the Holocaust* (New York: Vintage Books, 1997), p. 111. As Goldhagen's numerous critics have shown, his monocausal explanation of the Holocaust is seriously flawed; but his bibliography and summary of accounts of the German churches under the Nazis are useful. See especially pp. 106–14.

26. Guenter Lewy, *The Catholic Church and Nazi Germany* (New York: McGraw-Hill, 1964), p. 163; cited in Goldhagen, *Hitler's Willing Executioners,* p. 106.

27. How one might place Derrida in relation to this discussion is a complex question that I cannot adequately address here but which I must mention since a superficial or even not so superficial reading of his work, certainly since the turn to Levinas but also earlier, might see him as engaging in a similar "hyper-sublation" (I do not recommend the term, and I hope someone can suggest a better one). Some such charge was indeed already the substance of Rorty's critique of *"differance"* two decades ago. Derrida's famous essay "Before the

Law" in particular mixes Kant and the Freud of the primordial patricide in a way that seems parallel to what the Lacanians do, and Richard Beardsworth's reading of this mixture bolsters the feeling of such a parallel (*Derrida and the Political* [London: Routledge, 1996], pp. 30–31). Briefly, I would say that one must read this part of "Before the Law" in the context of the whole essay, which stresses as much the absolute historical contingency of the law in its phenomenalization (and not simply to deplore it, as Copjec and Rogozinski do) as it does the law's dimension of "withdrawal" from history. That is to say that in "Before the Law" Derrida is still practicing *deconstruction*.

28. For a comprehensive account of the tug-of-war between Right and Left over Nietzsche, see Steven E. Aschheim, *The Nietzsche Legacy in Germany 1890–1990* (Berkeley: University of California Press, 1992). Geoffrey Waite documents, and shrilly denounces, the widespread influence of Nietzsche on leftist thinking in *Nietzsche's Corps/e* (Durham, N.C.: Duke University Press, 1996). I have analyzed the contradictory pulls in Nietzsche's thought between his liberationist and fascist tendencies in *Nietzsche's Voice* (Ithaca, N.Y.: Cornell University Press, 1990), and more recently in "Dionysus Lost and Found: Literary Genres in Nietzsche and Lukács," in *Nietzsche, Philosophy, and the Arts,* ed. Salim Kemal, Ivan Gaskell, and Daniel W. Conway (Cambridge: Cambridge University Press, 1998).

29. See especially chapter 3, "Recognizing Responsibility," in Bernard Williams, *Shame and Necessity* (Berkeley: University of California Press, 1993), pp. 50–74. For a full-scale critique of the philosophical notion that "all genuinely moral considerations rest, ultimately and at a deep level, in the agent's will," see Bernard Williams, *Ethics and the Limits of Philosophy* (London: Fontana, 1985); quotation from p. 7.

30. *Shame and Necessity,* p. 69.

31. Ibid.

32. A more accurate philosophical account of how concepts of responsibility work would need to be more empirical in its approach, more respectful of the complexity of the diverse contexts within which these concepts are deployed. Williams makes the intriguing suggestion that "To a considerable extent, the idea that the Greeks thought very differently from ourselves about responsibility, and in particular more primitively, is an illusion generated by thinking only about the criminal law and forgetting the law of torts. We do argue legally, and in not so different a style [from that of the Greeks] in cases where damage follows from what someone unintentionally brings about" (ibid., p. 63).

3   Liquidating the "Nearly Just Society": Radical Evil's Triumphant Return

William L. McBride

Here is a local narrative. At the banquet marking the end of the summer 2003 World Congress of Philosophy, I happened to sit down next to a man from Asia, a person of great distinction and accomplishment, and we began exchanging observations concerning the current world situation. No doubt, he said, there was something about his Hindu upbringing that led him to think this way, but he had the feeling that there was an unusually strong upsurge of waves of evil in the contemporary world. I said that I, though unschooled in Eastern thought, shared very similar sentiments. I then thought immediately of this essay that I had promised to Alan Schrift and that I was finding so unaccustomedly difficult to write.

The problem is, how to grasp evil? Most efforts to do so, to go beyond superficial, virtually meaningless slogans such as "the Evil Empire" or "the axis of evil," almost inevitably fall short, sometimes ludicrously so. At the same time, however, there is a widespread, strongly felt need to reflect on it and to communicate about it. Evil is certainly very high on the contemporary philosophical agenda. There are good reasons for this, I believe, and it is worth the effort to try to understand and articulate them.

Religions, of course, as well as philosophies coming out of religious traditions, have made such an effort. Saint Augustine, to take one prominent example, devoted much thought to the question of evil, motivated in considerable measure by his conflicts with the Manichaeans as well as by his historical situation as observer of the decline of Rome. His well-known view was that evil is merely a "privation" of good, the product of human free will, not created by God, and certainly not, as the Manichaeans believed, coeval with God. A typical Augustinian refutation of the Manichaean "heresy," which loses something of its punch in the translation from a language that lacks articles into one that has them, reads as follows:

> You are quite correct in asking who is so blind mentally as not to see that the evil for any kind of thing is that which is contrary to its nature. But once this is estab-

lished, your heresy is overthrown. *For evil is not a* [sic] *nature if it is contrary to nature.* Yet you claim that evil is a certain nature and substance.[1]

Indeed, since for Augustine nature is a good thing, "not even the nature of the devil himself is evil, so far as it is nature; but perversity makes it evil."[2] It has been characteristic of many religions to attempt to incarnate evil in some imagined, often personified being called the devil, Satan, and the like; but Augustine's intellectual honesty here enables his readers to see just how problematic the conjuncture of this idea with the conviction that evil is simply (greater or lesser) absence of good turns out to be. If one has a sense, as my Asian collocutor and I do, that truly radical evil is abroad in the world, neither Augustine's devil—with his basically good, though of course dreadfully perverted nature—nor the entire millennial tradition characterizing evil as privation provides a satisfactory account of it.

For Kant, famously, evil is abroad in the world if only because *radical* evil is innate in each one of us, in human nature—though he hastens to explain that by "human nature" he means the subjective grounds for the exercise of freedom rather than something *opposed to* (moral) freedom, which is what the word "nature" more commonly means in his lexicon, by contrast with Augustine's. We are all born, Kant says, with a propensity to evil, though it is not the event of birth itself that occasions this propensity, and each of us must (and will!) freely choose to activate it in order for it to become operational, so to speak. The work in which Kant chiefly makes these assertions is entitled *Religion within the Boundaries of Mere Reason,* but as he attempts to explain the *origin* of evil, he falls back, at a crucial point, on the "historical narrative" of the Judeo-Christian scriptures, the story of Adam and Eve, by way of illustrating what he concedes is the ultimate inexplicability and "incomprehensibility" of the phenomenon in question.[3] Faced with the question of evil, then, Kant, the quintessential modern Enlightenment philosopher, is at once forceful (his prose becomes insistent and even somewhat florid as he elaborates on the radical evil within us) and yet confused, and he eventually confesses defeat.

On the whole, the cliché that much of modern Western philosophy after Kant, imbued as it mostly was with a spirit of optimism and belief in moral as well as technological progress, neglected the question of evil, or at least of radical evil, is true. Schopenhauer is an important counterexample, no doubt; and Nietzsche's case, with respect to this question, is an extremely complicated one that I do not wish to engage here. But it was possible for Simone de Beauvoir to assert confidently, and with considerable truth, at the end of the first chapter of *Pour une morale de l'ambiguïté:*

> In a metaphysics of transcendence, in the classical sense of the term, evil is reduced to error; and in humanistic philosophies it is impossible to account for it, man being defined as complete in a complete world. Existentialism alone gives—like religions—a real role to evil.[4]

So according to her, existentialism's preoccupation with evil sets it apart in modern Western thought.

But there is, in fact, considerable ambiguity in the way in which both Beauvoir and her colleague, Sartre, themselves deal with this question, as epitomized in their frequent, generally pejorative, allusions to "Manichaean" thinking. For them, and for a number of philosophers following them, the Manichaean is the demonizer who ascribes evil as a real force to some group—for example, Jews or Blacks—whose elimination would therefore, for him or her, be tantamount to the elimination of evil itself. But are not the anti-Semites and the antiblack racists (Lewis Gordon's term)[5] themselves being treated as deeply, even radically evil by these writers? Perhaps they *should* be; this, at least, is the implication of a significant book, *Sartre and Evil*, by Haim and Rivca Gordon,[6] who attest to what they regard as profound evil in the actions of their own Israeli government against the Palestinians.

Sartrean-style existentialism, as I have pointed out in the past, must in many ways be seen as an anticipation of postmodern thought—at least to the extent to which such an amorphous notion as "postmodernism" can be grasped.[7] If postmodern thought stands for anything, it seems to me, it stands for the rejection, as myths, of grandiose accounts of history construed as a progressive series of events resulting in a happy ending. Such myths, by contrast, reflected the spirit of modernity. That spirit, however, survived longer in some cultures and strands of thinking than in others. In particular, it had taken very deep roots in North America, as a result of a combination of many diverse factors: contingent facts of geography, including vast natural resources; the deliberate extermination and/or repression of potentially dissident putative *Untermenschen*, beginning with the so-called "Indians"; the enthusiastic cultivation of a peculiar "booster" or "cheerleader" mentality applicable to all aspects of life, from state to church to military hardware to sports teams; and so on. But modernist, happy-ending American nationalism, the product of all these convergent and frequently disconcerting factors, usually presented itself in a supremely self-confident, serenely untroubled, form. The most widely recognized philosophical expression of this spirit during the last third of the twentieth century was, I would argue, the work of the late John Rawls. This was most clearly the case within his chosen domain of political philosophy.

Rawls's chef d'oeuvre, *A Theory of Justice*, is often said to have revived this domain itself, which had previously been moribund. This is not quite accurate, for a number of books of political philosophy, especially in the Marxian tradition, had been published even in the United States in the 1950s and 1960s, prior to *A Theory*'s appearance. Nevertheless, by virtue of its ambitious and comprehensive nature, it achieved a notoriety that was warranted for its time. Rawls identified his work particularly with the Kantian tradition of ethics, but above all, though this was not greatly insisted upon until the writings of his middle period, with political liberalism, and in the last analysis, with political liberalism in its American form.

The methods and simple basic principles of Rawls's original theory have been regurgitated literally millions of times by now, in thousands of classrooms and conferences and articles; I do not intend to repeat them once more here. Rather,

I would like to step back and take an overview of his contribution in the light of our present themes of evil and radical evil. In fact, I already did suggest an overview of a sort that may still be relevant now when I chose as the title of a review that I wrote of *A Theory of Justice,* one of the very first published, "Political Theory *Sub Specie Aeternitatis:* A New Perspective."[8] This was intended to be ironic: to the extent to which Rawls was urging us, as he did in unwontedly poetic and reverential tones in his book's final paragraph, to aspire to achieve the "purity of heart" that would come from "see[ing] clearly and act[ing] with grace and self-command from this point of view"[9] of eternity, then there would, in fact, have to be something permanent and abiding—in other words, decidedly *non*-novel—about this perspective. (The perspective in question is that of the so-called "original position," outlined at the outset of the book and from which everything that has followed has presumably flowed, to which Rawls begins the final paragraph by referring once more.) The entire Rawlsian enterprise—like those of systematic political philosophers of the past such as Plato and Hegel— was characterized by considerable hubris. It was bound to attract, as it did, both enthusiastic adulators and severe critics. One of the best ways of grasping this hubris, it seems to me, is to consider Rawls's employment of the term, "a nearly just society."

As a philosophical theory with universalist aspirations, of course, Rawls's major work could not have been presented as *simply* an idealized version of American political structures. Significant allowances were made, for instance, for the theory's applicability within a variety of economies (as long as they are market economies), including, at least in principle, market socialism. And most readers would agree, I think, that Rawls's *intent* in formulating the so-called "difference principle" that was his core conclusion concerning the most just possible distribution of social goods was to advocate a narrowing rather than a widening of the gap between the wealthiest and the poorest individuals within a given society. (Just the opposite has occurred, as everyone knows, in the United States as well as on a global scale since the publication of *A Theory of Justice.*) Nevertheless, it soon becomes abundantly clear to the reader that the United States, Rawls's native country, is the actual society to which he is implicitly alluding throughout—as, for example, in his discussion of the need for a constitutional convention that opens the book's Part Two (of three).[10] Now there is nothing in principle wrong with this, to be sure—philosophers, and indeed writers in general, are well advised to anchor their work in their own lived experiences—but caution, as the cliché has it, is advised. In the nine sections (51–59) of the book in which the notion of a "nearly just society" comes into play, dealing with the duty to comply with an unjust law, civil disobedience, and "conscientious refusal" (of military service), Rawls's particularly strong focus on the American context, though it is understandable enough, especially in view of the tumultuous period of the sixties during which he was composing *A Theory of Justice,* should be regarded as quite *in*cautious—if only by virtue of his choice of the words, "nearly just," themselves.

Rawls, in fact, says very little about what precisely he means by a "nearly just" (or, sometimes, "reasonably just") society, except that it must be a democratic one, that it is "well-ordered" (one of his favorite expressions), and that it is possible that fairly blatant injustices may be found in it. He mentions, as examples of such, the denial to "certain minorities" of "the right to vote or to hold office, or to own property and to move from place to place."[11] It is obvious that these are serious injustices; the question is whether it makes sense to call a society in which they obtain a "nearly just society." The answer, I believe, is that it may *seem* to make sense if one is a member of the privileged majority. Rawls proceeds to lay down some fairly narrow guidelines for practicing, in a way that would be morally acceptable to him, civil disobedience with a view to altering these conditions.[12] We readers are led to suppose that, if Rawls's prescriptions are followed, there is likely to be a happy ending: the protested injustices will be removed, and justice will thenceforth more fully prevail in the "nearly just society."

The world of the early Rawls is a relentlessly reasonable one. He has no doubt, for example, that "in certain circumstances militant action and other kinds of resistance are surely justified." But, he goes on to say, "I shall not, however, consider these cases."[13] His is also, ultimately, a *good* world. The chapter immediately following the discussions of civil disobedience and conscientious refusal is, in fact, entitled "Goodness as Rationality." In it, Rawls elaborates his very pluralistic and individualistic conception of the good, according to which everyone is to pursue his or her own unique "plan of life." (This approach is obviously quintessentially modernist American, and it is not surprising that the recent recrudescence of communitarianism in political philosophy should have drawn some of its force from the reaction to Rawls, as epitomized in the work of his Harvard colleague Michael Sandel.) It is in one short paragraph in this chapter that *evil* makes its only appearance, as far as I know (and this observation is supported by the book's fairly comprehensive index). Here Rawls distinguishes among three types of not good men (*sic*): the unjust, the bad, and the evil. The basis of the distinction is motivation: the unjust man seeks legitimate aims such as wealth and security, but uses unjust means; the bad man revels in the sense of mastery over others that the exercise of arbitrary power gives him, although he does so for ends such as self-esteem and a sense of self-command that are in themselves good; whereas the evil man loves injustice in the form of humiliating and degrading others.[14] That is all that this 600-page book, one of the acknowledged classics of twentieth-century modernist thought, has to tell us explicitly about evil!

Thirty years later, to repeat what I wrote earlier, evil is very much on the agenda, as evidenced by the present volume. Rawls's beloved United States has been branded, notoriously by the late Ayatollah Khomeini but surely also by many others, "the Great Satan." In turn, its beloved (I jest) de facto president, Mr. Bush, has identified an anti-American "axis of evil"—a locution that, we are told, was chosen over a more pedestrian alternative precisely because of its theological connotations. What has happened to alter the landscape so drastically? Clues to answering this question may be found, I would like to suggest, in Rawls's short but significant late work, *The Law of Peoples*.

Let me clarify my strategy. Though highly flawed like all great works, *A Theory of Justice* was a great work for its time; *The Law of Peoples*, as I think most readers would agree, was not. (I say "was" rather than "is" because it originally appeared in essay form a full decade ago.) I am interested in Rawls's exegesis here only as a vehicle for exploring our theme of modernity and evil via this highly visible, highly regarded political philosopher, given that political philosophy is my own area of specialization and that I am convinced that evil, even radical evil, has its most salient manifestations today—as so often in the past—in the sociopolitical realm. (Hence, I am not interested here in discussing the evolution of Rawls's thinking through the middle period of his career, the period of the essays that constitute the volume *Political Liberalism*.) Between the lines, so to speak, of *The Law of Peoples*, I am further convinced, despite and indeed because of the fact that it is a less careful work than *A Theory of Justice*, are to be found very helpful insights into the phenomenon of evil in the modern world.

Rawls's concern in this book is to apply his theory of justice to the global arena, which is by no stretch of his or anyone else's imagination "nearly just." His approach, quite different in a number of respects from his earlier methodology, is to classify nonliberal societies in, as it were, a condescending order, the less-bad type being labeled "decent hierarchical peoples" (accompanied by the hint that there might conceivably be some other type of "decent" and therefore tolerable society of which he has not thought), and the worst being "outlaw states." In addition, he lists two other types that do not exactly fall within a rank ordering: "benevolent absolutisms," which honor human rights but have no democratic decision procedures, and about which Rawls says virtually nothing more; and "societies burdened by unfavorable conditions." That his made-up name for an imaginary "decent hierarchical society" is Kazanistan somewhat minimizes the need for us to deploy our own imaginations in order to suppose what type of country he may mean. The language used in discussing peoples who are "decent," but alas not quite as decent as we, is shot full of condescension, as I have indicated, or hubris of an unrelenting but still comparatively mild form. In my opinion, at any rate, it only flirts with evil and does not plunge us into it. Of quite another order, again in my view, is what Rawls says and implies about societies burdened with unfavorable conditions and about outlaw states.

To "burdened" societies, Rawls's advice is, basically, to suck it in. Suppose, he says, citizens of one such society experience feelings of inferiority toward citizens of another, more prosperous society. This would be onerous, he opines,

> *provided* that these feelings are justified. Yet when the duty of assistance is fulfilled [that is, once the wealthier societies have provided enough aid to stave off starvation in the poor ones], and each people has its own liberal or decent government, these feelings are unjustified. For then each people adjusts the significance and

importance of the wealth of its own society for itself. If it is not satisfied, it can continue to increase savings or, if that is not feasible, borrow from other members of the Society of Peoples.[15]

In any case, as he has already established, such societies' burdens are their own fault:

> I believe that the causes of the wealth of a people and the forms it takes lie in their political culture and in the religious, philosophical, and social traditions that support the basic structure of their political and social institutions, as well as in the industriousness and cooperative talents of its members, all supported by their political virtues. (p. 108)

He goes on to say that virtually any society in the world *could* become "well-ordered" if it acquired the proper attitudes and virtues and practiced a modicum of population control.

In short, when the erstwhile champion of distributive justice within single, well-ordered, nearly just societies like the United States comes to survey the current grossly unequal global distribution of resources, he is unsympathetic to the point of being simply insulting. In response, one is somehow reminded of the pathetic, simple-minded question that has so often been asked by ordinary US citizens in recent years: "Why do they hate us?"

When it comes to Rawls's treatment of "outlaw states" (or, as he sometimes writes, "rogue states"), the reader begins to sense a not merely condescending but deeply vindictive attitude on the part of the author himself. I certainly have no difficulty in agreeing with him when, early in the book, he characterizes Hitler's treatment of the Jews as "demonic madness" and traces it back to medieval Christian attitudes. But when he then immediately proceeds to contrast liberal and decent peoples, on the one hand, with unnamed contemporary "others" whose conduct is "wrongful, evil, and demonic" (p. 22), on the other, I sense an undertone of belligerent self-righteousness (undetectable, as I have noted, in the more Pelagian early Rawls) that is most troubling in its implications, especially in light of recent world events.

Throughout this *libellum,* Rawls exhibits a recurrent fascination with war. From the outset, while he insists, quite fatuously in my opinion, that "democratic" peoples never war with one another and says that nuclear weapons could be suppressed in a world of only liberal and decent peoples, he urges their retention in order to keep outlaw states "at bay" (p. 9). He does admit that the atomic bombing of Japanese civilian populations in World War II was wrong, even gravely wrong, but he endorses the possible use of such weapons in "supreme emergency situations" in the future. A few pages from the end, he again takes up the theme of war, asserting that "one does not find peace by declaring war irrational or wasteful, though indeed it may [*sic!*] be so, but by preparing the way for people to develop a basic structure that supports a reasonably just or decent regime" (p. 123).

All of this war talk might seem somewhat less problematic in a book on global relations (after all, modern international law theory began primarily, with Grotius, as an effort to define acceptable rules of warfare) if it were perfectly clear as to exactly which regimes count as outlaw states against which war may be justified, and which do not. But this is in fact far from clear, either in Rawls's book or in reality—apart from the perception that the nearly just United States, while it may occasionally have strayed beyond the limits (Rawls mentions the US government's covert subversions of the Allende, Arbenz, and Mossadegh regimes as definite examples, and its subversion of the Sandanistas[16] as a possible example), could never fall under this classification. Early modern France, Spain, and Austria-Hungary were outlaw states, according to him; Bismarck was not a statesman, whereas Washington and Lincoln unquestionably were. It all seems so neat, so foreordained—a supposedly theoretical category reinforcing preconceptions if not outright prejudices.

There is, in Rawls's book, at least one salient characteristic of an outlaw state that could serve as the (partial) basis of a definition: *expansionism:* "A liberal society cannot justly require its citizens to fight in order to gain economic wealth or to acquire natural resources, much less to win power and empire.[n] (When a society pursues these interests, it no longer honors the Law of Peoples, and it becomes an outlaw state)" (p. 91). Fair enough, except that the footnote referenced by the superscript reads: "Of course, so-called liberal societies sometimes do this, but that only shows that they may act wrongly." Blatant contradiction, sheer confusion, or simply special pleading? I leave the choice of label to you, dear reader.

In any case, what I discern through the pages of *The Law of Peoples* is a certain *pattern* of thinking that is both drearily familiar in one sense (it is the thinking, simply put, of the stereotypical privileged white American male intellectual) and yet capable of being viewed in a novel way in light of recent developments. Perhaps the words "power and empire" in the above citation from Rawls furnish the best key to this novelty as I perceive it: current US policymakers and their supporters feel far less hesitation than their predecessors about asserting that they seek power and empire—in the name, of course, of "liberal" values. (They may not like the *word* "liberal," but the *concept* behind it is one that they would claim to share, at some fundamental level at least, with Rawls.)

If Rawls were still alive, he might—I hope that he would, but I am not sure—express dismay at the arrogance and belligerence with which "rogue states," the US State Department formula that he himself, as I have noted, was not above deploying from time to time, are denounced and targeted. The claim to have a right to attack others preemptively at any time, anywhere, on the mere ground that they might themselves conceivably become attackers in the future, is patently, radically evil and is an invitation to the proliferation of further global evils ad infinitum. But some of the supercilious and denunciatory language and bellicose postures of Rawls himself, in *The Law of Peoples,* can be seen as anticipating, if not actually endorsing, that arrogance and belligerence. He had begun some years before to write about the special problems posed by intolerant fundamentalist religions, though he had very little if anything to say about the reasons why they were attractive to so many or about the social, political, and economic factors that help explain their rise; but he was apparently incapable of seeing the latent intolerance of self-righteous and self-professedly tolerant liberal democratic thinkers such as himself and of the actually existing state(s) that they glorified.

The atmosphere of radical evil that we experience, with a frisson, as cloaking the globe at the present time[17] has much to do with the hatred engendered by these mutual intolerances. Rawls's *intentions* may have been "good," meaning rooted in sincere self-righteousness; so may have been the intentions of the late Ayatollah Khomeini, to repeat the name of the one fundamentalist leader, among many, whom I mentioned earlier in this essay. So may even, for all I know, be the intentions of some members of the current US imperial leadership. All of them, not only Rawls, no doubt consider(ed) themselves both reasonable and rational (two terms that the middle-period Rawls found it important to distinguish). The problem is that the real presence of radical evil, however it is to be explained, is at any rate not explicable on the basis of mere intentions, much less by the absence of rational calculation.

Kant, in his confused chatter about the rooting of radical evil in human nature (but of course not "human nature" as it is usually understood, as an unfree given), and in his conclusion that it is ultimately inexplicable and "incomprehensible," seems somehow to have realized this much—even though it goes against the grain of his entire ethical theory, for which the agent's intention is so crucial. Rawls, on the other hand, when, as we have seen, he tried to identify what is meant by an "evil man" and to distinguish this type from the "unjust" and the "bad" man, based his definition on motivation alone. In short, as a self-professed Kantian moralist, he failed ever to seriously put into question the intentionalist, rationalist illusion. Without questioning this illusion, to wit, that there is one universal and in principle thoroughly knowable scheme of rationality, one cannot hope even to *begin* to grasp the nature of evil, and one therefore becomes a good candidate for serving as its unwitting instrument.

Here is one final local narrative, which no doubt many others besides myself could recount. Once, in a city far from my home, I twisted my ankle severely. The pain was intense, and walking very difficult. Someone attending the same conference as I was attending offered, somewhat deferentially lest I be contemptuous of "superstition," to treat my condition with reiki meditation. I agreed unhesitatingly: I harbored no prejudices that would cause me to eschew what could not be explained in terms of my own conventional conceptions of rationality, and the treatment committed me to no action on my part other than patient sitting. It worked—not to perfection, which at any rate I had been told not to expect, but quite well. I have no idea why: it remains, to me, inexplicable and "incomprehensible."

To move from the trivial to the cosmic, it is also ultimately inexplicable and "incomprehensible" that radical evil is abroad, even apparently triumphant, in today's world of rampant global hubris and injustice. But some *hint* as to the reasons for this may be gleaned, as I have tried to show, by reflecting on what type of society it is that preens itself on being, in the words of one of its most articulate cheerleaders, "nearly just."

Notes

1. Augustine, *The Catholic and Manichaean Ways of Life,* trans. Donald A. and Idella J. Gallagher (Washington, D.C.: Catholic University of America Press, 1966), p. 66; emphasis mine.
2. Augustine, *The City of God against the Pagans,* trans. W. C. Greene (Cambridge, Mass.: Harvard University Press, 1960), book xix, ch. xiii, p. 177.
3. Immanuel Kant, *Religion within the Boundaries of Mere Reason,* trans. Allen W. Wood and George di Giovanni (Cambridge: Cambridge University Press, 1996), pp. 64–65.
4. Simone de Beauvoir, *The Ethics of Ambiguity,* trans. Bernard Frechtman (New York: Citadel Press, 1994), p. 34. I use the French title in my text because of the extremely misleading nature of the English title.
5. Lewis Gordon, *Bad Faith and Antiblack Racism* (Atlantic Highlands, N.J.: Humanities Press, 1995).
6. Haim and Rivca Gordon, *Sartre and Evil: Guidelines for a Struggle* (Westport, Conn.: Greenwood Press, 1995).
7. William L. McBride, "Sartre and His Successors: Existential Marxism and Postmodernism at Our *Fin de Siècle,*" *Praxis International* 11, no. 1 (April 1991): 78–92.
8. William L. McBride, "Political Theory *Sub Specie Aeternitatis:* A New Perspective," *Yale Law Journal* 81, no. 5 (April 1972): 980–1003.
9. John Rawls, *A Theory of Justice* (Cambridge, Mass.: Harvard University Press, 1971), p. 587.
10. "The idea of a four stage sequence is suggested by the United States Constitution and its history" (ibid., p. 196, n. 1). I have been told, by someone who knew Rawls, that he was very enamored of that history.
11. Ibid., p. 372.
12. As Jeffrey Paris has shown in a magisterial review of Rawls's intellectual evolution as manifested in his *Collected Papers,* Rawls tended always to impose a severe onus on anyone making broader calls for social justice that might threaten the existing order. See his "After Rawls," *Social Theory and Practice* 28, no. 4 (October 2002): 679–99.
13. *A Theory of Justice,* p. 368.
14. Ibid., p. 439.
15. John Rawls, *The Law of Peoples* (Cambridge, Mass.: Harvard University Press, 1999), p. 114. Page numbers in the text are to this work.
16. This is the famous case, it will be recalled, in which the US government's mining of the principal harbor of Managua was brought by the Sandanista regime to the International Court, which found that this had indeed blatantly violated international law; whereupon the US government declared that it would simply not recognize the validity of the Court's decision. If "outlaw

state" *is* a meaningful term in the international context, is it not obvious that it is applicable here?

17.   As I hope I made clear in my initial anecdote, such perceptions may be widely shared, but they are difficult if not impossible to verify by any objective methods. In my own experience, the most intense period of sensing radical evil occurred during the last weeks preceding the US government's attack on Iraq in Spring 2003, as it became clear that no rational argument or expression of worldwide public opinion or even personal pleas from the pope and other religious leaders would dissuade those committed to "pre-emptive" aggression from their intent to "shock and awe" their human targets, using their overwhelming weaponry.

4 Violence and Secularization, Evil and Redemption

Martin Beck Matuštík

We pray to be delivered from all evil; we hope that we can avoid temptation to do iniquity and that evil deeds will be wiped clean with the rites of atonement, fasting, or pilgrimages to holy places. But in our prayers and hopes, do we comprehend what is *evil?* Do we grasp how *radical* is the "radical evil" that darkens our intellect and weakens our will?

In his late essay, "Religion within the Boundaries of Mere Reason," Kant argues that evil must be imputed to the weakness of human will. This fact attests to the dignity of human freedom and the rational will's innate orientation to do good. Building on Kant, with Kierkegaard's distinction between aesthetic and ethical in mind, I will consider that there is nothing redemptive or holy in war on evil. Yet by translating the religious mode of sin into the moral language of radical evil, does not Kant muddle the issue? Relying on Kierkegaard's religious grasp of evil, I want to consider that there is nothing wholly secular about violence. Finally, I will meditate on some postsecular consequences of radical evil.

Kant on "Radical Evil"

Kant laments the fact of "radical evil" in international politics. When we consider "the state of constant war" among "civilized peoples" and how they "have also firmly taken it into their heads not to get out of it," then we become aware of the fundamental contradiction between our promulgated moral principles and the realpolitik. In his "Religion" essay, he presciently described the disdain that is expressed for the relevance of the United Nations at the start of the twenty-first century: "So *philosophical chiliasm,* which hopes for a state of perpetual peace based on a federation of nations united in a world-republic, is universally derided as sheer fantasy as much as *theological chiliasm,* which awaits for the completed moral improvement of the human race" (6:34).[1] A telling footnote says that the human race is guided by the raw progress of nature through force rather than by the other-regarding categorical imperative to treat humans as ends in themselves:

> So long as a state has a neighboring one which it can hope to subdue, it strives to aggrandize itself by subduing it. It thus strives for . . . a state constitution in which

all freedom would necessarily expire. . . . Yet after this monster . . . has swallowed up all its neighbors, it ultimately disintegrates all by itself. [And] instead of striving after a union of states (a republic of free federated peoples), in turn begins the same game all over again, so that war (that scourge of the human race) will not cease . . . (6:35)

Kant admits the "incomprehensible" (6:44) reality of radical evil—hateful distortions of friendship, cruelty and savagery, sectarian violence, warfare among states—only to save humans from misanthropy, indeed, to bid them instead to become enlightened through tolerance (6:33). Good and evil originate in human free will as a choice of fundamental maxims we give ourselves, and we alone are their authors (6:21–22, 25). Such is the price for the dignity of human will, and there is no other "*beginning in time*" of evil than its subjective origin in our lived will (6:42).

Intellect and will suffer a certain propensity or weakness that predisposes humans to adopt evil rather than good maxims to guide their conduct. Kant attributes this propensity, not to some original depravity, but to "*the good or evil heart,*" that is, the fragility, impurity, and perversion of our actions (6:29–30). One can be called "evil *by nature*" only in a derivative sense (6:32), since acts of free will alone, not persons as such or races, can be imputed good or evil (6:31). We cannot observe maxim giving in others; we can hardly even detect its upsurge within our free will; so we do not have access to the originating ground of *all* such maxims in a person. *Ergo,* "the judgment that an agent is an evil human being cannot reliably be based on experience" (6:20). Evil cannot destroy human dignity because evil arises from the willing act, not from human sensuousness or from reason that is never cut off, says Kant, from respect for the moral law within. Sensuous desires offer us too little to qualify for free human acts, and reason holds too much ideality to qualify for radical evil. So we may not root radical moral evil in the core of rational humanity, for that would transform any one of us into "a *diabolical* being" (6:35). "[D]espite a corrupted heart" the human person can "always" possess "a good will" (6:44).

In a move to save the human dignity of evildoers, Kant softens the radicalness of evil insofar as it could never shatter the ability to sustain free will *as* good will. In attending to moral evil, how should we grasp the radicalness of its root? Kant calls only the "*perversity* of the heart" "*evil.*" By locating the radical root of evil in human "depravity" (*Bösartigkeit*) in something that does not prevent me from repenting myself back into ethical life (6:37), he avoids calling this root the "*malice*" (*Bösheit*) of willing. He absolves the legislative will (*Wille*) that never wavers in its respect for the law and assigns the root of evil to free choice of the lived will that is never fully coincident with itself (*Willkür*). Radical evil—this "foul stain of our species" (6:38)—never destroys our respect for the moral law within, and Kant shies from admitting this possibility out of fear of crippling rational freedom's access to moral light. That one could "incorporate evil *qua* evil for incentive into one's maxim" and *do* things "*diabolical*"

(6:37), but still remain human, not a "*diabolical* being" (6:35), Kant rejects without explanation.[2]

War on "Radical Evil"

Can war on evil promise redemption without grasping what evil is? Waging a war on evil one has not understood can be just as stupid as trying to destroy the ring of power in J. R. R. Tolkien's trilogy *The Lord of the Rings* by thinking that some good folks can safeguard the ring by attacking it with a hammer. Any naive externalization of evil proves to be dangerous in that it is attached to its own ignorance. No more needs to be said of Tolkien's story, which has become a great movie hit but whose point remains lost on the crowd. In what follows, I want to question the very notion of *war on evil*, whether it is defined in political terms (evil empire, axis of evil, evil ruler) or sacral terms (jihad on Great Satan, evil people targeted by a suicide bomber).

The significance of Kant's foregoing discussion is that it exposes all externalizations of evil as *morally* deficient. If a discourse on evil fails to be moral in Kant's sense, it certainly cannot be religious in Kierkegaard's sense either. This conclusion would be true regardless of whether or not we embarked on translating Kierkegaard's religious categories into secular ones. Those who externalize evil become doubly removed from religious categories even prior to any attempt at translation: first, one fails to account for the origin of evil in human will, thereby falling behind the ethical to aesthetic sense of 'evil'; and second, since one cannot root out evil at the core of the human self by projecting it outside of free will, one wages a war of annihilation on projections.

Kierkegaard helps us distinguish between the aesthetic and ethical significance of evil. He agrees with Kant that good and evil are categories only imputable to free will. Good and evil arise for human beings with the question of their radical self-choice—What am I? What shall I become? To pose the question with absolute earnestness delivers me from aesthetic drift into an ethical stage of existing where good and evil qualify the mode of all my willing. This movement from stage to stage is not like a pledge of allegiance to this or that domain or flag or cause; it requires inward (existential) self-transformation of my willing. Kant's moral point of view presupposes responsible individuals who no longer flow with the immediacy of external (sensuous) identifications but who become the autonomous origins of all value-positing.

An aesthete might consider boredom to be the root of all evil, and he might embark on an elaborate method of self-evasion and external change. An aesthetic war on evil would be akin to a rotation method of crops (Kierkegaard, *EO* I:291)[3]—perhaps a regime change—but with no existential grasp of good and evil. The external, even though religiously inflected public discourse on evil not only fails to grasp Kierkegaard's view of religiousness, but also the Kantian moral significance of radical evil: wars on evil are but the aesthetic rotation of likes and dislikes. But "an aesthetic choice is no choice. . . . [T]o choose is an intrinsic and stringent term for the ethical" (*EO* II: 166). The aesthetic choice, by being purely external, gets lost in immediacy and multiplicity but with no inner "transfiguration" of willing (167). The external assault on evil shows certain "aesthetic earnestness," so we do get taken in by public moralizers. And especially in public externalizations of the enemy, "evil is perhaps never as seductively effective as when it steps forth in aesthetic categories." The ethical earnestness should preclude one from speaking of "evil in aesthetic categories." Yet we only need to study "the predominantly aesthetic culture of our day" that values such talk of evil. Consider a discourse on evil that produces in the speaker an eye-twinkle of excitement (the nether side of boredom that moves the speaker as well as pleases the crowd) when describing an execution of the criminal or destruction of the enemy. Mass culture provides a platform to "moralizers [who] rant against evil in such a way that we perceive that the speaker, although he praises the good, nevertheless relishes the satisfaction that he himself could very well be the most cunning and wily of men but has rejected it on the basis of a comparison with being a good man" (226).

Significantly, Judge William, the ethicist in Kierkegaard's *Either/Or,* does not even "assume a radical evil" in his radical either/or choice between aesthetic and ethical ways of life. Judge William, even as he admits that one can repent oneself back into ethical life, stops short of considering Kant's late preoccupation with human incapacity to freely sustain good will. "Radical evil" is discussed by the pseudonymous authors created by Kierkegaard's for his later ethico-religious works because, if understood under the category of sin, it posits religious existence for the first time. Judge William confines himself to showing the difference between a life without any ethical axis and one that is self-governing (*EO* II: 174f). The aesthetic discourse on evil, loudly wishing God's wrath on evildoers, cannot root out evil, since it lacks the category of inwardness posited by ethical self-choice. The lack of inwardness leads to relations of "leveling reciprocity" (*TA* 63). The crowd is untruth, regardless of whether it is secular or sacral. An aesthetic, crowd-pleasing notion of evil embodies social evil in its own right: "The distinction between good and evil is enervated by a loose, supercilious, theoretical acquaintance with evil" (*TA* 78).[4]

This brings me to the second degree: through externalizing evil in political and religious discourses, one becomes removed from religious categories. That Kant concedes the radical perversity of the human heart while protecting the dignity of the human person is an advance over many a contemporary discourse on evil. He resists all attempts to demonize evil that would either assign it a face or brand as evil some group, sect, or people and then rally others to annihilate the evil brand by purifying the earth externally. Evil deeds also certify human dignity, for Kant even a dignity of a terrorist or tyrant, precisely in qualifying their evil choice as an act "against the [moral] law." By committing even an inhuman evil act, one does not thereby become a nonhuman species or vanquish the moral law within. "The human being (even the worst) does not repudiate the moral law, whatever his maxims, in rebellious attitude (by revoking obedience to it)" (6:36). The propensity to radical evil must be sought "in a free power of choice." "This evil is *radical,* since it corrupts the ground of all maxims. . . . Yet it must equally be possible to *overcome* this evil, for it is found in the human being as acting freely" (6:37). The political name for overcoming sectarian violence is a procedurally enacted tolerance to disagreement and an institutionally anchored league of nations based on perpetual peace.

Kant saves humans from having to demonize the face of evil. He warns us that by externalizing our struggles against evil, we have not attended to its root in human freedom. It is in free will—hence in the security council of a league of nations—where all struggle must be waged while standing armies yield to the normative procedures of perpetual peace. Violence enacted against evil externally breeds more evil. Strictly speaking, there are no evil empires/empires of Satan, no axes of evil/jihads against evil, no brand names or faces of evil. There is only an evil will. The league of nations, not war, therefore, should allow us to cultivate the public meaning- and will-formation through political dialogue and just procedures of international law. Preemptive or unilateral (nondialogic) acts against the imagined faces of evil make it impossible to overcome at its root the international propensity to radical evil—for Kant this root lies in human willing. Wars easily disguise empire-striving or factionalism under projections of evil they want to annihilate.

Discourse on evil followed by war on evil cannot promise redemption without grasping the root of evil. By externalizing evil, one remains doubly ignorant of what one wants to overcome. First, one deceives by employing religious language about external evil; then the aesthetic chatter about evil is followed by a failure to act morally. External war is an aesthetic rotation of the same. Second, when war on evil targets the faces of evil, human beings are demonized as nonhuman. Wars purify by outward cleansing, if not annihilation, of all deemed nonhuman. We know that this is a fantasy projection because war that begins with aesthetically abstracted or unchanged human beings "nonetheless creates more evil men than it takes away" (6:35). There is nothing redemptive or holy in war on evil.

"Radical Evil" within the Boundaries of Mere Reason?

A poster from a New York worldwide antiwar demonstration on February 16, 2003, proclaimed that if you want to be a cowboy, you've got to be smarter than the cows. Kierkegaard's religious Anti-Climacus says as much in his phenomenology of despair: "A cattleman who (if this were possible) is a self directly before his cattle is a very low self"; one gains "infinite reality" in "the self directly before God" (*SUD* 79). Ranting about evil, sin, and God aesthetically does not make one a self even ethically; indeed, one acts stupider than the cows.

Can any self-assessment of radical evil that wants to stay within the boundaries of mere reason, because it does not acknowledge its willfully bound free will, curb the existential roots of violence? Is violence a phenomenon that can be cured through enlightened forms of tolerance? Or must it be admitted that there is nothing wholly secular about violence? If violence betrays at its core religious significance, we need to determine what has been lost with the translation of the religious category of evil as sin into the moral significance of radical evil and into its rational overcoming. Can the discursive, moral and political, translation of religious contents—including Kant's translation of sin into a truce between unwavering enlightened respect for moral law and ongoing perversion of human willingness to obey it freely—arrest the impetus to violence that arises from radical evil?

Kant should not have equivocated the origins of evil choice by translating "sin" as "depravity" that could be overcome in time with our power of repentance into the light of reason and good will (6:39, 41–43). To await "a *revolution* in the disposition of the human being . . . and so a 'new man' . . . a kind of rebirth, as it were a new creation . . . and a change of heart," this Kant cannot postulate even morally. He invokes a gratuitous cooperation of "reflective" faith with available grace, but he does so without grasping how radical evil robs intellect and will of their natural light and willingness—how we become more confused by the very use of rational light, more bound by our free will (6:47, 52f.). Kant's human-all-too-human way of talking about the epistemic and moral effects of "sin" hides the *radical* root of radical moral evil.

Perhaps our present age will shrug its shoulders at wanting to preserve religion, even within Kant's limits of human reason, as at best past its time, and at worst, boring. Nobody cares about *rational* religion anymore, certainly not atheists; to be sure, not fundamentalists. Kant (6:43) and Kierkegaard agree that evil, just as freedom, is a rationally inscrutable and self-propelling existential whole, a moment of leap (*CA* 21, 50, 30, 112, 161; *SUD* 106f.).[5] Yet the enlightened notion of rationalized evil is both existentially counterintuitive and historically falsified: radical evil in the post-Kantian age has remained anywhere but within rational boundaries. If human evil as we know it in the last hundred years has been transgressing all rational frames, then is there anything wholly secular about violence? The radicalness of radical evil must be clarified outside of the safe boundaries of mere reason.

Kant fears to name as "diabolical" radical evil that humans bring into the world. He aims to preserve the dignity of human self-legislative reason and good will as more originary than the propensity of actual free will to do evil. He keeps open the metaphysical access of even corrupted free will to moral repentance, as if grace always and already sustained progress and transformation of the human race.[6]

Kierkegaard acknowledges sin as the beginning of religious life. Derrida reaches the same conclusion when he says that "the possibility of *radical evil* both destroys and institutes the religious."[7] De Vries views this at once Kierkegaardian and Derridean-Levinasian difference from Kant in that "the 'spiritual' [the best] and the 'demonic' [the worst] occupy [structurally] the same 'space'."[8] Yet religiously speaking, despair grasped as sin is essentially a category that cannot be translated into secular or even moral language without softening the issue of radical evil altogether. The sin-category discloses the radical limit of repenting oneself back to the ethical sphere of existence by the light of one's reason and the moral reformation of free will. But this category still does not explain why radical evil—such as genocide or indiscriminate warfare—in humans should be said to reach "diabolical" intensities.

Kant shuddered at the possibility of a "diabolically" free human act: If I am unable ever to choose evil freely as my maxim, then I can never act, strictly speaking, "diabolically." With Kant, humans are safely off the "diabolical" hook. For this reason and contrary to this argument, it is not Kant who in the end saves human dignity by confining radical evil within the boundaries of mere reason. It is Kierkegaard who finds, in the dreaded capacity of humans to despair, the depth of human excellence (*SUD* 14f.). In order to become a self smarter than the cows and to speak about evil better than a cowboy would, one must acknowledge that one's existence unfolds before the infinite spirit. Kierkegaard saves human dignity, not by downplaying the possibility of "diabolical" extremes of human freedom (Kant's solution to the problem of evil), but rather by looking this possibility squarely in the face. This "diabolical" possibility attests in the same measure to the greatest intensity of human existence. By calling the most radical form of evil a defiance of unconditional love, Kierkegaard does not devalue the self to a nonhuman status. Rather, he builds on the Kantian moral basis for human dignity and then goes beyond Kant: Kierkegaard shows the greatest expansion of human dignity to lie in the category of "the theological self" (*SUD* 79). For Kierkegaard, the radicalness of radical evil inheres existentially in the possibilities of a human spirit that can say yes or no to the offer of unconditional love. To be "diabolical," then, is to reject emphatically the gift of creation, forgiveness, and love; this is "diabolical" because there is no rational explanation for a human person who wants to exist in defiance of the loving cosmos. Such defiance is at once a fully human expression of freedom and yet is no longer confined within the boundaries of mere reason. The despair of defiance does not render such a person nonhuman; nonetheless, to will to be oneself despairingly is to defy that the very ground of existence consists of love. Defiance makes no sense without this relationship of the rational and free self to the offer of unconditional love. It is precisely this rejection of such an offer that marks the "diabolical" extreme of human freedom. Paradoxically, then, the despair of defiance, the very "diabolical" possibility, attests to the most human and spiritual core of selfhood. The redemptive overcoming of evil lies, for Kierkegaard, in accepting unconditional love for oneself. Because he considers the radical evil of my acts as no longer confined within the bounds of mere reason, he can now confront evil at its root in one's despair. Far from externalizing evil (rejecting the aesthetic version of evil) and, with Kant, decidedly opposed to the dehumanization of evildoers (accepting the moral argument against the cowboy approach to evil), Kierkegaard's acknowledged possibility of "diabolical" freedom testifies to the spirit-self. The spirit-self embodies the most dignified humanity because therein one exists directly before God.

In reverse, aesthetic discourses on evil must be judged as masked forms of defiance that fall behind Kant's rational hope in moral *metanoia*. Aesthetic discourses on evil are always and already forms of demonic usurpation. When theft of fire from heaven hides behind a religiously flavored external war on evil, it becomes an act of willed ignorance about its own despair. At its highest pitch, the belligerent willingness to wage external war on evil is an act of defiance. The cowboys who wage external wars on evil, parading in religious costume and without grasping evil and yet bereft of minimal ethical capacity for repentance, disrespect even cows who are God's creation. Willed stupidity is "diabolical."[9]

I can draw a twofold conclusion from these findings. First, one cannot be defiantly related to an empty and meaningless cosmos. Defiance means that one always and already knows in one's heart what is being rejected and yet rejects that very certainty of the gift. In mythology, devils are not portrayed as intellectual atheists; they are spirit beings who insist on existing unloved and unloving. Hell is portrayed as a state of despair, not as intellectual doubt about God. Humans too despair in the most deep recesses of their spirit-self about accepting the unconditional gift of love—that is, that I exist before infinite spiritual reality, that my life without anxiety and despair is possible, that unconditional love is my redemptive possibility. Spirit-reality endows human free will with the possibility of choosing radical evil for its own sake and yet retaining human dignity. Kant did not consider this possibility seriously enough, and in his haste to protect us from the "diabolical" use of freedom, he diminished human dignity. In the first step out of despair, my enlightened reason and repentance yield to an acknowledgment of my defiantly despairing will.

Second, violence at its existential roots is neither aesthetic nor ethical, but spiritual disorder. External wars on despair and the rational forms of tolerating and resolving conflicts cannot suffice to heal this disorder. In the second step out of despair, after owning my defiance and thus willing to be myself, I yield to detachment from my despairing willing to be myself.

Concepts such as violence, evil, and redemption are related yet distinct religious categories that cannot be translated into secular languages without watering down the radicalness of radical evil. Yet this untranslatability does not diminish the dignity of rational and moral beings. By refusing to set the fact of evil within the boundaries of mere reason, by grasping what it is we pray for when we want deliverance and purification, we are able to restore greater dignity to humans than in the confines of cowboy wars on evil or mere tolerance of conflict. I have considered the issue of evil immanently in a reverse order: Can enlightenment tolerance deter sectarian conflicts? Can perpetual peace be achieved by secular means alone? If both answers were 'no,' then modern ethnic, nationalist, and religious violence must be grasped as postsecular phenomena. This situation calls, in turn, not for more secular translations, but rather for a religious critique of the public discourses on violence, evil, and redemption: *a redemptive critical theory*.

I started with a suspicion that modern translations of religious contents into moral procedures—that is, secularization of sin—could resolve the problem of sectarian violence through tolerance alone. I questioned the claim that with the modern secularization of worldviews we have overcome the sectarian conflict of beliefs. With Kierkegaard's aesthetic, ethical, and religious senses of evil, I defended two theses about violence and evil against two claims about secularization and redemption: (1) there is nothing redemptive or holy in external war on evil, and (2) there is nothing wholly secular about violence.

Postsecular Consequences of "Radical Evil"

The process of secularization gradually translates sacred or traditional beliefs into publicly redeemable validity claims, thus overcoming the problem of intolerance and violence.[10] Yet if the outcome of this process is a degree of emptiness that renders human existence unlivable, can the vanishing point of secularization offer a true path to uprooting sectarian intolerance and violence? Another way of posing this question: "Is secularized consciousness capable of living without redemptive hope?" Can humans exist without wonder and mystery? Can humans flourish without inhering in the cosmos that receives them and in that embrace stimulates their freedom to find their vocation? What is the dimension of time and space that secular consciousness opens for us? While there is no issue here about deflating the rational argument for tolerance, ultimately the possibility of uprooting violence must go to the heart of intolerance, which arises even in secular existence from willed forms of despair. The answer to the question, "Is secularized consciousness capable of living without redemptive hope?" is not whether it wants to keep rooting out the most entrenched source of violence, but if it *can*.

The twentieth century witnessed unparalleled violence inflicted by secular societies. Our fascination with retributive death-dealing and war, our desire to purify the world of all evil—these are hardly secular ambitions. If modern violence inflicts wounds at the core of a fully secularized consciousness, how can the argument for rationally achieved tolerance carry the day? How can secularization be an answer to violence at the heart of secularized consciousness? The argument for tolerance addresses one side of the issue, but it fails to reach the core of violence in secularized consciousness. The side that the argument does address well is how to resolve the clash of belief systems or of civilizational values. The process of secularization is a self-correcting process of learning whereby we come to view our differences without the need to annihilate or assimilate them. Even secular consciousness can learn to exist with the religious one; thus, tolerance can flourish even in postsecular societies where different belief systems coexist with a fully secularized consciousness. Believers can learn from the process of secularization of the value of tolerance, as they must vie for their autonomy on procedural grounds of secular society.

But violence can and does arise at the heart of a fully secularized consciousness. Violence arises in postsecular societies that did have their share of sectarian hatred. Does it not mean, then, that there are dimensions of violence not curable on the path of secularization? If that is so, what can secular translation alone do to cure violence, especially the ongoing need for retribution, revenge, and war? If an impetus to violence comes from newly sacralized rage against human finitude, disease, fallibility, death, then how can secularization bring us more sobriety?[11]

If violence has to do with the need to purify oneself and the world of evil—if evil is defined as human finitude and mortality—there is nothing entirely secular about such violent flight from this evil.[12] By calling violence a sacralized rage against the evil of finitude and death, I do not mean that all religions are motivated by hate. On the contrary, I am saying that secular integrations are not sober about the sources of their ongoing violence.

In all religious traditions there is another route to sobriety: admit my finitude and death; face my own inability to sustain free existence; hope for redemption but first give up my heroic rage against the cosmos for inflicting on me the evil of my finitude and death. Therein lies the nonviolent core of great spiritual traditions. It leads by way of divestment, detachment, openness to the cosmos, acceptance of one's vocational place in the larger unknown of the mysterious universe, self-forgiveness of one's finitude and even mortality, yielding to the sources of unconditional love, and embracing the works of such love as a way to healing all that suffers.

To curb our propensity for violence on the other side of secularization— whether or not we actually coexist in postsecular societies with a mix of religious and secular attitudes or live already in postmodern fundamentalist revivals— requires a spiritual corrective to both religious and secular validity domains alike. Such a corrective would fund the core motive and intuition behind what I would like to call *redemptive critical theory,* or *redemptive critique.* Any postsecular redemptive reality must come to terms with human finitude and death— without inflicting pain and violence on others in the process of escaping mortality and without needing to purify the world of such projected and feared evil. This redemptive reality is postsecular because it affects both secularized and religious consciousness; still it is a redemptive reality rather than a belief system because no present validity domain knows how to secure redemption without reproducing the attraction and terror of death-dealing violence.

Intolerance is at bottom a claim that my or our way is the ultimate path to redemption for others to follow. This arrogant blind spot does not bypass secular consciousness. Redemptive reality cannot be a validity claim—whether one means a belief proposition about redemption or raises claims to be "redeemed" in public discourse. Our waiting and working to hasten the realization of the not yet cannot depend on any validity domain, even the messianic one. The redeemed reality is not won by redeeming an unconditioned claim.

We do not own the shape of redeemed reality; we can only come to exist in it. Such reality is, after all, a matter of gift, grace, faith, hope, and love. Yet in redemptive criticism, we are not left resting in some quietist paralysis. On the contrary, we must actively engage the false religious beliefs in the ultimate shape of the gift as well as the secular translations that all such false beliefs can be redeemed now in the form of public discourse on the criticizable validity claims. There is a double acoustical illusion (*PF* 49–54) that issues from religious belief claims about redemption as well as their secular translations. Redemptive criticism would serve to deter the violence of these twin illusions, a violence they inevitably inflict on others. But this would be a deterrent without calling for retributive death or holy war.[13]

Notes

1. References to Immanuel Kant, "Religion Within the Boundaries of Mere Reason" (1793), will be cited parenthetically by marginal numbers of the German edition of Kant's works. *Religion and Rational Theology,* trans. and ed. Allen W. Wood and George Di Giovanni (Cambridge: Cambridge University Press, 1996), pp. 55–215.

2. On contemporary discussions of radical evil relevant to my discussion, see Joan Copjec, ed., *Radical Evil* (London: Verso, 1996), p. xv; Jacques Derrida, *Given Time: I. Counterfeit Money,* trans. Peggy Kamuf (Chicago: University of Chicago Press, 1992), p. 165 n. 31; idem, "Faith and Knowledge: The Two Sources of 'Religion' at the Limits of Reason Alone," in *Acts of Religion,* ed. Gil Anidjar (London: Routledge, 2002), pp. 48–53, 77, 100; Ronald M. Green, *Kierkegaard and Kant: The Hidden Debt* (Albany: State University of New York Press, 1992), pp. 64–68, 156–80, 193–95, 273 n. 113; María Pía Lara, ed., *Rethinking Evil: Contemporary Perspectives* (Berkeley: University of California Press, 2001); Keiji Nishitani, "What Is Religion?" in *Religion and Nothingness,* trans. Jan Van Bragt (Berkeley: University of California Press, 1982), pp. 22–30; Jacob Rogozinski, "It Makes Us Wrong: Kant and Radical Evil," in *Radical Evil,* ed. Joan Copjec (London: Verso, 1996), pp. 30–45; Paul Ricoeur, *Figuring the Sacred: Religion, Narrative, and Imagination,* trans. David Pellauer, ed. Mark I. Wallace (Minneapolis: Fortress Press, 1995), chaps. 4, 11, 14; and Hent de Vries, *Religion and Violence: Philosophical Perspectives from Kant to Derrida* (Baltimore, Md.: Johns Hopkins University Press, 2002), pp. 102–22, 156, 160–75.

3. References to Kierkegaard's texts will be made parenthetically, using the following abbreviations:

CA: *The Concept of Anxiety,* ed. and trans. Howard V. Hong and Edna H. Hong (Princeton, N.J.: Princeton University Press, 1980).
EO: *Either/Or, Part I and Part II,* ed. and trans. Howard V. Hong and Edna H. Hong (Princeton, N.J.: Princeton University Press, 1987).
PF: *Philosophical Fragments,* ed. and trans. Howard V. Hong and Edna H. Hong (Princeton, N.J.: Princeton University Press, 1985).
SUD: *The Sickness Unto Death,* ed. and trans. Howard V. Hong and Edna H. Hong (Princeton, N.J.: Princeton University Press, 1980).
TA: *Two Ages: The Age of Revolution and the Present Age. A Literary Review,* ed. and trans. Howard V. and Edna H. Hong (Princeton, N.J.: Princeton University Press, 1978).

4. See also Martin J. Matuštík, *Postnational Identity: Critical Theory and Existential Philosophy in Habermas, Kierkegaard, and Havel* (New York: Guilford, 1993), Part III.

5. Cf. Green, *Kierkegaard and Kant,* pp. 160–63, 64f.

6. On Kant's fear of the "diabolical," see Derrida, *Given Time,* p. 165 n. 31, and "Faith and Knowledge," p. 49; de Vries, p. 171.

7. Derrida, "Faith and Knowledge," p. 100.

8. De Vries, p. 162; cf. pp. 105, 108f, 170f.

9. Derrida traces the sense of "diabolical" cruelty and unforgivable evil that "calls for forgiveness," and that "Kant does not want to acknowledge," to *bêtise,* or stupidity, in *Given Time,* p. 166 n. 31. Cf. Kierkegaard, who, in *The Sickness unto Death,* calls sin a willed or motivated form of ignorance, i.e., stupidity.

10. Jürgen Habermas, "Zum Friedenspreis des deutschen Buchhandels: Eine Dankrede," delivered October 14, 2001, at Frankfurt's Paulskirche on the occasion of receiving the Peace Award of the German Publishers; printed in *Süddeutsche Zeitung,* October 15, 2001. English translation: "Faith and Knowledge," in *The Future of Human Nature,* trans. Hella Beister and Max Pensky (Cambridge: Polity Press, 2003), pp. 101–115.

11. When I posed this question to Habermas in the fall of 2002 at the Northwestern conference to honor Charles Taylor, he had nothing to say.

12. See Ernest Becker, *Escape from Evil* (New York: Free Press, 1975).

13. The redemptive reality does not deliver us to a messianic figure who signals radical apocalyptic change. Such apocalyptic change often suffuses desire to rid the earth of all evil and leads to outward heroic projects to do the same in the name of the expected change. The redemptive messianic reality has at once a prophetic and existential structure: Humans in their drama must decide on the course of action, and they alone must learn to curb their desire for the mastery of the unknown reality. As Sandor Goodhart suggested to me in a conversation on this topic, redemption arrives to us when we have worked out all issues of responsibility in our freedom, when, in that freedom, we no longer need to master the apocalyptic change by pursuing evil outwardly. Then redemption issues in concrete existence when the apocalyptic messiah no longer needs to be posited as a value or heroic project. I discuss how the prison abuses in Abu Ghraib reveal the dangers of "heroic projects" like the US war on terror in "America's Prayer," *Open Democracy,* June 3, 2004 at www.opendemocracy.com/debates/article-3-77-1938.jsp.

5   Disenchantment and the Persistence of Evil: Habermas, Jonas, Badiou

Peter Dews

It is easy to understand why Hannah Arendt, as a philosopher of German-Jewish origin, felt compelled to declare in 1945 that "the problem of evil will be the fundamental question of postwar intellectual life in Europe."[1] But, as Richard Bernstein bluntly observes in his book on Arendt, "she was wrong. Most postwar intellectuals avoided any direct confrontation with the problem of evil."[2] Bernstein, however, seems to regard this merely as a curious omission or failing on the part of intellectuals after the Second World War. Correspondingly, he treats Arendt's continued preoccupation with the problem of evil as requiring philosophical clarification, but not as fundamentally problematic. Yet this is surely mistaken.

To the contrary, I want to suggest that the supposed failure of postwar intellectuals was, in fact, the response to a deep cultural and intellectual dilemma. On the one hand, we often feel impelled to resort to the notion of evil in describing events such as those that occurred at Auschwitz—no other term seems adequate to our sense of the violation of the most elementary ethical conditions of a human existence. Yet on the other hand, in the disenchanted and predominantly secularized West, the religious assumptions—however implicit—that gave the notion of evil its place in our thinking about the world, as the violation of a divinely sanctioned order, are no longer shared by the majority of people. This is a dilemma that Arendt herself was forced to confront.

In February 1951, she sent Karl Jaspers a prepublication copy of *The Origins of Totalitarianism*. In their correspondence, resumed after a long hiatus enforced by the Second World War, the two philosophers had, of course, engaged in intense discussion of recent events in Europe and of the nature of the Nazi regime. Arendt had prefaced the book with an epigraph from Jaspers, and he immediately sent back a brief letter thanking her. He expressed his eagerness to come to grips with the whole work and praised the foreword and conclusion, at which he had already glanced. But he ended his letter with an enigmatic question: "Hasn't Jahweh faded too far out of sight?"[3]

In her reply to Jasper's question, Arendt admitted that traditional religion—

whether Jewish or Christian—held nothing for her. But she also affirmed: "I make my way through life with a kind of (childish? because unquestioned) trust in God (as distinguished from faith, which always thinks it knows and therefore has to cope with doubts and paradoxes)."[4] But this reply seems hasty and inadequate. One cannot help feeling that the blitheness of the trust in God that Arendt expresses here is incompatible with her own sense of the moral catastrophe of totalitarianism. After Auschwitz, one might ask, what kind of relation to God could there be that would *not* be fraught with doubt and paradox?

I

In what follows, I want to examine how this tension between a moral vocabulary and the deeper convictions required to nourish and sustain it can be found in the work of three leading thinkers of the present and the recent past: Jürgen Habermas, Hans Jonas, and Alain Badiou. The basic philosophical orientations of these thinkers are quite divergent. Their work offers, one might say, three contrasting answers to the problem of how ethical reflection can be sustained in the face of the traumas of the twentieth century. Yet I believe it can be shown that each oeuvre displays, in different ways, an intellectual strain that may be symptomatic of our culture in general. But before beginning, we must take a brief backward glance toward the late eighteenth century. For it seems clear that Immanuel Kant must be regarded as the first formulator of the modern problem of evil, and hence as the first cartographer of this terrain.

In a relatively late work, *Religion within the Limits of Reason Alone,* Kant introduced the notion of "radical evil." This expression has often been misunderstood as referring to particularly horrendous forms of moral violation, and in fact this is how Arendt takes the term in *The Origins of Totalitarianism.* But what Kant means by "radical evil" is simply an evil that lies at the very root of human nature. On his account, human beings have a "propensity to evil," an intrinsic tendency to prioritize their particular interests over the universalizable requirements of the moral law. In fact, no immoral act could ever occur had not human beings made a timeless "choice" to allow the precedence of self-centered interests over moral duty. But the pervasiveness of this "perversity" of the human heart, which runs against our own equally intrinsic "predisposition" to respect the categorical imperative, then confronts Kant with a dilemma. For if the human will is intrinsically corrupt by virtue of our fundamental choice of an "evil" nature or intelligible character, how could it ever reverse the inverted priority of particular and universal and set itself back on the path to purity?

Kant finds that the only way to address this question is by resorting to a religious vocabulary. As he writes in the "General Observation" appended to Book 1, "Reason, conscious of her inability to satisfy her moral need, extends herself to high-flown ideas capable of supplying this lack, without, however, appropriating these ideas as an extension of her domain."[5] More specifically, Kant argues that the moral conversion that we cannot achieve through our own efforts must be regarded as a gift of grace. But at the same time, we cannot rely on grace or even anticipate it, for to do so would be to deny the obligation to strive for moral self-transformation through our own efforts. Hence, Kant reaches a paradoxical conclusion:

> Even the hypothesis of a *practical* application of this idea [of grace] is wholly self-contradictory. For the employment of this idea would presuppose a rule concerning the good that (for a particular end) we ourselves must *do* in order to accomplish something, whereas to await a work of grace means exactly the opposite, namely, that the good (the morally good) is not our deed but the deed of another being, and that we therefore can *achieve* it only by doing nothing, which contradicts itself. Hence we can admit a work of grace as something incomprehensible, but we cannot adopt it into our maxims either for theoretical or for practical use.[6]

It is scarcely surprising that, despite this cautious relation to traditional religious concepts, some of Kant's more progressive contemporaries regarded him as having betrayed his commitment to the Enlightenment in his book on religion. In a letter to Herder, Goethe wrote that Kant had "criminally smeared his philosopher's cloak with the shameful stain of radical evil, after it had taken him a long human life to cleanse it from many a dirty prejudice, so that Christians too might yet be enticed to kiss its hem."[7] The judgment that the concept of evil that Kant proposes is essentially a Christian residue, a reformulation of "original sin," has been repeated up to the present day. Most contemporary Kantians, for example, appear to believe that they can provide a reworked version of Kant's rational grounding of morality without referring substantively to the concept of evil.

II

The work of Jürgen Habermas is a good example of this approach. For though Habermas has pioneered the dialogical reformulation of Kant's moral philosophy in his "discourse ethics," he has had little to say about the question of evil. His whole effort has been directed toward developing an account of the normative bases of morality that appeals only to shared human communicative capacities and is therefore independent of any religious perspective on our moral nature. But if Habermas's silence is understandable from a purely philosophical point of view, it is less so in terms of the deep political motivation of his life's work. For Habermas's thought as a whole can be seen as a response to the moral disaster that befell the German nation in the form of Nazism. In autobiographical discussions he has described the forging of his basic political and moral convictions amidst the ruins of Germany immediately after the war. A teenager at that time, Habermas's outrage and distress was aroused by the repressive normalization of German society, the refusal to engage honestly with what had occurred. Philosophically, Habermas's efforts have always been directed toward the reconstruction of a different German intellectual tradition, or rather the recovery of a countertradition, strongly Judaic in its sources of inspiration, that can be opposed to the antirationalism and regressive antimodernism—that "Teutonic brew of vague and deep thoughts," as he has described it, that has been such a dominant strain in the history of German thought. For Habermas, in other words, an emphatic rescue and defense of the Enlightenment heritage is to provide one of the essential bulwarks against the possibility of a return to the horrors of the past.

It is difficult not to sympathize with this project and its motivation. But at the same time, one cannot help asking: If the moral structures of modernity are vulnerable to the kind of disintegration that occurred under Hitler, what gives Habermas the confidence that the universalism of modern moral consciousness can indeed become stably anchored and will remain steadfast even in the face of adverse social and economic developments in the future? Habermas himself has recently stated that the growth of the economic underclass, if left unchecked, will result in what he terms a "moral erosion of society . . . which cannot help but damage the universalistic core of any republican community."[8] But given the possibility of such regression, one can ask a further question: Do not the moral catastrophes of the twentieth century highlight a potential for breakdown in the ethical capacities of human beings, a susceptibility to perversion that must be reckoned with in *any* philosophical perspective? Is Habermas being short-sighted in assuming he can develop a theory of ethics based on the notion of communicative consensus, while screening out all questions concerning our fundamental moral constitution?

A version of this question can also be posed at the level of Habermas's discourse theory. For on his account, such a theory can only demonstrate the *possibility* of a universalistic moral point of view. It cannot prescribe the content of morality, which is dependent on everyday intuitions, but only a procedure of discussion for settling disputes when consensus breaks down. "The moral intuitions of everyday life," Habermas states at one point, "are not in need of clarification by the philosopher."[9] At the same time, in less formal contexts, Habermas has spoken of the fate of what he terms a "primal anthropological trust," "an underlying layer of solidarity in the face-to-face relations of human beings" on which we rely despite all the "bestialities of world history." This basis of trust, he suggests, was destroyed by the gas chambers, since "the monstrous occurred, without interrupting the calm respiration of everyday life."[10] It might be noticed that this destruction of anthropological trust is also central to Arendt's account of the unprecedented character of what occurred under the Nazis. In her book on the Eichmann trial she writes:

> Just as the law in civilized countries assumes that the voice of conscience tells everybody "Thou shalt not kill," even though man's natural desires and inclinations may be murderous, so the law of Hitler's land demanded that the voice of conscience tell everybody: "Thou shalt kill," although the organizers of the massacres knew full well that murder is against the normal desires and inclinations of most people. Evil in the Third Reich had lost the quality by which most people recognize it, the quality of temptation.[11]

In Habermas's case at least, reliance on the ethical fabric of everyday life that, on his own admission, *may* have become hopelessly corrupted indicates an unresolved problem—one that has been seized on by his colleague Karl-Otto Apel. With a fervor that ultimately springs from his own response to the traumas of German history in the twentieth century, Apel argues against Habermas that it is not adequate simply to demonstrate the *formal* possibility of a universalistic moral viewpoint. The existence of an obligation to adopt and promote this point of view must also be demonstrated philosophically. For Apel, one must be capable of "affirming through rational insight the universal validity claim of a postconventional discourse ethics of responsibility."[12] Apel's basic philosophical proposal, which he repeats in many variations, is that anyone who seriously puts up for discussion the question "Why should I be moral?" has already de facto recognized the moral norms that make it possible to achieve an answer through discussion.[13] These are the norms of equality and reciprocity of participation that are the preconditions of dialogue oriented toward achieving a true consensus.

To this criticism Habermas replies that the universal rules of discourse are not *moral* norms and that the crucial role of morality in human life cannot be *grounded* philosophically. At best, the existential meaning of morality, its capacity to inspire action, can be elucidated through what Habermas terms "the world-disclosing power of prophetic speech, indeed of every innovative language that initiates a better form of life, a more self-aware conduct of life."[14] Yet it is striking that Habermas seeks to guard against any contamination of philosophical discourse by prophetic speech, stressing that "world-disclosing arguments, which bring us to see things in a radically new light, are not *essentially* philosophical arguments."[15] This is strange, because one might have assumed that—even for Habermas—it would be far less risky to entrust the integrity of moral life to a conceptually filtered, rather than a philosophically unmonitored prophetic speech. Thus the strictness of Habermas's distinction between philosophical and religious discourse at this point highlights his insistence on what he terms the "*methodological atheism* . . . of every philosophical appropriation of essential religious contents."[16]

In fact, Habermas's current philosophical position is characterized by a distinctive division of labor. On the one hand, he is convinced that philosophy must be able to survive on conceptual resources that are compatible with our situation in a disenchanted world. As he puts it: "The basic concepts of religion and metaphysics had relied upon a syndrome of validity [i.e., a fusion of cognitive and evaluative claims—P.D.] that dissolved with the emergence of expert cultures in science, morality and law, on the one hand, and with the autonomization of art on the other."[17] But on the other hand, he realizes that the meaning of the moral life can be illuminated, and moral motivation sustained, only by drawing on the traditions, including the religious traditions, of a culture. As he writes: "I do not believe that we, as Europeans, can seriously understand concepts like morality and ethical life, person and individuality, or freedom and emancipation, without appropriating the substance of the Judeo-Christian understanding of history in terms of salvation. . . . Others begin from other traditions to find their way to the plenitude of meaning involved in concepts such as these."[18] In other words, under the conditions of a pluralistic culture, our fundamental moral vocabulary cannot afford to remain *dependent on* specific religious doctrines or sources of revelation, although it may continue to be *energized by* them. The task of philosophy is to translate religious insights and impulses into terms that are capable of a shared discursive justification.

III

But can this task be carried through? The work of Hans Jonas, another thinker exemplifying the tensions I outlined at the beginning, might give cause to doubt it. Whereas Habermas proposes a "translation programme" for religious discourse, Jonas is a believer. An early pupil of Heidegger and lifelong friend of Hannah Arendt, he developed, in some of his later writings, a speculative and confessedly mythical account of God's relation to the world, specifically in response to the unprecedented evil that befell the Jewish people in the twentieth century. Jonas's studies in biology and cosmology led him to the view that it is impossible to account for the evolution of life—from its most primitive stages up to the fully reflexive consciousness of human beings—without presupposing that some implicit spark of freedom and awareness was already present at the beginning of creation. Hegel too, of course, has this idea, with his conception of nature as commencing from the extreme point of the self-alienation of mind. But for Jonas, Hegel's account of the ensuing process is intolerably optimistic: "The disgrace of Auschwitz," he affirms, "is not to be charged to some all-powerful providence or to some dialectically wise necessity, as if it were an antithesis demanding a synthesis or a step on the road to salvation."[19] In place of Hegel's account, Jonas suggests that, at the beginning of things, God "abandoned Himself and his destiny entirely to the outwardly exploding universe and thus to the pure chances of the *possibilities* contained in it under the conditions of space and time. Why He did this remains unknowable. We are allowed to speculate that it happened because *only* in the endless play of the finite, and in the inexhaustibility of chance, in the surprises of the unplanned, *and* in the distress caused by mortality, can mind experience itself in the variety of its possibilities. For this the deity had to renounce His own power."[20]

One crucial consequence of this conception is that God cannot be reproached for the failure to intervene in order to prevent the horror of Auschwitz. For God has handed over responsibility for history to human beings, and both the nameless evil of the Holocaust and the solitary, miraculous acts of devotion and sacrifice that mitigated against it must be attributed to human beings alone. This does not mean, however, that God stood by indifferently as the moral catastrophe occurred, like the divine watchmaker of eighteenth-century deism. On the contrary, Jonas's God is not merely a suffering and becoming divinity, but also a *caring* divinity. Jonas writes:

> This I like to believe: that there was weeping in the heights at the waste and despoilment of humanity; . . . "The voice of thy brother's blood cries unto me from the ground": Should we not believe that the immense chorus of such cries that has risen up in our lifetime now hangs over our world as a dark and accusing cloud? that eternity looks down upon us with a frown, wounded itself and perturbed in its depths?[21]

In some respects, Jonas's approach appears superior to that of Habermas, since it avoids the latter's discomfiting split between the rational procedures of philosophy and the "semantic resources" of the religious tradition. It does so by developing an account of evil that is self-confessedly mythical and yet not—at least in Jonas's view—merely fictional. As he writes: "Such is the tentative myth which I would like to believe 'true'—in the sense in which myth may happen to adumbrate a truth which of necessity is unknowable and even, in direct concepts, ineffable, yet which, by intimations to our deepest experience, lays claim upon our powers of giving indirect account of it in revocable, anthropomorphic images."[22] From the point of view of Habermas's Critical Theory, however, Jonas's approach must, in its turn, give cause for concern. For if such a mythical narrative can communicate "truth," even in an oblique form, then to conform to the expectations of modernity, this truth must be translatable into more generally accessible and acknowledgeable terms.

Although Habermas himself has not commented on Jonas's myth, a response *has* been offered by his colleague Albrecht Wellmer, who in some respects pushes the commitment of Critical Theory to "post-metaphysical thinking" further than Habermas himself thinks wise to go. Wellmer's response is in many ways powerful and of direct relevance to our central topic. In his essay "Jonas's Myth of the God who Suffers and Becomes," he argues that since, as Jonas himself admits, the mythic imagery of his account cannot be transformed into a new *metaphysics* that could actually *support* moral claims, it is more plausible to interpret Jonas's speculations as the "metaphorical *expression* of an ethical self-understanding, rather than as its possible foundation."[23] Wellmer writes: "My suspicion is that, insofar as it can be retrieved in philosophical-conceptual terms, Jonas's myth of a God caught up in becoming is indistinguishable from a position of radical finitude. What makes this myth of a becoming God, who externalizes himself in the world so convincing—by contrast with all positive theology—is that it takes the finitude of human beings seriously and thereby takes up a basic theme of the modern, post-Nietzschean critique of metaphysics."[24] Thus, for Wellmer, Jonas's account of a God who surrenders to plurality and contingency can be translated into what he calls a "thesis of radical finitude," namely, that "it is intrinsic to the concept of mind that it be connected to individuated—finite—particular beings; indeed, in such a way that the conditions of naturalness and finitude are not only limits of the human mind and human possibilities, but *at the same* time and *indissolubly* the conditions of everything that we call 'mind,' 'knowledge,' 'truth,' 'good will,' or even 'linguistic meaning.'"[25]

Wellmer finds confirmation of this interpretation in certain arguments that Jonas himself develops—in his well-known essay "The Concept of God after Auschwitz"—against the onto-theological conception of God. Jonas suggests, for example, that the notion of absolute power is logically incoherent, since "power meeting no *resistance* in its relatum is equal to no power at all: power is exercised only in relation to something that itself has power."[26] Similarly, Wellmer argues, all the idealizing notions of metaphysics—absolute power, absolute freedom, even Habermas's ideal speech situation—must succumb to a thought of radical finitude in which contingency and negativity remain essential, insuperable conditions of the positive and the ideal.

Toward the end of his essay, Wellmer then tries to show that, if followed through, the thought of radical finitude—that he takes Jonas to be expressing in mythical form—must block the possibility of transforming Jonas's imagery into a conceptually coherent metaphysical position. For example, Jonas obviously has to concede that the *possibility* of evil is contained in God, but he insists that this is only a possibility, else the notion of God's goodness—that he regards as essential—would be lost. But, Wellmer enquires, why does Jonas speak only of the possibility of evil? In accordance with the thought of radical finitude, must one not posit the *reality* of evil, in order to get any grip on the thought of a countervailing goodness?

The question is a penetrating one, for it raises crucial questions concerning the relation between mythical and conceptual modes of discourse, and how exactly an equilibrium is to be struck between them. Jonas often appears to believe that merely confessing the mythical character of his speculations will immunize them against conceptual dissection, yet it is undeniable that his myth gives no adequate account of the relation between finitude as such and moral evil. Undoubtedly, this is a deficiency in Jonas's account, though in fact the issue is addressed in some of the sources on which he tacitly draws, such as the thought of Schelling. But once we have seen what is at issue in Jonas's myth, then the question of finitude can be turned back against Wellmer. For in the last analysis, there is something strangely complacent about his "thesis of radical finitude." As we have seen, Wellmer writes as though the decoding of Jonas's myth would result in an unproblematic notion of "conditions of naturalness and finitude [that] are not only limits of the human mind and human possibilities, but *at the same* time and *indissolubly* the conditions of everything that we call 'mind,' 'knowledge,' 'truth,' 'good will,' or even 'linguistic meaning.'"[27] But to put matters in this way not only reveals a surprising insensitivity to the concerns of past thought, but almost seems to represent an abandonment of philosophy as such. For it is precisely the finite, natural beings' capacity to grasp truths that appear to transcend any spatial or temporal context, understand meanings whose objectivity seems independent of any psychological process of comprehension, and so on, that—through the ages—has aroused the perplexities with which philosophers have grappled. Extravagant and abstruse as Jonas's speculations may be, it requires only a little sympathy to see that their elaboration is driven by the pressure of genuine problems.

Against this it might be objected that, however genuine and enduring *some* of Jonas's problems may be, his central concern of reconciling evil and the existence of God must surely be regarded as generated by outmoded theistic assumptions. So it is fascinating to find that Wellmer's "position of radical finitude" in fact produces a version of the same "problem of evil." As we have seen, Wellmer suggests that the reality of evil—or the existence of the "non-good," as he terms it—is implied by the "finitude of the conditions under which alone we are able to use the concept of the ethically good." But he also hastens to add that we evidently cannot include something so "radically evil" as Auschwitz in this reality, for this would make it a condition of the good. Yet Wellmer makes no attempt to explain how the radically evil is to be distinguished from the merely evil or the non-good, so as to avoid such a morally destructive interdependence (significantly, Wellmer himself employs the word "blasphemous" in this context).

In fact, Wellmer finds himself in a dilemma. For he feels *morally* compelled to exclude a qualitatively distinguished "radical evil" from his general account of the contrastive meaning of concepts. But this raises the question of how such "radical evil" is itself to be identified, and here Wellmer has two equally unpalatable options. He can either claim that radical evil is recognized intuitively, in which case we can ask why this might not also be possible in the case of other concepts. Or he can claim that radical evil is recognized by virtue of its opposition to its own special contrastive partner, which we could call the "radically"—perhaps "unconditionally"—good. Neither solution sits well with Wellmer's other commitments, most obviously his rejection of absolute principles of any kind. We must conclude, it seems, that while Jonas's self-consciously mythico-religious discourse is undeniably problematic, as Wellmer insists (and Jonas's himself acknowledges that such discourse can no longer be taken simply at face value), it is not as straightforward as Wellmer assumes to ease our modern intellectual discomfort by providing a "radically finite" translation of such discourse. There remains something resonant, yet resistant to the secularizing impulse, in Jonas's approach to evil.

IV

But what if the problem lay with Wellmer's insistence on "radical finitude"? One might argue, after all, that the very term, if it is intended to suggest exclusive, unqualified finitude, is inconsistent with Wellmer's contrastive theory of concepts. Does not the appeal to radical finitude necessarily evoke a notion of the infinite, even if only as that from which we are cut off, as that of which we moderns are deprived? This is, in effect, the view of Alain Badiou. In his short, polemic book, *Ethics: An Essay on the Understanding of Evil,*[28] Badiou seeks to develop an account of evil applicable to the contemporary world. But as one might expect of a former Maoist, whose initial points of reference were Lacan and Althusser, he strives to do so within a framework that is antireligious, indeed, explicitly atheistic ("There is no God"). Furthermore, Badiou implies that to be truly antireligious, one must go beyond the complicity between finitude and transcendence that he regards as a pervasive mark of post-Heideggerian thought. This is why he attacks so vehemently the thought of Emmanuel Levinas, which has exerted such a powerful influence on the "turn to ethics" within contemporary European thought. Badiou argues that Levinas's appeal to a transcendent alterity as the source of ethical obligation puts ethics beyond philosophical deliberation. In fact, it also reveals ethics, as conventionally understood, to be an essentially religious notion, since the universalist aspiration of the modern discourse of "human rights" must also rely on an ultimately transcendent support. In response to the objection that Levinas's ethics is based precisely on the *singularity* of the face-to-face relation, Badiou points out that, for Levinas, "there can be no finite devotion to the non-identical if it is not sustained by the infinite devotion of the principle to that which subsists outside it. There can be no ethics without God the ineffable" (p. 22). In short, Levinas's orientation toward the divine cuts across all historical, social, and cultural difference; his thought is traduced when used in support of a vague, multiculturalist celebration of the "Other."

On Badiou's account, then, any universalist ethical orientation is suspect. And since he rejects such universalism, he also opposes what he calls "the idea of a consensual or a priori recognition of evil" (p. 61). Badiou goes on to argue that, in contemporary thought, the Nazi extermination of the European Jews has been set up as the paradigm of transgression of the moral law, as the very embodiment of "radical evil." But as he points out, the focus on one historical event, however monstrous, has contradictory effects. On the one hand, the particular crime of the final solution undergoes a "*mise en transcendence*" (p. 63); it becomes the "measure without measure," entirely comparable to Levinas's notion of the "Altogether-Other": "What the God of Levinas is to the evaluation of alterity (the Altogether-Other as incommensurable measure of the Other), the extermination is to the evaluation of historical situations (the Altogether-Evil as incommensurable measure of Evil)" (p. 62). But at the same time, the final solution also becomes the standard against which all other evil is assessed; it becomes the standard of comparison: "As the supreme negative example, this crime is inimitable, but every crime is an imitation of it" (p. 63).

From his resolutely atheist standpoint, Badiou proposes to give a different account of the nature of evil. The first surprising feature of this account, however, is that in many respects it is close to the Kantian thought that Badiou takes himself to be opposing. For Badiou rejects the notion of evil as the outcome of an overriding animal impulse. As he writes, "[Evil] must be distinguished from the violence that the human animal employs to persevere in its being, to pursue its interests—a violence that is *beneath* Good and Evil" (p. 66). In this respect, Badiou's thought remains within the Kantian lineage, where evil is regarded, not as weakness but as something willed, as the expression of a perversity in willing: "If Evil exists, we must conceive it from the starting point of the Good. Without consideration of the Good, and thus of truths, there remains only the cruel innocence of life" (p. 60). As this statement suggests, Badiou's basic image of human beings is also reminiscent of the Kantian picture (and indeed, I would argue, the Levinasian one). We are beings torn between two extremes, recalling Kant's distinction between the realm of necessity and the realm of freedom. These poles Badiou characterizes in terms of the opposition of "ordinary interests and disinterested interest," of "human animal and subject," and even of "mortal and immortal." But one crucial difference from Kant lies in the fact that Badiou does not also align these polarities with the distinction between particular and universal. On the contrary, he claims that "truths" only appear as singular; hence, "the only genuine ethics is of truths in the plural—or, more precisely, the only ethics is of processes of truth, of the labor which brings some truths into the world"(p. 28).

Now this claim raises an important question. For in the case of Kant, and of post-Kantian idealists such as Hegel and Schelling, evil is understood in terms of an inversion of principles that sets the particular above the universal. But in Badiou's case, truth itself is portrayed as a singular emergence, so that inversion, if it occurs, cannot take place in quite the same way. In fact, Badiou identifies three forms of evil. First, evil can consist in the *terror* produced by commitment to what he calls a "simulacrum" of truth. Such terror occurs when the supposed breakthrough of truth is related to the "closed particularity of an abstract set" (p. 74) rather than to the unspecifiable "void" that it reveals at the heart of a specific situation. Thus the breakthrough of the National Socialist "revolution" was addressed to the German *Volk;* it did not raise a claim to broader significance by negating the particularity of the situation from which it emerged. Second, evil can consist in the *betrayal* of a truth, a lack of the nerve and commitment required to pursue its implications as far as they will go. Finally, evil occurs in the form of *disaster* when the power of a truth is absolutized, in other words, when there is a failure to acknowledge that the situation in which a truth has emerged cannot be rendered fully transparent, that a truth-process cannot entirely appropriate, through nomination, its own contingent context.

It will be apparent that in Badiou's definition of his first form of evil, *terror,* there is in fact a gesture toward universality. Terror arises when a proclamation of truth is addressed to a determinate audience, rather than being addressed "to all" (p. 76). Thus, Badiou writes: "Every invocation of blood and soil, of race, of custom, of community, works directly against truths; and it is this very collection [*ensemble*] that is named as the enemy in the ethic of truths" (p. 76). At the same time, Badiou's third form of evil seems to consist precisely in the universalization of a truth, made possible by its detachment from its original context through an act of appropriation, of naming. As Badiou writes: "The Good is Good only to the extent that it does not aspire to render the world good. Its sole being lies in the situated advent of a singular truth. So it must be that the power of a truth is also a kind of powerlessness" (p. 85). And he continues: "That truth does not have total power means, in the last analysis, that the subject-language, the production of a truth-process, does not have the power to name all the elements of the situation." Hence, given this assumption, "every attempt to impose the total power of a truth ruins that truth's very foundation" (p. 83). This is the form of evil that Badiou describes as "*disaster*."

I will leave aside Badiou's third category of evil, *betrayal*, since I do not believe that it captures a genuine feature of evil. By "*betrayal*" Badiou means the failure to live up to and sustain the strenuous demands of a truth. For Badiou, truths occur in four fundamental domains: poetry, science, politics, and love. Hence, betrayal might take the form of falling out of love, for example, or of failing to pursue the implications of a novel scientific or political insight because of the personal cost. But while such events may exemplify various forms of human defeat and debility, I cannot see that they necessarily result in what we would call evil. I believe the real substance and the real tension in Badiou's account lie in his descriptions of terror and disaster.

Essentially, Badiou describes as "disaster" the appropriation by a truth of its own context or situation, which he regards as being—at its core—unnameable. But arguably, he only has to enter this caveat, because he is ultimately in search of truths that are both substantive and disruptive, on the one hand, and yet in some way generalizable, on the other. Badiou describes everyday communication as the circulation of a tissue of "opinion" that is capable of neither truth nor falsity and that is pierced through and disorganized by the emergence of a new truth: "Every truth, as we have seen, deposes constituted knowledges, and thus opposes opinions. For what we call *opinions* are representations without truth, the anarchic debris of circulating knowledge" (p. 51). This means, of course, that a new truth cannot be judged or assessed by any preexisting criteria. Indeed, Badiou draws an even stronger conclusion: "What arises from a truth-process . . . cannot be communicated. . . . In all that concerns truths, there must be an *encounter*. The Immortal that I am capable of being cannot be spurred in me by the effects of communicative sociality, it must be *directly* seized by fidelity" (p. 51).

There are numerous issues raised by this account. Most obviously, in view of the vocabulary that Badiou employs, it is hard to understand how he can maintain that his viewpoint is antireligious. It seems clear that for him the encounter with truth is an experience of being "claimed," of being torn away from one's everyday finite concerns toward some transcendent dimension. For Badiou, someone caught up in a truth process is "simultaneously *himself*, nothing other than himself, a multiple singularity recognizable among all others, and *in excess of himself*, because the uncertain course of fidelity *passes through him*, transfixes his singular body and inscribes him, from within time, in an instant of eternity" (p. 45). Secondly, Badiou's account or terror, as a form of evil, centers around the notion of a "simulacrum" of such a truth process. And, he says, "'Simulacrum' must be understood here in its strong sense: all the formal traits of a truth are at work in the simulacrum. Not only a universal nomination of the event, inducing the power of a radical break, but also the 'obligation' of a fidelity, and the promotion of a *simulacrum of the subject*" (p. 74). As we have seen, in the case of terror, the subject interpellated into being by the irruption of truth is a simulacrum because the address is confined to a specific group—in the case of the Nazis, this was the German *Volk*.

Given this account, it can be plausibly claimed that not only Badiou's account of truth but also his account of evil has a religious dimension. For terror consists in the perversion of substituting a particularized appeal for the universal appeal that truth implies, and yet following the simulacrum with all the zeal that would be appropriate if it were a genuine truth. But this definition also raises the question of how Badiou can *define* the universal appeal of truth, establish a reliable criterion for distinguishing truth from simulacrum. And here he runs into difficulties. For he affirms that "there is not, in fact, one single Subject, but as many subjects as there are truths, and as many subjective types as there are procedures of truths" (p. 28). This makes it difficult to see how there could be, *in principle*, a universal address of truth, contrasted with the simulacrum, since there is no "all" to which such an address could be directed; there are only singular subjects called into being by the situated, particularized processes of truth.

At this point, in fact, Badiou falters. Seeking to define what is objectionable about the violent exclusivism of simulacra of truth, he writes: "However hostile to a truth he might be, in the ethic of truths every 'some-one' is always represented as capable of becoming the Immortal that he is. So we may fight against the judgments and opinions he exchanges with others for the purpose of corrupting every fidelity, but not against his *person*—which, under the circumstances, is insignificant, and to which, in any case, every truth is ultimately addressed" (p. 77). But if every truth is ultimately addressed to human beings as "persons," then Badiou's religiously tinged stress on the singular unmediated irruption of truth seems to go by the board. He acknowledges implicitly that the spread of a truth must be mediated by the capacity of individuals to reflect and reason for themselves—and this is an essentially modern, Enlightenment conception of truth. Furthermore, Badiou's third definition of evil, as "disaster," appears to confirm this reading, since what the definition implies is that the attempt to impose a substantive conception of the Good without restraint, without reference to its contingent origin as a conception, will inevitably result in violence.

Far from offering an antireligious or "atheist" account of evil, then, Badiou's philosophy is suspended between a discourse that is strongly religious in tone and inspiration, and a discourse that draws on the resources of a secular universalism. At the start of his book, Badiou vigorously attacks what he regards as the debased "piety" of the modern language of human rights; and his ostensible aim is to wrest ethical discourse free from tacit religious assumptions. But in fact, his *Ethics* vividly substantiates the view—a view that we have also found confirmed by the work of Habermas and Jonas—that there is an inescapable tension between religious and secular orientations in modern culture's confrontations with evil.

Notes

A short section of this essay has appeared in a different form as "'Radical Finitude' and the Problem of Evil: Critical Comments on Wellmer's Reading of Jonas," in María Pía Lara, ed., *Rethinking Evil: Contemporary Perspectives* (Berkeley: University of California Press, 2001), pp. 46–52.

1. Hannah Arendt, "Nightmare and Flight," in *Hannah Arendt: Essays in Understanding 1930–1954*, ed. Jerome Kohn (New York: Harcourt Brace, 1993), p. 134.
2. Richard J. Bernstein, *Hannah Arendt and the Jewish Question* (Cambridge, Mass.: MIT Press, 1996), p. 137.
3. Hannah Arendt and Karl Jaspers, *Briefwechsel 1926–1969*, ed. Lotte Köhler and Hans Saner (Munich: Piper, 1985), p. 201. Unless otherwise noted, all translations from the German are my own.
4. *Briefwechsel*, p. 202.
5. Immanuel Kant, *Religion within the Limits of Reason Alone*, trans. Theodore M. Green and Hoyt H. Hudson (New York: Harper and Row, 1960), p. 48.
6. Ibid., p. 49.
7. Cited in Gordon E. Michalson Jr., *Fallen Freedom: Kant on Radical Evil and Moral Regeneration* (Cambridge: Cambridge University Press, 1990), p. 17.
8. Jürgen Habermas, "1989 im Schatten von 1945. Zur Normalität einer künftigen Berliner Republik," in *Die Normalität einer Berliner Republik* (Frankfurt: Suhrkamp, 1995), pp. 186–87.
9. Jürgen Habermas, "Discourse Ethics: Notes on a Program of Philosophical Justification," in *Moral Consciousness and Communicative Action*, trans. Christian Lenhardt and Shierry Weber Nicholsen (Cambridge, Mass.: MIT Press, 1990), p. 98.
10. Jürgen Habermas, "Die Grenzen des Neohistorismus," in *Die nachholende Revolution* (Frankfurt: Suhrkamp, 1990), p. 150.
11. Hannah Arendt, *Eichmann in Jerusalem: A Report on the Banality of Evil* (New York: Penguin, 1977), p. 150.
12. Karl-Otto Apel, "Normatively Grounding Critical Theory Through Recourse to the Lifeworld? A Transcendental-Pragmatic Attempt to Think with Habermas against Habermas," in *Philosophical Interventions in the Unfinished Project of Modernity*, ed. Axel Honneth et al. (Cambridge, Mass.: MIT Press, 1992), p. 157.
13. Karl-Otto Apel, *Diskurs und Verantwortung* (Frankfurt: Suhrkamp, 1992), p. 448.
14. Jürgen Habermas, "Erläuterungen zur Diskursethik," in *Erläuterungen zur Diskursethik* (Frankfurt: Suhrkamp, 1991), p. 189.
15. Ibid.

16. Jürgen Habermas, "Transzendenz von innen, Transzendenz ins Diesseits," in *Texte und Kontexte* (Frankfurt: Suhrkamp, 1991), p. 129.

17. Jürgen Habermas, "Metaphysics after Kant," in *Postmetaphysical Thinking: Philosophical Essays,* trans. William Mark Hohengarten (Cambridge, Mass.: MIT Press, 1992), p. 17.

18. Ibid., p. 15.

19. Hans Jonas, "Mind, Matter and Creation: Cosmological Evidence and Cosmogonic Speculation," in *Mortality and Morality: A Search for the Good after Auschwitz,* ed. Lawrence Vogel (Evanston, Ill.: Northwestern University Press, 1996), p. 188.

20. Ibid., pp. 189–90.

21. Hans Jonas, "Immortality and the Modern Temper," in *Mortality and Morality,* p. 129.

22. Ibid., pp. 127–28.

23. Albrecht Wellmer, "Der Mythos vom leidenden und werdenden Gott. Fragen an Hans Jonas," in *Endspiele: Die unversöhnliche Moderne* (Frankfurt: Suhrkamp, 1993), p. 253.

24. Ibid.

25. Ibid., p. 254.

26. Hans Jonas, "The Concept of God after Auschwitz: A Jewish Voice," in *Mortality and Morality,* p. 139.

27. Wellmer, "Der Mythos vom leidenden und werdenden Gott," p. 254.

28. Alain Badiou, *Ethics: An Essay on the Understanding of Evil,* trans. Peter Hallward (London: Verso, 2001). Parenthetical page numbers in the text are to this edition.

6   How Rape Became a Crime against Humanity: History of an Error

Debra B. Bergoffen

The Other Error

The title of this essay shamelessly plagiarizes Nietzsche's "How the Real World at Last Became a Myth: History of an Error" of *Twilight of the Idols*. Telling the story of that error, Nietzsche condenses the history of philosophy into six theses. These theses, none of which is more than a few sentences, track the processes by which the idea of a real world loses its credibility, trace the operations through which the loss of the real world also destroys the idea of an apparent world, and describe the ways in which the disappearance of these worlds opens the way for the world of Zarathustra, a phenomenal world beyond appearance and reality. I steal this title to do something different. The error I trace is not the error of identifying rape as a crime against humanity but the errors of *not* seeing rape in this way. Through this title, I follow the trail by which the crime of rape loses its status as an apparent crime, as only *apparently* a crime against women, and becomes recognized as a real crime, not just against women but against humanity. Lacking Nietzsche's talent, it will take me nine theses to do this.

1. The patriarchy of our life world is particular to a monotheist configuration of subjectivity.
2. This configuration, following the idea of the monotheistic One, allows for an absolute, autonomous subject made in the image of God and identified as man, and an inessential other subject, woman, whose subjectivity is taken up with the task of reflecting, confirming, and recognizing the truth of man. (Man and woman stand to each other as God and his people.) The sexual difference represents the negative and positive valences of the one.
3. With the death of God, these subjectivities lose their grounding. The one can no longer assert its exclusive claims to be the subject.
4. The ghost of God survives God's death. The patriarchy of the one perpetuates itself through appeals to the one of truth, humanity, etcetera.
5. The recent judgment of the UN Yugoslavia War Crimes Tribunal threatens the ghost's power. In finding that three Bosnian soldiers who raped

and sexually enslaved Muslim women were guilty of crimes against humanity, the court pointed to the end of the era/error of the absolute and inessential other subjects and opened the way for the formation of subjectivities according to the two of the sexual difference.

6. In a life world structured by the two of the sexual difference, the subject's reference to the universal of humanity is not lost. As subjects who are recognized as sexually different in their subjectivity, they discover their shared embodied vulnerability. The one of humanity is now grounded in this shared difference.

7. Within the social contract of the absolute one and his inessential other, woman's difference, coded as lack, survives only to the extent that it is aligned with and protected by an essential subject. Men's and women's subjectivities are configured as the distinctions of the powerful and the vulnerable, the protector and the protected, the potential attacker and the potential victim.

8. The social contract of the sexual difference calls upon the virtue of trust. As all subjects are vulnerable to each other, as no subject is identified as essentially vulnerable and no subject is coded as being immune from the possibility of becoming a victim, we recognize our common destiny by institutionalizing the value and virtue of trust. No Delilahs. No protection rackets.

9. After the death of God, at the end of the reign of his ghost, the possibility of the end of patriarchy is announced in a court verdict that finds the crime of rape to be a crime against humanity because it violates the bond of trust demanded by the sexual difference and required for the justice of a life world that recognizes the embodied, sexed two of human subjectivity.

Were I Nietzsche, I could leave it at that. Not being Nietzsche, I will take up the task of making this clearer. Though I turn to Nietzsche's *Twilight of the Idols* for the title of this essay, I look to his "Madman" of *The Gay Science* to ground its arguments. Here, I turn to a question I've asked in different ways in different contexts throughout the years: What does the death of God mean for the life of patriarchy? More precisely, what is the relationship between a world anchored in the idea of a monotheistic God and the patriarchal practices of that world? What part does the death of God play in ending the history of this error by which the possibility of identifying rape as a crime against humanity is foreclosed?

Nietzsche's is not the only voice I appeal to in delineating this history. Simone de Beauvoir and Luce Irigaray are crucial. Beauvoir provides the category of the inessential other. Irigaray alerts me to the question of sexual difference, the question she identifies as the crucial question of our age. Enlisting these three voices, undoing this history of the error of monotheistic patriarchy translates into a series of questions: Can the category of the inessential other, the bedrock of monotheistic patriarchy, survive the death of God? Is the death of God the condition of the possibility of the sexual difference becoming the question of our age? Can we mark the reign and end of patriarchy by the way in which rape, wartime rape and domestic rape, is coded, prosecuted, and punished?

The Madman's Ghost

Carrying the message of God's death into the marketplace peopled by atheists, Nietzsche's madman finds himself playing the role of the jester. He is the object of ridicule and jeers. That believers would find this messenger mad is one thing, but what can Nietzsche mean by telling us that *atheists* are ignorant of this cataclysmic event? The answer to this question lies, I think, in Nietzsche's distinction between God, who is dead, and his ghost, who still travels among us. This God-ghost, like the shade of Hamlet's father, is an insistent presence. It exerts an influence that will not be stilled unless and until we act.

The Madman sings a requiem for God's ghost. Nietzsche asks something else of us. It is not enough to play the role of the atheist, the one who no longer believes in the religious trappings of the idea of God. We must get to the heart of the matter of God. We must give up the monotheistic idea of truth: the idea of truth as One, as Absolute. We must abandon the idea of a real world. Philosophizing with his hammer, Nietzsche demands the end of metaphysics. He also offers a transvaluation. After the death of God and the reign of his ghost, we will find ourselves in a world of gods; a world where the excesses of life proliferate in the truths of perspectivism. Only after giving up the ghost of God can we understand that, like the reality-appearance distinction, which disappears once the real world becomes a fable, the threat of relativism evaporates once God's ghost is abandoned. Perspectivism multiplies truths by dismantling the binary reasoning by which some truths are relegated to the status of the negative—the truth of women, for example. It does not render the term *truth* inoperative. When a people call something true, they direct us to a way of life. Nietzsche evaluates truth claims by assessing whether what a people call truth, whether their way of life, affirms life or negates it. Strange as it sounds, Nietzsche argues that there are ways of life that denigrate the very forces that sustain it. He calls such life forms nihilistic and rejects their truth claims. Minimally, it is a matter of the principle of contradiction. In more Nietzschean language, it concerns the will to power.

Multiplying the Truth of Humanity

So long as God or his ghost lives, men can claim to be Man. Declaring themselves to be created in the image of The Absolute, they can claim to be the absolute of humanity. Given that within the monotheistic world there is only room for one truth of humanity, instantiations of the human that do not reflect the image of man back to himself are identified as inadequate. Thus the Aristotelian; the Jewish, Christian, and Islamic; the social contract; the Freudian psychoanalytic distinction between man—humanity in its full positivity—and woman—humanity in its inadequate form, its evil seductive form, its incompetent citizen form, its castrated mutilated form. Men claiming to be Man, the absolute, contest each other's claims to authority. They insist that the truth is one and that they embody it. Thus they subjugate, oppress, and enslave each other. Oppressors and oppressed alike, however, recognize that subjugated men carry the threat of rebellion. Men, whatever their current status vis-à-vis other men, are poised to take up the position of the One.

Beauvoir notices that the subjugation of women to men is neither explained by nor captured in this Hegelian drama of violence.[1] Among men the position of master and slave follows the vicissitudes of history. Men of different tribes, nations, races, and religions take on the mantle of master or find themselves in the position of the slave according to the circumstances of their times and technologies. No such historical shifts are recorded as having occurred between men and women. Unlike the male Other who, when his claims to being fully human are rejected in the name of race, nationality, religion, or class can call upon his status as a man, the Absolute, to rebel against his oppression, woman, having no claim to embody the human, is not positioned to contest her inferior status. She is not the Other who has been robbed of her status as an absolute subject by those who have the power to politically enforce their claim to be the Absolute of humanity. She is inessential other, the one whose inadequacy as a subject is eternally inscribed in the order of things so long as that order is structured according to the law of the Absolute One. As inessential other, woman as woman's truth is the truth of the mirror. She can participate in the monotheistic world of truth if she reflects men's truth as Man back to him. The truth of her existence, her body, her way of engaging the world, will become the absence of the fullness of his truth. As his negation, she will not activate the dialectic. She will freeze it. Being what he is not, she will confirm the truth of who he is (the "you're so strong" syndrome).

The law of the Absolute One requires a certain decision on our part. For women to be woman, the Inessential Other, the one unfit to enter the dialectic of history, we must accept an account of the human that trivializes the sexed body. We can do this either by equating the human with the soul, the consciousness, the mind, where the body per se is devalued, or by reducing the human to a bodily materiality whose sex is irrelevant. Maintaining this decision, we can be proper monotheists or good humanists. We cannot, however, be good phenomenologists. Once we become good phenomenologists, we will notice what Beauvoir noticed: concrete human beings are sexed. They exist as either male or female.[2] (I leave the problematics of this assertion aside for now.) We come to Irigaray's conclusion: The question of the sexual difference is the question of our age. There are two truths of humanity. The ethical, political question concerns the meaning of this doubled truth of the human condition. It becomes a matter of determining how the sexual difference that constitutes us as human contains the conditions of an ethics and a politics of justice.[3] The search for the truth and meaning of man drops out as a meaningful question. It is replaced by the question: What is the meaning of the sexual difference in its being as the truth of the difference and in its demand that we respond to the one who is different?

[*A Note too important to be relegated to a footnote:* None of this is meant to imply that patriarchy and monotheism are necessarily synonymous. I am speaking, as Nietzsche taught me to speak, of a particular form of monotheism and its particular form of patriarchy. Patriarchy has thrived and thrives in nonmonotheistic socialities. These forms of patriarchy require an analysis appropriate to their specific understandings of the relationship between truth and woman. Moreover, monotheism, the commitment to one God/Truth, need not necessarily insist on a singular truth of humanity embodied as male. There are two Genesis accounts of the creation of humanity. One (the rib story) justifies patriarchy. The other (the simultaneous creation) does not. In announcing the death of God, Nietzsche celebrated what he hoped would be the end of the era (error) of resentment. From his point of view, monotheism and resentment are different faces of the same relationship to life. He may have been wrong. It may be that the patriarchy of monotheism is the sexed expression of the resentment that characterizes our current mode of monotheism. Defining resentment as a degradation of life, Nietzsche critiqued the monotheistic preference for eternal over finite life as nihilistic. Designating women, the embodiment of the human that births and sustains life, as the inessential other also falls under this nihilistic category. Nietzsche could not envision a non-nihilistic monotheism. He may have been wrong. He may have missed the difference between Christendom and monotheism. I tread a more cautious path. Irigaray may be right. A monotheism that rejects the category of the inessential other and calls us to an ethic of sexual difference may be possible. *End of note.*]

Crimes against Humanity

The idea of a crime against humanity is relatively recent. The idea of considering rape a crime against humanity is as new as yesterday. The concept of a crime against humanity is a legacy of World War II. The war crimes tradition could not cope with the unimaginable criminalities of the Third Reich. A war crime can only exist in the context of interstate armed conflict. It refers to criminal behavior between enemy states. The criminality of the Final Solution could not be addressed in this way. This lawless violation of people's humanity was ordered and legitimated by the Nazi regime. No wartime enemy was involved. Here the state's war machine was turned on its disavowed own. The category of a crime against humanity was created to deal with this unprecedented viciousness. The criminality of a crime against humanity is established by the content of the act—for example, torture—not its context, for example, a state of war between perpetrator and victim. Developed in response to a then-unimaginable evil, it was surely hoped that there would be little need to appeal to this concept once the Nuremberg trials were concluded. What was once an unimaginable evil is now a too-frequent reality. Talk of crimes against humanity is familiar. The crime against humanity charge is now a fixture of international law.[4]

The Bosnian–Serb ethnic cleansing strategies drove the court to see that traditional understandings of war crimes laws, where rape per se was not identified as a crime against humanity, could not adequately address the aggression in the former Yugoslavia. The court's ruling changed the status of rape in two respects. First, it identified it as a unique form of torture that had to be treated in its own right. Second, it determined that rape could no longer remain unacceptable in principle but forgivable in practice. The judgment called our attention to the fact that rape has been the ignored, the tolerated war crime.[5] It has been the crime that is invisible (few if any women bring "credible," "audible" charges), innocent (boys will be boys, the pressures of war and all that), and unavoidable (something like collateral damage). A court's judgment rendered this fact unacceptable.

Torture was always included among the list of crimes identified as a crime against humanity. Rape, until the 2001 Hague Tribunal dealing with the war crimes of the former Yugoslavia, was considered to be covered under the general category of torture. In convicting three former Bosnian-Serb soldiers of crimes against humanity, The Hague court was specific: their crime was rape and sexual slavery, a specific form of torture, not torture in general. In formulating its judgment in this way, the court indicated that rape needed to be identified as a crime against humanity in its own right, that viewing it only as a species of torture failed to capture the specificity of the way in which this crime violates our humanity.

The court's determination was influenced by the fact that these rapes were part of a concerted campaign of genocide. As part of its genocidal strategy, the Bosnian-Serb command employed different forms of torture. They marked rape, however, as crucial to the success of their program of ethnic cleansing. Under these circumstances, calling rape torture and leaving it at that would have missed the specificity of the criminal violence. It may also be the case that the court (headed by a female judge, who insisted that reports of rape be thoroughly investigated, that those accused be brought to trial, and in short, that rape be taken as seriously as other criminal acts) brought a gendered eye to the evidence before it and that this eye saw what a "neutral" eye would not notice: rape, insofar as it is a neutral phenomenon, is a crime that can be committed by men or women against women and men. Within patriarchal socialities, however, rape is a crime committed by men against women. The statistics are clear: in our world rape is a gendered crime. It cannot be adequately addressed through the gender-neutral concept of torture.

In declaring a male soldier's rape of a civilian woman a crime against humanity, the court's ruling brings the realities of sex and gender to the idea of the human. It determines that it is in her particularity as a raped woman that an embodied sexed being can represent the human in its universality. It found that violating a woman's sexual integrity was a crime not only against this particular woman but through her against the species in its humanity. It confronts us with the matter of the relationship between the particular and the universal. In rejecting the patriarchal equation that only the male = the human, the court does not offer us an inversion, the female = the human; it asks that we forgo both equations for a concept of humanity that considers the human in the particularities of its sexual differentiations. In this, it directs us to examine how the violence of the patriarchal sexual difference can be challenged, resisted, and rejected.

Genocidal Rape: Deploying Women's Bodies as Weapons of War

I am arguing that a specific court case and verdict, referencing a specific set of crimes, has broad implications for our legal, political, and social understandings of what is meant by a crime against humanity. I am proposing that these implications, read through Nietzsche's history of an error and death of God, Beauvoir's concept of the inessential other, and Irigaray's question of sexual difference, direct us to reconceive the concept of humanity. I am contending that the necessity of invoking the concept of humanity to establish the credibility of the idea of a crime against humanity does not require conceiving of humanity as a One, and that the appeal to justice embedded in this concept of a crime against humanity requires attending to the sexual difference inherent in the human condition. The argument appeals to the particulars of the Bosnian-Serb crime of ethnic cleansing.

I read this crime, its conception, its strategies, its effectiveness, as taking up the logic of patriarchy and pushing it to the limit.[6] The strategy is effective because it correctly identifies and aims at patriarchy's Achilles' heel. It takes advantage of the fact that though the fabric of a patriarchal society is woven through its women, patriarchy positions its women as inessential others. As inessential, their identity and value is derived from and dependent upon the men whose names they bear. The women are said to lack independence and power. They are coded as vulnerable and weak. The success of the Bosnian-Serb strategy, however, suggests that it is not the weakness of the Muslim women, but the vulnerability of a society that refuses to acknowledge the essential role of its women—that is, of a society that determines that women's bodies and actions are extensions of men's intentionalities—that allows rape to become a weapon of war. Rape could render the men impotent so long as their status as subjects depended on their identity as protectors of women. The Muslim patriarchy did not attend to the ways in which denying women the status of the subject created the conditions whereby "their" women's bodies could become weapons of war. The Trojan horse had to be brought into the enemy city. The Bosnian Serbs were saved the trouble.

The Bosnian-Serb command saw itself devising a war strategy grounded in Muslim psychology. A proposal called the Ram plan first establishes "ethnic cleansing" as official government policy in 1991. The objective is to occupy

Croatian territory and Bosnia-Herzegovina and to control the area where Muslim fundamentalism is strong. The plan calls on local militia groups to create unrest in order to provoke calls for intervention. During these meetings, psychologists and experts in psychological warfare provide analyses of Muslim communities that conclude that community morale and will can be undermined *only* if the point where the religious and social structure is most fragile is attacked. They identify this point as the women, especially adolescents and children. Attacking the young women, these psychologists assert, will create confusion, fear, and panic. It will trigger a Muslim retreat from the targeted territories. They propose that the Ram plan be combined with a propaganda campaign that comes to be called the Brana plan. The objective of both plans is to provoke "spontaneous" flight. The Belgrade meeting identifies a commander for this new military operation against noncombatant women and children and decides that the chain of command should be as small as possible. Secrecy, it seems, is important. Late in 1991 reports of death/rape camps reach Zagreb. The plan seems to have been put into effect immediately. There are also documents from commanders in the field to politicians reporting that the "cleansing" of the Bosnian territories and the psychological attacks on the Muslim population is succeeding and should be continued.[7]

The tactic of ethnic cleansing was a strategy of state-ordered terror. Men, women, and children were tortured and killed. At their meetings in Belgrade, however, the Bosnian-Serb command determined that driving a people from its land also, and essentially, required something more specific—the rape, the sexual enslavement, and if possible, the forced impregnation of the women. It is also significant to note that though men were summarily killed, taken out and shot, sometimes tortured and then killed, women were often publicly raped before they were killed. Often they were not killed. As raped bodies, they were as good as dead to their communities.

The Bosnian Serbs tied the success of their genocide campaign to Muslim psychology. They did not see themselves as sharing this Muslim psychology. They did not notice that in using women's bodies as weapons of war, and especially in adopting a policy of rape as a practice of coerced impregnations, condemning Muslim women to birth "chechnik" babies (the idea, accepted, it seems, by both the Muslim and Serb communities, being that the identity of the child is given by the father), and endorsing policies of sexual mutilations that would destroy the women's ability to become mothers of Muslim children, the Serb command was replicating its own view of women's bodies as weapons of war.

In October 1992, the Serbian ruling party, the Serbian Socialist party, the Serbian Academy of Arts and Sciences, and the Serbian Orthodox Church published a document titled "Warning." This document saw the high birth rate of Albanians, Muslims, and Romanians as a threat to the Serbian nation. Responding to this threat, it declared that Serbian women had a responsibility to serve their nation by reproducing.[8] In 1994, Patriarch Pavle, leader of the Serbian Orthodox Church, denounced women who do not have children as the "White

Plague." He called their refusal a sin against themselves and their nation. These women would be responsible for reducing Serbs to an ethnic minority, bereft of sufficient soldiers necessary for the nation's survival.[9] Whether they looked at Muslim or Serb women, the Bosnian Serbs saw the same thing: women were reproductive bodies; and as reproductive bodies, they were classified as weapons of war. As enemy bodies, women's reproductive capacities had to be destroyed or put to the service of the Serbs (the forced pregnancies). As Serb bodies, they had to contribute to the war machine.

The Serbs share more than this with their Muslim enemies. The genocidal rape strategy targeted women's bodies in order to destroy the men. A raped woman signifies the failure of her men. They did not or could not protect her. In civilian rape cases, this law of patriarchy can be fudged. The woman can be found to be at fault. She wore provocative clothes. She was where she should not have been. She led the rapist on. Her no was really a yes. If she is at fault, he is absolved of his role of protector. His manhood is secure. The case of genocidal rape is unambiguous. Her rape is his fault. Rape her, demoralize him. How can a man consider the place where he failed to protect his mother, sister, wife, daughter his home? Witnessing the nullification of his property rights in his women, he is made to understand that all of his property rights are lost. Better get out. That was the message the rapes were intended to carry. It got through. The Serb command did not need experts in Muslim psychology to teach them these tactics. They share this "protection" code of honor with their enemies. Muslim and Serb confront each other as patriarchal doubles.

The particular ways in which the rapes were committed were important to their overall strategic goal. Their effectiveness depended on "maximizing shame and humiliation not only to the victim but also to the victim's community."[10] Thus, investigators note common patterns in the rapes. They occur in conjunction with other efforts to remove the targeted ethnic group from the region. To heighten the shame, the rapes occur in public in front of family members or are witnessed by other detainees. Family members are forced to rape each other. Young women, virgins, educated women, and prominent members of the community are targeted. Many perpetrators say they were ordered to rape. Gangs of rapists subject women to multiple rapes.[11] There are also reports that the rapes were routinely videotaped.[12]

Their public staging was crucial to the rapes' genocidal effectiveness. As publicly performed, they engage the power of the spectacle of violence to construct and formalize subject positions.[13] The decision to commit the rapes in public signals that the Bosnian Serbs intended to inscribe their power on the bodies of Muslim woman, and through this inscription to shape the ways in which Muslim women and men experienced themselves. The women probably learned nothing new about themselves. The vulnerability to being raped, the status of potential victim, is the horizon of a patriarchal woman's life. But the public rapes were not directly targeting the women's subjectivity. It was the men's subjectively as essential that needed to be refigured. The violence inflicted on "their"' women's bodies was intended to humiliate them. It was directed at transforming them from absolute subjects into abject ones.

The Court Speaks

The genocidal rape campaign invoked the power of the spectacle of violence to rework the subjectivities of Muslim men. Following the logic of the power of the spectacle, but allowing that discursive spectacles also have the power to constitute subjectivities, I see the 2001 Hague Tribunal—the trial, the verdict, the transcript—as a discursive public spectacle. Its invocation of the language of crimes against humanity and its rejection of the defense claim that the rapes could not be categorized either as torture or as a crime against humanity challenge patriarchal subjectivities. In identifying a crime against a woman's body as a crime against humanity, the court's discourse challenges the legitimacy of the inessential other as a subject position. It invites us to conceive of the universal—humanity—through the sexual difference of the human. It asks us to refigure our concepts of subjectivity.

In identifying rape as a crime against humanity and categorizing it as a distinct species of torture, the court's ruling affirms the principle of embodied subjectivity. It goes beyond past rulings on torture, however, in attending to the sexed realities of embodiment and in insisting that violating a *woman's* sexual integrity is a crime against humanity, "the second most serious category of international war crimes after genocide."[14] Before this ruling, the standard against which evidence for or against the charge of a crime against humanity was measured was the normative "neutral" (i.e., the unmarked male) body. Using this body as a measure, torture, understood through the criteria of physical pain, was identified as a crime against humanity. Appealing to this criteria, rape too was classified as a crime against humanity. Prior to this decision, however, to be convicted of rape, evidence of violence was necessary. Once evidence of violence was established, the rape victim, like the torture victim, could be recognized as having her humanity violated; for like the torture victim, she too could establish that she had suffered physical pain and injury.

Appealing to this understanding, the defense counsel argued that the prosecution did not prove that the alleged victims of rape were exposed to any severe physical or psychological suffering—that rape in itself is not an act that inflicts severe bodily pain and therefore that no crime against humanity occurred.[15] In effect, the defense argued that if the court wished to include rape in the category of crimes against humanity, it would have to identify rape with violence and pain, and that if the court defined rape without reference to violence and pain, it could not establish rape as a crime against humanity. Given accepted definitions of crimes against humanity, there was nothing amiss in the defense lawyer's logic. The argument failed, not because the court refused the defense lawyer's reasoning, but because it refused traditional definitions of crimes against humanity.

This court took a different position. It identified an act as rape, a crime against humanity, whether or not there was evidence of violence or physical pain and injury. It decoupled the idea of forced entry from the idea of painful entry. In doing this, it exposed the injustice of judgments that claim to speak to the issue of human rights but that ignore the relationship between the universal right to be respected as human and the specificity of the sexed body through which we live our humanity. What may be true for men—a crime against humanity occurs when the body is subjected to violence, injury, and pain—may not always be true for women. Women's humanity, the court ruled, can be criminally abused even if they have not been subjected to physical violence, injury, or pain.

In finding that rape does not have to be represented as an act of physical violence to be condemned as a crime against humanity, the court spoke to the issue of sexual difference. The effect of its speech is threefold. First, it exposed the fallacy of treating the masculine body as the universal body. Second, it directed us to identify the woman's body as the mark of the universal. Third, it directed us to the intersections of difference and universality; for it is not as the universal body, but as the specifically sexed body, that the woman's body is seen as speaking of our shared human condition. The court's ruling shows us that in coding women as particularly vulnerable, patriarchy is both right and wrong: it is right in that women's vulnerability is specific to their lived bodies; it is wrong in that vulnerability is a human, not a sexed, condition. Men's bodies, too, are vulnerable. We have long recognized the injustice of the cut that breaks the body open. The court demands that we see the violation of the opening already inscribed in the body as equally criminal.

Politically speaking, rape is a crime that violates the social contract. Not all social contracts are the same. The specific ways in which rape is seen as violating the social contract tells us how different social contracts are instantiated. Keith Burgess-Jackson identifies three social constructs of rape. Two are of interest here. One is the conservative construct, where rape is understood as trespass, an appropriation and use of a man's property without his consent. In this construct, the criminality of rape lies in its violation of a social contract grounded in male authority. This contract, by establishing women as valuable property belonging to men and situating women as requiring the protection of the men who possess them, forms male subjectivity around the idea of the protector.[16] This conservative contract grounded the Yugoslav–Muslim community. It seems to have also been the ground of the Bosnian-Serb community.

In the liberal social contract construct, the criminality of rape is found as a violation of the principle of consent. Here the social contract takes the woman's individuality as a given. It is no longer a property right that is violated, but a right to autonomy.[17] The liberal contract and concept of rape as a crime appears to step out of the patriarchal frame. Critics, however, have pointed to the ways in which the liberal criteria of consent continue to reflect patriarchal values.[18] It is possible to read The Hague court's judgment as a case of a war strategy based on a conservative understanding of rape colliding with a court invoking a liberal theory of rape. But things are not this clear; for though the court appeals to the liberal concept of autonomy and integrity in some of its verdict, its ruling sometimes appeals to a conservative understanding of rape.

In signaling that the traditional defense of rape in times of peace and war—"boys will be boys"—and the specific wartime defense—"I was only following orders"—are no longer acceptable, the court appeals to two principles. One refers to men and their responsibility to women; the other refers to women and their rights. The first, elegantly put by Judge Florence Mumba, states, "In time of peace as much as in time of war, men of substance do not abuse women."[19] The second, more radical principle, links women's dignity to their "fundamental human right to sexual self-determination."[20] The first principle reinforces the conservative patriarchal social contract. The second may either be read as a reiteration of the patriarchal liberal social contract or as something more radical. I read it as something more radical; for unlike liberal rape law proceedings, which too often tie criteria of consent to the man's belief that consent was given, the court looked at the matter of consent from the women's point of view. When the men claimed that consent was given, it asked whether the conditions of the believed consent were consistent with conditions of possible consent. It determined that the power relationship between a civilian woman and an enemy soldier was such that consent in any meaningful sense could not have been given. Under these conditions, mistaking submission for consent was criminal.[21]

By pursuing this more radical line of the court's ruling, we are able to add to Burgess-Jackson's three social contract indexes of rape (conservative, liberal, radical) a fourth: a social contract where rape is identified as a crime against humanity. This category relies on the liberal and radical concepts insofar as they reject the conservative construct of woman as the inessential other (the liberal in theory, the radical in fact). It relies on the radical concept insofar as it identifies women with the specificities of their situations. It veers away from the radical understanding, however, in appealing to the Enlightenment principle of humanity. This ambiguity, I think, is the promise of the court's ruling. For if the liberal concept of rape shows us how the death of patriarchy leaves behind its ghost in the concept of autonomy, the radical concept may go too far in rejecting the idea of the universal.

The challenge that the court articulates so clearly is this: How can we invoke the political power of the concept of humanity (without which we have no basis for insisting on such things as human rights or calling some things crimes against humanity) without calling up the ghost of patriarchy (the Enlightenment ideal of the asexual human one)? How can we appeal to the concept of the sexual difference, with its power to create a world where the ghost finds no sustenance, without seeming to reinvest patriarchy, which is grounded on the insistence on the sexual difference, with its powers and without losing the concept of humanity? Between Irigaray's ethic of sexual difference and The Hague court convictions, we are provided with some answers to these difficult and troubling questions. The court and Beauvoir are clear on this: positioning woman as the inessential other is unsupportable on ontological, ethical, political, and legal grounds. They are less clear, however, regarding the implications of, and resources for, remedying the injustice of this subject position.

Irigaray is unambiguous. Women and men are other to each other. Their shared humanity is not an argument against their irreducible difference. Their irreducible difference is not an argument against their shared humanity. Irigaray's ethics of sexual difference holds on to this tension between the singular and the universal. It appeals to the emotion of wonder in the Cartesian sense, as the emotion that takes delight in the otherness of what it encounters without attempting to possess or appropriate it, to speak of a radical democratic politics that encodes the sexual difference in policies of equity rather than equality.[22] The court, I think, shows us the legal way of designating women's difference under the sign of the universal.

Invoking the Concept of Trust

Irigaray speaks of wonder; the court speaks of crimes against humanity. I would like to invoke the concept of trust. The reinscription of women's and men's subjectivities called for by the court and Irigaray requires that we exist before each other in the difference of our vulnerabilities to each other. To acknowledge the wonder of the sexual difference is to accept the obligation of otherness. This is not an obligation to care for each other. It is not an obligation to protect each other. It is an obligation to not exploit the vulnerability of the other's difference. It is an obligation to let the other be in their unique form of finitude. There is nothing secret about our distinctive and shared vulnerability. The torturer, those who plan genocide campaigns, and the rapist are not privilege to any esoteric knowledge. Their criminality lies not only in the particulars of their violence but in breaking the bond of trust through which we must live our obligation to let the other be. Our vulnerabilities are an open secret. We cannot protect ourselves from each other by camouflaging them in ideologies that designate some of us as vulnerable and others as not. We can, however, begin to free ourselves from the proliferation of crimes against humanity if, instead of fleeing our bodily vulnerabilities, we appeal to our mutual vulnerability to create a social contract of trust where human rights are respected. From the perspective of this social contract, the crime against humanity of the Bosnian-Serb soldiers was their failure to accept the obligations of the bonds of trust. Paraphrasing Judge Mumba, "Men and women of substance do not violate the trust that makes the justice of the ethics of sexual difference possible."

To see the court's ruling as moving us toward this reinscription of subjectivity, we also need to consider the extent to which these rapes were judged to be crimes against humanity because they were part of the strategy of genocide. If it is the case that it was not the principle of sexual and bodily integrity that triggered the crimes against humanity judgment, but rather the genocidal context of the rapes that grounded it, then the concept of a crime against humanity has yet to confront the issue of the unmediated relationship between the particular and the universal. Bringing Nietzsche, Beauvoir, and Irigaray to the court's verdict pushes it in this direction.

It's been considerably more than six theses and a few pages. Considerably more could and should be said. The ambiguities of the court case, the continued effect of the ghost of God, both keep the absolute subject in play. Despite its ambiguities, however, the court's findings give us the language, the precedent, and the direction for challenging the error that blinds us to the way in which rape, once it is recognized as a crime against humanity, directs us to reinscribe our subjectivities within a social contract where justice speaks a language beyond the good and evil of patriarchy.

Notes

1. Simone de Beauvoir, *The Second Sex,* trans. H. M. Parshley (New York: Random House, 1989), pp. xxii–xxiii.
2. Ibid., pp. xx–xxi.
3. Luce Irigaray, *An Ethics of Sexual Difference,* trans. Carolyn Burke and Gillian C. Gill (Ithaca, N.Y.: Cornell University Press, 1993), pp. 5–19.
4. See M. Cherif Bassiouni, *Crimes against Humanity in International Criminal Law* (The Hague: Kluwer Law International, 1999).
5. Theodor Meron, *War Crimes Law Comes of Age* (Oxford: Clarendon Press, 1998), pp. 205–6.
6. Beverly Allen, *Rape Warfare: The Hidden Genocide in Bosnia-Herzegovina and Croatia* (Minneapolis: University of Minnesota Press, 1996), p. 39.
7. Ibid., pp. 56–61; see also Todd Salzman, "Rape Camps, Forced Impregnation, and Ethnic Cleansing: Religious, Cultural and Ethical Responses to Rape Victims in the Former Yugoslavia," in *War's Dirty Secret: Rape, Prostitution, and Other Crimes Against Women,* ed. Anne Llewellyn Barstow (Cleveland, Ohio: Pilgrim Press, 2000), pp. 70–71.
8. Salzman, "Rape Camps," p. 65.
9. Ibid., p. 66.
10. Allen, *Rape Warfare,* p. 47.
11. Ibid., pp. 77–78.
12. Ibid., p. 34.
13. Gail Mason, *The Spectacle of Violence: Homophobia, Gender, and Knowledge* (London: Routledge, 2002), p. 27.
14. Editorial, "A Landmark Ruling on Rape," *New York Times,* 24 February 2001.
15. See Marlise Simons, "Bosnian War Trial Focuses on Sex Crimes," *New York Times,* 16 February 2001.
16. Keith Burgess-Jackson, *Rape: A Philosophical Investigation* (Aldershot: Dartmouth, 1996), p. 44.
17. Ibid., p. 49.
18. Ibid., pp. 54–55, 207.

19. Quoted in Marlise Simons, "Three Serbs convicted in War Time Rapes," *New York Times,* 24 February 2001.
20. Judgment of trial chamber II in the Kunarac, Kovac and Vukovic case. Retrieved 22 February 2001 from www.un.org/icty/6.
21. Ibid., 461, 4.
22. Irigaray, *Ethics of Sexual Difference,* pp. 72–82.

7 Ways of Winning: The Costs of Moral Victory in Transitional Regimes

Robert Meister

The War Is Over

Soon after my arrival in South Africa in 1998, I found myself across a dinner table from an Afrikaner MP, a member of the African National Congress (ANC) who had been released from prison in 1989 to negotiate the return of the exiles. His counterpart in that negotiation was the officer who had tortured him. "Not mentioning this," he said, "was hard for both of us. For me, what made it easier was that we had won."

Winning had made it psychologically possible for him to meet his former torturer daily without acknowledging their shared past. It allowed him, and other ex-combatants, to work with former enemies to bring about the transition to ANC rule while believing that, eventually, there would be full disclosure of what was done to them and their dead comrades. Agreeing to unconditional amnesty as the price of peace would still be difficult for many ANC leaders who had suffered during the struggle, but many came to believe that an amnesty conditioned on confession would be less an act of forgiveness than an exercise of power, less a decision not to prosecute than a pardon for those who were already self-condemned.[1] It could even be another way of winning—a moral victory over enemies who had already lost politically.

But what of those more passive victims of apartheid who had not yet "won" in the obvious sense of assuming power from their former oppressors? Could a Truth and Reconciliation Commission (TRC) grant these noncombatants a moral victory without also granting them material justice? "That is the question," my interlocutor agreed.

From its inception, the TRC attempted to answer this question by articulating a coherent conception of what it would mean to have won a legitimate struggle against injustice. Its stated goal was to mark South Africa's transition from a period of struggle over apartheid to a "new future" based on the creation of a shared "Human Rights Culture."[2] This goal embodied the growing belief of many who had advocated a South African revolution that what happened instead would be better, even morally, than what might have been achieved through successful armed struggle.[3]

What happened instead, however, was a negotiated compromise in which the ANC achieved majority rule without militarily defeating the white minority. The broadest terms of the compromise are well described by the historian George Fredrickson:

> [T]he entrenchment of market capitalism and the recognition of most existing white property rights was the price that had to be paid to open up the political system to Africans by some means short of actually driving the whites from power after a prolonged and bloody revolutionary struggle. . . . Major reform, with revolutionary implications for the racial status order but not for the character of other social and economic relationships, is one way to describe what has taken place in South Africa . . . [4]

The legislation establishing the TRC effectively gave it two years to transform this political compromise into a moral victory over apartheid.[5] Its central assumption was that the struggle against apartheid had been won, and that the nation as a whole could *realize* that victory by achieving a consensus that the apartheid was an evil that must never be repeated.[6] The TRC's core mission was thus to define the appropriate moral attitude toward an evil that had been morally (if not militarily) defeated. What could it mean to *have won* a moral victory of this kind? Is "having won" consistent with pursuing the agenda for which the liberation movement struggled? Or must that agenda be transformed in the name of "living on?"[7] As the symbolic end of apartheid—and the beginning of a new Human Rights Culture—the TRC had to enact a moral logic of "having won" that differed from the way those still engaged in righteous struggle would imagine the forward-looking task of "winning." The stress on personal forgiveness in discussions of the TRC has diverted attention from the more complex political notion of *victory* as a moral relationship to evil, and from the ways in which a moral victory over evil requires a belief in its pastness.

This essay concerns the moral and political cost to South Africa of achieving a consensus that the past was evil. Does it require, also, a consensus that for purposes of justice the evil is now past? Would continuing to struggle against the effects of past evil have cost the anti-apartheid movement its historical opportunity for moral victory and closure? Or is "closure" itself the liberal ideology that allows past evil a secure afterlife?

These questions lead us beyond South Africa and the TRC to the moral logic of the *fin de siècle* Human Rights Culture. Human rights are on the global political agenda today because in most parts of the world revolution is not. This opens a historic opportunity to convince many who once condoned political repression (or looked away) that a liberal consensus on human rights will be a benign successor to the counterrevolutionary project they no longer need. The question I will pose throughout this essay is whether the Human Rights Culture is also a benign successor to the revolutionary project. Is something more required in order for the politics of reconciliation to be a way of winning for victims of oppression who once hoped for revolutionary change?

Victims as Victors: The Revolutionary Idea of Justice

The *un*reconciled victim—the victim-as-revolutionary—was a central figure in twentieth-century political thought. Revolutionary ideologies (whether Marxist or not) typically had both a theory to show that human suffering has beneficiaries and a practice intended to provoke those beneficiaries into siding with the perpetrators when their benefits are threatened.[8] Victims would thus achieve the heightened "consciousness" necessary for self-liberation by recognizing the beneficiaries of injustice as would-be perpetrators. For these unreconciled victims, justice itself henceforth becomes a continuing struggle—not merely to defeat the evil regime, but also to eliminate its unjust consequences.

Even after the perpetrators of injustice have been defeated (both politically and morally), the unreconciled victim will see struggle against the remaining beneficiaries of injustice as unfinished business of the revolution. Justice, as the outcome of revolutionary struggle, would consist of the final victory of the unreconciled victim over the remaining beneficiaries; from this perspective, anything short of victims' justice is a compromise or a defeat.

The revolutionary notion of "winning" is well exemplified in books like William Hinton's *Fanshen,* which describes in great detail the effort in Maoist China to root out the effects of centuries of oppression, both cultural and material, by a systematic program of economic redistribution and political reeducation that treats even the most minor beneficiaries of past oppression as would-be perpetrators.[9] In the process of "settling accounts" with such persons, the Revolution is able to enlist former victims as retroactive combatants against an evil that has already lost. *Fanshen* vividly demonstrates how a postrevolutionary concept of justice-as-struggle can be part of the project of liberation itself.

In contrast, the postwar literature on release from concentration camps illustrates how little liberation can mean if it is *not* imbued with a sense of justice-as-struggle. Hannah Arendt tells us that for passive victims of atrocity, the experience of release can produce feelings of profound depression and even shame.[10] This phenomenon is also described by Primo Levi, who notes that, at the moment of liberation from Nazi death camps, only those who had thought of themselves as combatants felt joy.[11] Historians and journalists have described the early encounters of rescued victims and defeated perpetrators in the aftermath of atrocity as a state of sullen coexistence without acknowledgment or insight. The ethos that they describe is not a form of reconciliation but a moral depression beyond rage or guilt.[12]

These historical accounts of passive liberation suggest that one important function of revolutionary justice is to allow former victims to construct themselves as combatants after the fact. Unlike the passively "saved" victims of

Primo Levi's Auschwitz, the unreconciled victim of revolutionary theory is not depressed, because the war is never over. His initial victory against the active perpetrators of oppression is just the beginning of the struggle against the passive beneficiary of oppression. The unreconciled victim thus rejects any feelings of embarrassment for the shame of the defeated enemy by coming to believe that the real enemy poses a continuing counterrevolutionary threat that will destroy him if it is not finally eliminated. The moral reality of this threat is well understood by the unreconciled victim because it is, in fact, his own projected desire to fight on but is re-experienced as a fear of the enemy's desire to destroy him. This process of "projective identification" defends the unreconciled victim from experiencing destructive feelings as his own and enables him to introject an idealized fantasy of revolutionary omnipotence—the fantasy of victims capable of liberating themselves from evil forces on which they do not depend and with which they will not have to coexist hereafter.[13]

In stressing this point, I want to acknowledge that any revolution may be unsure of final victory, and that even the most successful revolutions have real enemies. I am concerned here, however, with the moral logic of continuing to press the who/whom question as a way of winning. Most revolutionary movements, to a greater or lesser degree, portray postrevolutionary justice as a form of militant struggle against the return of past evil, and most will need to demonize some present representatives of that past in order to make the struggle real. Even if initially successful revolutions did not have enemies, they would need to create them—and they do.

In practice this often means that such revolutions will treat the continuing beneficiaries of past evil as would-be perpetrators—counterrevolutionary threats—and that some beneficiaries will react to this apparently unjust treatment by *becoming* enemies of the revolution. The struggle for revolutionary justice will thus continue until the ongoing beneficiaries of the old regime cease feeling threatened by the new. But this, for the unreconciled victim, would represent both a moral and material defeat. The unreconciled victim must thus repudiate the "merely moral" victory that is there to be claimed—for him, the danger of moral defeat is always real. It will have already occurred if he gives up the struggle for material justice; it may yet occur if he pursues that struggle until the revolution discredits itself.

The political trajectory of revolutionary justice is thus to create enemies until it is eventually defeated by the enemies it creates—first morally, and then politically. The constitutional purpose of the TRC was to take South Africa off this trajectory once and for all.[14] On the threshold of power, the ANC understood that in revolutionary justice the victim is to become victor; the problem with this concept is that nothing counts as winning except continuing the fight.

Deconstructing Victimhood: Liberal Justice

How, then, could the TRC attempt to reconcile the moral attitudes that made South Africans capable of engaging in righteous struggle with the moral attitudes that would make them capable of ending it? The answer is relatively simple. If the category of unreconciled victimhood is constructed by the ultimate refusal to distinguish between the perpetrators and beneficiaries of evil, then it can be deconstructed in the aftermath of struggle through institutional practices that reinstate such a distinction. This is the essence of the TRC's project of justice-as-reconciliation, the purpose of which is to delegitimate and marginalize the "unreconciled victim" of revolutionary theory who sees the beneficiaries of oppression as would-be perpetrators and who wages righteous struggle against perpetrator and beneficiary alike.

Justice-as-reconciliation replaces the unreconciled victim of revolutionary theory with the victim who was morally undamaged by past oppression. This lack of moral damage is demonstrated by the victim's retrospective willingness to distinguish, after all, between perpetrators and beneficiaries. The passive beneficiary of injustice can identify fully with the victim, much as the comfortable reader of a literary melodrama is expected to identify with the victim of the social injustices therein portrayed. The condition of this identification is to distinguish between all other grievous injuries done to victims and the distinctively moral kind of damage that would make victims capable of doing injustice in their turn, and thus incapable of legitimate rule.[15]

According to this liberal script, passive beneficiaries of social injustice will not feel guilt, but will rather identify with the innocence of idealized victims whose ability to transcend their suffering reveals that they were never really a threat. This new social compact between undamaged victims and passive beneficiaries presupposes that the unreconciled victim has been damaged by the past and that the beneficiaries of past evil would have been justified in hearing that victim's voice as a threat. Reconciled victims, however, get to "win" in this liberal scenario and to be relatively safe, but only on condition that they demand little more than this from their putative victory. For them, moral victory must be victory enough.

The acknowledgment and repair of moral damage on the part of victims reverse the logic of "consciousness raising" through which unreconciled victims might have become revolutionaries in the period when evil still ruled. It foregrounds reconciliation as a moral (and not merely political) imperative that is no less part of our conception of justice than the capacity for righteous struggle against injustice.[16]

In the aftermath of struggle, the liberal project of "transitional justice" systematically distinguishes between the perpetrators and beneficiaries of past injustice, and refuses to treat one as the other. By making, or acknowledging, these distinctions, former victims can show themselves to have been morally undamaged by their suffering in a way that reassures the continuing beneficiaries of evil that they will not be treated as perpetrators. Those unreconciled victims who remain are marginalized as criminals or terrorists—the moral equivalent of those "extremists" on the other side who play on the fears of beneficiaries that they will be victimized in their turn.

This idea was centrally at stake in what may have been the defining moment of the TRC's public hearings: the appearance of Winnie Mandela. To many South Africans, black and white, she represented the unreconciled victim for whom the anti-apartheid struggle was not yet over. The agenda of her hearing was to demonstrate that she was also (therefore?) morally damaged—a genuine victim whose persecution had made her capable of criminal behavior in her turn. Time and again, Archbishop Tutu pleaded with her to admit her moral damage, and each time she responded with reserve.[17] The overall effect was to construct her as the very figure that the TRC meant to marginalize. She now represented the implicit antitype of Nelson Mandela, the reconciled and morally undamaged victim who was fit to rule.[18] The greatest appeal of justice-as-reconciliation does not lie in its fuzzy notion of "forgiving," but rather in the fact that it has a clear notion of "winning": something the revolutionary model of justice lacks.[19]

We are now in a position to better appreciate the sense in which the TRC portrays reconciliation as a historically specific form of justice rather than a compromise with injustice. If its underlying project is to deconstruct revolutionary victimhood, then success depends upon the specific truth to be established when its official procedures are done. The particular truths that can lead to reconciliation are those that enable previously unreconciled victims to distinguish once again between the perpetrators and beneficiaries of past evil, and thus permit continuing beneficiaries to believe that, henceforth, unreconciled victims will be on the same moral footing as unreconstructed perpetrators. To live on after systemic evil, to survive it, might seem to require that surviving beneficiaries be allowed to live *off* that evil without being deemed to have revived it.

The crucial, and controversial, assumption here is that an evil *can* be truly dead even if its beneficiaries continue to prosper from it. Those of us who are troubled by this assumption will find it natural to respond by reverting to the revolutionary logic of justice as struggle described earlier: "The evil still lives," we will say, "so the struggle continues." This response may be appropriate in South Africa, where by some measures, the level of social inequality is now greater than under apartheid. If the vast majority of South Africans continue to suffer from the effects of racialized exploitation, then perhaps the project of justice-as-reconciliation is an ideological means of preserving those effects without resort to overt repression.[20] I will later suggest that there is merit in this critique if we can make it without reverting to the logic of unreconciled victimhood.

My point, thus far, is that we should not underestimate the power of this revolutionary/counterrevolutionary logic. Beneficiaries of injustice can and will fear that everything could be taken away by victims who treat them as perpetrators; victims, in their turn, will often come to fear persecution at the hands of those from whom they demand greater equality. Continuing this psychology of struggle can idealize each potentially threatened group in the eyes of its members and thus keep solidarity alive. This is often an effective defense against the anxiety that former victims will feel about the difficulty of coexisting with one-time persecutors, and vice versa.[21] If, however, continuing to struggle is the *only* possible defense against anxiety about the end of struggle, then there can be no permissible outlet for reparative impulses on either side. For the very idea of struggle to make moral sense, *something* has to count as having won. Otherwise, justice-as-struggle will always be insufficient.

What, then, is the appropriate attitude to take toward the already-defeated? The justification of the former struggle is not in itself sufficient to answer this question: We cannot continue to fight those who have already lost without ultimately discrediting ourselves. How, then, is a just war (or other righteous struggle) to end? Both judgment and mercy are possible ways of ending such a struggle from a position of moral superiority. They are the biblical attitudes of God—equally appropriate alternative responses to a defeated evil.

Reconciliation is a third way of living with defeated evil, but it is not always a form of moral victory. In many circumstances, reconciliation may even be difficult to distinguish from compromise and moral defeat. To avoid this difficulty, the proponents of justice-as-struggle would permanently deny the victims their moral victory over apartheid as long as its material aftereffects remain. They thus pursue a path in which victory is evanescent and the danger of moral defeat is present at every turn. This is the critique that revolutionaries characteristically make of reconciliation, the chosen path of the ANC after the release of Nelson Mandela in 1990.

The TRC *Report*

Viewed politically, the TRC's *Report* represents the ANC's abandonment of its revolutionary goals as a way of winning the armed struggle that began after Sharpeville in March 1960. The TRC could not accomplish this, however, by simply portraying the ANC as the victor in a righteous struggle—there was too much compromise for that, and no decisive battle. Rather, the *Report* found a moral victory for the ANC in its willingness to renounce the logic of righteous struggle in order to confront the moral damage inflicted on those who followed its strategy of making South Africa "ungovernable" in the mid-1980s.

The fundamental challenge of the *Report* was thus not merely to decide "who won" the struggle that had recently ended, but also to end the struggle proactively by redefining what it would mean to have won. Through the TRC's approach to reconciliation, the victims of apartheid would be promised a moral victory, at least, with possible economic benefits to come. The TRC's *Report* is fundamentally an effort to seize that moral victory and to distinguish it from the political and economic compromises that also occurred.[22]

Archbishop Tutu makes this clear in the *Report*'s Foreword:

[T]he bulk of victims have been black and I have been saddened by what has appeared to be a mean-spiritedness in some of the leadership in the white community. They should be saying: "How fortunate we are that these people do not want to treat us as we treated them. How fortunate that things have remained much the same for us except for the loss of some political power." Can we imagine the anger that has been caused? . . . Should our land not be overwhelmed by black fury leading to orgies of revenge, turning us into a Bosnia, a Northern Ireland or a Sri Lanka?[23]

This comment illustrates the degree to which the moral logic of revolution and civil war lies behind the rationale for reconciliation as the Archbishop conceives it. He had famously said at Chris Hani's funeral in 1993, "We are marching toward victory." But the real victory was to be "a victory of peace and reconciliation over the violence and alienation of apartheid."[24] Now, in October 1998, Tutu had come to declare that the victory had been won and that the absence of reprisal was a sign of moral superiority on the part of those who struggled and suffered, a moral superiority that seals their right to rule.

This is a form of Christian politics, but it should not be confused with the Christian self-abnegation that Nietzsche dismissed as "slave morality." Rather, Archbishop Tutu was proposing a peculiarly Nietzschean Christianity, a Christianity in which the goodness of those who suffered is and ought to be humiliating to those who stood by. The Archbishop intends this *Report* to show that whites were saved without deserving it and that nonwhites, particularly blacks, were their saviors. What is the appropriate moral attitude of the saved? The Archbishop's argument is that a feeling of relief is not enough, that humility and contrition are also necessary.[25]

This would be a victory for blacks of a distinctively moral kind—establishing once and for all that the evil of apartheid was an affront to the goodness of blacks. TRC Commissioner Wynand Malan, in stating his "Minority Position," objects to precisely this aspect of the majority's view—in effect, its core argument—as *ultra vires* because it is a religious and moral claim about political communities rather than a finding of fact about individuals. In this respect, he believes, the *Report* participates in the divisive logic of apartheid itself.[26]

Commissioner Malan has indeed located a central question about the majority's approach, although not quite the one he identifies. The *Report* implies that the moral superiority of the black community is to be established through self-restraint, a refusal to rule as it had been ruled. Does this mean that redistributive initiatives, if there are any, must come from *white* beneficiaries of apartheid, rather than being imposed by majority rule? Does it mean that redistribution by majority rule will only be legitimate when there are enough black beneficiaries of the new order to pay a significant share? Would the black majority sacrifice the moral superiority that the *Report* confers upon them if they were to demand more now at the expense of whites?

These are not questions that the *Report* directly answers. Despite its multivocal tone, it carefully avoids the moral relativism that Malan believes to be the only way forward—the recognition that in a land of "multiple truths" bygones must finally be bygones. There is, however, a thread of argument in the *Report* that Malan seems to miss, a recurring concern with the question of *moral damage* and its relevance to the democratic legitimacy of ANC rule.

This concern with moral damage is intertwined with the separate thread of argument by which the Commission defends itself against the charge that it was an ANC tool. Perhaps the most widely noted aspect of the *Report* was the Commission's decision to include the ANC among the perpetrators of human rights violations, and the ANC's subsequent effort to suppress the *Report* that it had commissioned.[27] The precise issue here was whether the *Report's* moral endorsement of the ANC's militant struggle against apartheid should have put the violence of the liberation movement in a category different from the acts of violence committed in support of the regime.

Following the news accounts of ANC objections to the *Report,* I read it with a particular focus on the question of moral equivalence between the perpetrators of violence on each side of the revolutionary struggle. The argument it gives is very subtle and is dispersed throughout the five volumes. It is, however, one of the paramount achievements of the TRC, and it deserves more careful notice than it has thus far received. Let me here sketch the main points as they bear upon the tension between justice-as-struggle and justice-as-reconciliation discussed above.

- Apartheid was a crime against humanity, and the struggle to overthrow apartheid was a just war.[28]
- Not all violent acts committed in furtherance of that just war were themselves just.[29]
- This does *not* imply a moral equivalence for the excesses of each side. The violence of the powerful is far less excusable than the violence of the powerless, because the powerful have affirmative duties to protect the citizens of the nation.[30]
- One effect of crimes committed by the powerful is to hystericize protest—which weakens the distinction between symptoms of powerlessness (like crime and group violence) and effective means of resistance.[31]
- The moral damage suffered by powerless victims is one of the deepest harms of the experience of gross injustice,[32] and it is deepened further by the acts that must sometimes be committed in struggle against injustice. The ANC (and also Inkatha) would not have committed or condoned such crimes but for the struggle against apartheid.[33]

This analysis has clear implications for the present generation of ANC leaders as legatees of the apartheid state:

- The thirty-year revolutionary struggle against apartheid will have brought to power resistance leaders who have become potentially capable of misrule.
- They must also be capable of confronting and healing their own moral damage so that the nation can know that it is not ruled by potential murderers.
- Only in this way, can the nation as a whole view this particular aftermath of evil as a salvation rather than a punishment.

In a fundamental sense the *Report* is, as its critics charge, a legitimation of ANC rule. What is remarkable, however, is the form of that legitimation. The TRC does not argue that ANC rule will be legitimate because it was the victor in a righteous struggle. Instead, the TRC bases the legitimacy of ANC rule on its willingness to renounce the logic of struggle and to confront the moral damage inflicted by that logic on all those who followed its "ungovernability strategy." This was clearly not the legitimation that then Deputy President Mbeki wanted, but President Mandela, in accepting the TRC's *Report* "with all its imperfections," may have recognized that it gave the ANC both penance and absolution.

The task before the TRC was thus extremely delicate. Its final *Report* had to make the crimes of the ANC and the apartheid government morally equivalent after the struggle without conceding that they were morally equivalent while evil still reigned. This is a difficult line to draw, but one that was necessary in order to establish that the ANC is *now* morally undamaged by its persecution, and thus fit to rule.

In the extensive literature on "transitional justice," there is nothing like the TRC *Report* in its scope, its critical self-awareness, and its understanding of its place in a process of reconciliation that it regards as never-ending. The *Report's* approach to national recovery can be dismissed as an alternative to justice only if we hold fast to the model of justice-as-struggle. Otherwise, it arguably reflects an alternative *conception* of justice based on the undamaged, rather than the unreconciled, victim.[34] Although the TRC's approach to transitional justice acknowledges the need for economic redistribution, it presupposes a deep discontinuity between the moral impulses that demand the eradication of past injustice and those that allow us to create a consensus that the evil that produced such injustice is truly past.[35] The former follow the moral logic of just war; the latter, the logic of reconciliation and peacemaking. From this perspective, the Human Rights Culture that is generally sought in the aftermath of evil regimes is not merely a political compromise with injustice that is necessary in order to end a righteous struggle. It rather reflects a nonrevolutionary conception of transitional justice as something other than a first step toward redistributing the illegitimate gains of past oppression. We must thus consider whether this liberal successor to the revolutionary idea of justice is plausible on its own terms.

The Transition to Liberalism

There is now a large and growing literature on the transition to *liberal* democracy after periods of state-sponsored oppression.[36] A common theme in this literature is that successful transitions depend upon constructed narratives that allow the victims and beneficiaries of past injustice to share their fear of reenacting past struggle.[37] This theme, as I have written elsewhere,[38] is an effort to replace the moral logic of agonistic struggle with a moral logic of common survivorship and collective rebirth. The point of survivor's justice, thus conceived, is to go forward on a common moral footing—not because the past has been forgiven or forgotten, but because continuing to struggle against an evil that is gone is no longer appropriate, and may be morally equivalent to reviving it.

In the present essay, I have gone on to interpret transitional liberalism as a surrogate for the forms of revolutionary and counterrevolutionary politics that dominated the second half of the twentieth century. South Africa's TRC was, by design, a culmination of this *fin de siècle* project.[39] It followed the example of previous truth commissions in reducing the politics of revolution and counterrevolution to the moral psychology of violence and the fear of violence. Critics of the TRC correctly state that it was not required to embrace this limited conception of its role: its mandate explicitly permitted it to consider the cumulative social injustice produced by apartheid (which began in 1948) and by earlier forms of racialized exploitation as the *context* of the revolutionary and counterrevolutionary violence that occurred between 1960 and 1994, the period of the TRC's official mandate.[40] This period begins with the Sharpeville massacres of 1960, the moment when the anti-apartheid movement embraced the strategy of revolutionary armed struggle. Within its mandated period, the TRC focused further on 1978–89,[41] the years immediately following successful communist revolutions in Mozambique and Angola (1974), Cambodia and Viet Nam (1975), and massive unrest in Soweto (1976). These events had made it possible for the Botha government, which came to power in 1978, to recast the defense of apartheid in South Africa as a "total strategy" against the "total onslaught" of global communism. By the late 1970s, South Africa's State Security Council (SSC) had, as part of its "total strategy," embraced the same extralegal tactics of state terrorism, torture, and murder that were practiced by other US-supported authoritarian regimes toward the end of the Cold War. These were the techniques that were later condemned as "gross" violations of human rights by truth commissions set up to promote democratic transitions in Latin America and elsewhere.[42]

The TRC thus dealt with precisely those aspects of apartheid that had most in common with other "securitocratic" responses to revolution (and in the Eastern Bloc to counterrevolution) during the final years of the Cold War. An implicit conclusion of the *Report* is that whites had reason to fear the consequences of majority rule in 1976 when they believed South Africa was in danger of becoming another Mozambique or Angola.[43] Perhaps for this reason, the responsibility of the Reagan and Thatcher governments for supporting Botha's "total strategy" was never addressed by the TRC. Its final *Report* went no farther with this issue than the Latin American truth commissions, which never explicitly rejected the proposition that a real threat of communist revolution might have excused extralegal repression by the state as the lesser of two evils.[44] By the 1990s, the generally accepted precondition for creating a new Human Rights Culture was the repudiation by the left of its revolutionary aims. Nonwhites in South Africa were thus allowed their moral victory over apartheid only after whites had "won" the Cold War.[45] In the vast and growing literature on transitional liberalism, there is virtual agreement that if the new Human Rights Culture is to take hold, *non*victims are the constituency that must be persuaded that the past was evil. The live questions concern *their* fears of empowering those who suffered in the old regime.

What would it take to persuade those who merely benefited or stood by, that in the minds of victims, the struggle against past evil has come to an end? This question underlies the plethora of recent books on creating a Human Rights Culture. The answer today almost always involves either trials or truth commissions. Significantly, the relative "success" of these alternatives is judged less by how effective they are in exposing and discrediting the most egregious perpetrators than by the procedural assurance the "rule of law" affords to those with more attenuated responsibility that they will not be subject to reprisal.[46] In this respect, the addressees of both truth commissions and trials are almost always the beneficiaries and victims of the collective injustices that were the context of "gross human violations" against individuals.[47]

We must note, however, that the survivor stories that appear in the great documents of transitional liberalism, such as the *Nunca Más* series and the TRC *Report,* are almost never *about* the victims and beneficiaries of systemic injustice as such. They are rather about a narrow class of victims (those who suffered physical torment) and a narrow class of perpetrators (their active tormenters). Although one might argue that focusing on these particular atrocity stories merely puts a human face on collective injustice, much of the recent writing on human rights in political transitions explicitly rejects this interpretation as incompatible with reestablishing (or establishing) the "rule of law." The rule of law in the aftermath of evil is expressly meant to decollectivize both injury and responsibility, and to redescribe systemic violence as a series of individual crimes.[48] Punishment or amnesty will then appear as forms of closure —either one of which may be appropriate in particular circumstances, and both of which are preferable to collective reprisals.[49]

The point of this now-familiar story of liberal transitions is to reduce the broad spectrum of collective injury to individual acts of cruelty and to suggest that the root of such cruelty may lie in the willingness to treat individuals as representatives of collective evil.[50] Beneficiaries of past injustice are expected (when the story works) to identify with individual victims (or at least with their pain) and also to see themselves *as* victims, now that they know the "truth" about the regime they once condoned.[51] (If they still identified with perpetrators, the story would not have worked.) Those who suffered because of group oppression are expected, in their turn, to identify with the innocence of passive beneficiaries who were *not* perpetrators, and who would never again condone the acts of perpetrators out of fear of what the victory of victims might mean.

Former beneficiaries are almost always broadly aware of the harms and cruelties done to victims—how could they not be? But they may also believe that the victims of such cruelty must have been morally damaged by their experience and therefore be capable of even greater injustice in return. The primary problem here is not that the beneficiaries of past evil are inclined to deny that its victims were degraded in a material and physical sense, but rather that they are inclined to believe that these victims must have been degraded morally as well. These beneficiaries may be willing to fight on (even to the death), not because they believe that their cause is just, but rather because it has made them justly hated by an enemy whose triumph they would now have even greater reason to fear.

In a sense, the project of "transitional liberalism" in South Africa is to make this fear inexpressible in public political discussion. To give the fear its due, however, we should remember Socrates' argument that the *only* harm that is done by injustice is to make its victims capable of injustice. From this it followed that rule by damaged victims after a revolution is a paradigmatic form of misrule. We need not agree with Socrates that moral damage is the only harm of past injustice to see it as a genuine harm that can strike fear into the hearts of beneficiaries, especially those who believe themselves to be justly hated. In the South African context, Rian Malan, in *My Traitor's Heart*, has identified this underlying attitude in himself, the quintessential "Just White Man" who resisted the regime. His point is that all South African whites were morally damaged in the struggle over apartheid by the belief that blacks could justly hate them. For some, this damage took the form of tolerating an otherwise abhorrent regime; for others, it was expressed in the delusion that they could cleanse themselves by opposing it.[52]

At its core, the project of transitional liberalism presupposes the near-universality of moral damage in periods of gross injustice and the consequent need for a form of justice in which all parties are more concerned with repairing this damage in themselves than with demanding or receiving restitution. Christianity provides the two moral templates for the problem of transitional justice thus conceived. It first asks victims of evil to recognize themselves as would-be perpetrators; it then requires all who would be saved to identify themselves as passive beneficiaries of gross injustice—the ultimate injustice that Christ himself suffered on the cross.

This Christian message bears a close resemblance to the "truth"—the moral truth—to be established in recent liberal transitions by truth commissions or human rights trials. According to this truth, passive beneficiaries were saved (often without deserving it) because of the moral qualities exhibited by victims whose experience of suffering did not make them threats after all. Once this "truth" has been entrenched in political culture, the reconciliation of passive beneficiaries and morally undamaged victims can be accomplished, as we have seen, by splitting-off and demonizing the irreconcilables on both sides—the "terrorists" and "fanatics" who must now be identified and condemned because they are still living in the past. The public's intolerance of those who fight on strengthens the political consensus that the evil is past. By promoting this consensus, both truth commissions and trials offer salvation to the passive beneficiaries and all others who were *not* perpetrators and who may themselves come to identify with rescued victims. The achievement of a Human Rights Culture marginalizes those on both sides who are still willing to fight on by establishing a shared understanding of what the past *will have been* so that a return to struggle would be equally reprehensible on all sides. To have established a consensus of the rule of law is to create a future moral equivalence between those unreconciled victims who advocate acts of terrorism against beneficiaries of the old regime and extremists on the other side who incite the fears of beneficiaries that they will be so treated if they do not look the other way at reports of vigilantism. Human rights in the new dispensation are based, not on past suffering, but on the transcendence of suffering.

In this respect, the foundational premise of the *fin de siècle* Human Rights Culture is "never again"—the replacement of a politics of cruelty and the fear it inspires with a fear of fear itself.[53] What victims and beneficiaries tend to share in the new liberal dispensation is a commitment not to revive the former relationship between victims and perpetrators by confusing those who were morally responsible for past evil with those who were merely lucky enough to benefit from it. To be sure, the literature on the emerging Human Rights Culture takes the overt form of a debate about whether truth commissions or political trials are most conducive to a posttraumatic culture of respect for human rights.[54] But that debate should not obscure the shared goal of both procedures, which is to construct a public narrative of the history of individual victims and perpetrators that will replace a politics rooted in the collective fear that beneficiaries have of former victims.[55]

Justice between Times

But what follows from this struggle for the soul of the nonvictim in an emerging Human Rights Culture? Is relieving him of guilt an alternative to structural reform, or a precondition? To what extent may structural reform collectively disadvantage the vicarious beneficiaries of a past evil (e.g., through reverse discrimination), and in what situations would structural reform be experienced and symbolized as a collective (and perhaps vicarious) punishment that treats all nonvictims as perpetrators?

Writers on transitional liberalism disagree about the compatibility of providing political reassurance to nonvictim groups and promoting critical self-reflection on their responsibility for the past.[56] Is it really necessary to choose between these aims? they ask. If so, which choice would be most likely to reduce the defensiveness of those whose interests were broadly served by a past regime that has lost its moral purchase? This question is often raised in discussions of whether, and where, to draw a boundary between mere bystanders and passive beneficiaries of the old regime. Will the general exoneration of all nonperpetrators be more conducive to national "healing" than a result that inculpates those whose interests were served?[57] Or is the project of identifying and measuring the persistent effect of unjust advantage essential to the task of making whole a divided nation?

In transitional liberalism this redistributive project can never be rejected in principle and can never be pursued in practice.[58] The problem is always that in states recovering from traumatic histories, distributive justice will inevitably have a retributive side. The Human Rights Culture is thus essentially a period of grace in which redistributive claims in the name of victims are indefinitely deferred to the extent that they would appear to exact retribution from fellow-survivors who now also reject the past as evil and have thus been "saved." In a sense, this grace period presents itself as a special time—the time it takes to complete the past time, the time before accounts can finally be settled.[59] This special time, however, can be of indefinite duration: its lesson is that we are never in more danger of relapsing into the patterns of the past than when we believe we have recovered from history.[60] From this perspective, the victim's demand for justice *now* can always be rejected as an idolatry of the present—a belief that we are already living at the privileged moment of judgment when the past can be put safely behind us. To reject this idolatry is to demystify the present, which now (and always) appears as a time between times—the past time of suffering and the time of redemption yet to come.[61] Permanent recovery requires that those who happened to come out ahead acknowledge as evil the practices that produced their present advantage. Yet it also leaves much of that advantage in place insofar as the absence of a redistributive politics demonstrates, both morally and psychologically, the capacity of former victims to regard the evil as past and to get on with their lives. In a "recovering" nation, former victims of the old regime cannot attempt to win without challenging the consensus that the historical evil is truly past. In contrast, the passive beneficiaries of a defeated evil have a lighter burden—they have no need to defend a past that former victims still need to attack.

The broad position that I am here calling transitional liberalism has been referred to by different names. Supporters sometimes refer to it as the "Human Rights Culture" or "the decent society" (as opposed to the just society), or simply "the liberalism of fear."[62] The essence of this position is to build a consensus on the moral values by which a nation of survivors will judge the past, a consensus that tends to work against efforts to portray the aftereffects of evil as symptoms of its continuing presence.

Thus described, transitional liberalism has little moral plausibility as a self-sustaining position. Its appeal depends on describing the revolutionary alternative as a kind of hell in which the worst atrocities are always committed by victors with the consciousness of victims in the name of final judgment.[63] Yet transitional liberalism is itself merely the suspension of a final judgment that must remain forever possible: constant vigilance is required to prevent relapse into the patterns and practices of the past. Justice-as-reconciliation thus authorizes and presupposes the very wish for revolutionary justice that it seeks to censor. It relies on fantasies of genocidal guilt and punishment that will remain potent enough to suggest that the project of recovery may never end. Instead of "burying the past" to avoid reliving it, transitional liberalism is haunted by a past that it fears will return. The result is a constitutional discourse that enshrines the logic of historical transition in much the same way that the discourse of the personal "recovery movement" makes permanent the logic of incurable disease.[64]

In consciously posttraumatic regimes, as we have seen, former victims can't win unless they are willing to settle for a moral victory (a story) as victory enough. This is *not* the expected result of the Rawlsian theory of justice, with its "maximin" principle benefitting the worst-off. In the model of "justice-as-reconciliation," however, the "worst-off" are also, and more importantly, *victims* —and the most relevant issue is whether their demand for benefits will return society to the logic of revolution and civil war from which it has so recently escaped. The "worst-off" citizens of states recovering from a traumatic past will thus be effectively barred from demanding redistribution if in making such demands they must first represent themselves as the unreconciled "victims" of past evil. For this reason, justice-as-reconciliation is in important ways *reconciliation to continuing inequality* as a morally acceptable aftermath of past evil.

I want to stress this point while giving comparable stress to the fact that it is not the whole story. In the liberal model of justice-as-reconciliation, it becomes politically acceptable to struggle over how the victims' suffering will be *remembered,* provided that the struggle over the past is sharply distinguished from the ordinary politics of gain and loss. This split perspective distinguishes transitional liberalism as a way of reconciling the "survivors" of past injustice from reactionary liberalism that denies the reality of victimhood itself.

I am not, however, satisfied with the notion that justice-as-reconciliation is merely a "transitional" form of liberalism—distinct both from a Rawlsian liberalism that promises social equality and from a reactionary form of liberalism that blocks most attempts at achieving equality. Suppose, for a moment, that *all* liberalism is based on fear of the moral logic of justice-as-struggle. We might then say that liberalism needs victims to keep that fear alive, but that it does not know quite what to do with their sense of injustice.

Liberalism thus needs victims of a particular kind—victims who no longer identify beneficiaries as potential perpetrators and who would come to feel that any attempt to identify perpetrators, as such, is a form of demonization.[65] To base a redistributive claim on past victimhood would be to identify those who must pay as responsible (at least vicariously) for the past in a way that is incompatible with Rawlsian principles. Whenever the "worst-off" speak as "victims," the advancement of liberal values will preclude extensive redistribution that might have been justified on Rawlsian principles in a society without traumatic history. Rawlsian justice must never be retributive: it is not in its very conception a way of winning.[66]

The foregoing critique of transitional democracy is not new. For Karl Marx, liberal democracies are always transitional in the sense that feudal oppressors have been morally defeated (or "put in the past"), even while the beneficiaries of that oppression continue to prosper. Class analysis began as a way to think about this problem, and I believe that something like it needs to be reinvented as a way to address the specific historical conditions of liberal regimes in the emerging Human Rights Cultures that are replacing authoritarian regimes.[67]

A class analysis of transitional democracy would, in my view, focus on the ways in which this form of government rules not only in the name of the victims of past injustice but also in the interests of the beneficiaries. These beneficiaries seek to legitimate their continuing power on the basis of both repugnance for the perpetrators of past evil and fear of being ruled by its morally damaged victims. A class analysis of this type of ruling ideology would seek to reestablish the link between the backward- and forward-looking faces of a liberalism that must always represent itself as "transitional."

Class analysis, however, will not be enough without a new look at the moral imperatives that underlie it. I began this essay with the premise that the liberal model of justice-as-reconciliation is defective because it does not allow the historical victims of conquest and oppression to win (unless they accept a moral victory as victory enough). This criticism makes sense from the moral perspective of "the transition to socialism" in which the former victim will be victorious in the end. We have seen, however, that in the literature on transitions to liberalism, justice-as-reconciliation represents both a deconstruction and a critique of the revolutionary model of justice as a continuing struggle for final victory. If the critique of transitional liberalism is that past victims never win, the liberal response can now be that in revolutionary justice nothing counts as winning other than the perpetuation of struggle itself. In transitional liberalism the victims can, at least, enjoy their moral victory. But what is this moral victory, and how does it relate to justice in nations, such as South Africa, that are recovering from a history of systemic repression?

Mock Reparation?

The moral logic of the TRC's *Report* recognizes that the fear of genocidal punishment (and the residual hate that follows from it) will be difficult to eliminate if the beneficiaries of past evil see themselves as susceptible to future victimization when the full extent of past atrocity is known. To avoid this scenario, the TRC has attempted to redirect rather than eliminate the hate and fear that both the perpetrators and beneficiaries of past oppression may harbor toward their former victims. Its proceedings have allowed the beneficiaries to identify themselves as fellow-survivors and hence transform their latent guilt into a sense of shame over their impotence in evil times.[68] Some previously unreconciled victims have in turn become capable of embarrassment for the shame of past oppressors, and have thereby relinquished the desire to carry on old struggles until material justice has been achieved.[69]

This is a psychologically plausible approach to the concerns of *whites* in South Africa. The journalist Rian Malan suggests that all South African whites, regardless of politics, defend against their anxieties about punishment and rescue by splitting off their fantasies of good and bad victims of apartheid, which are then projected onto blacks.[70] In a sense, the work of the TRC builds on such split-off fantasies of genocidal punishment by allowing the good victims (Nelson Mandela) to rescue the beneficiaries from the bad victims (Winnie Mandela). Americans should have no difficulty understanding this view of what it means to be an Afrikaner (African). Throughout US history, "playing Indian" and fearing Indians has been part of what it means to be an "American."[71] The Indians were (in our national fantasy) "split" into idealized objects with whom we identified, and persecutory objects whom we eliminated or controlled. Through these forms of identification and projection, "we Americans" permit ourselves to keep our conquered territory. Malan's remarkable book, *My Traitor's Heart*, suggests that Afrikaner tribal identity was never based on an abstract belief in white superiority as such, but rather on a similar white anxiety. The method of coping is also similar: an idealization of the "good" African with whom one can identity, and a fear of being slaughtered by the "bad" African, who must be either eliminated or controlled.[72]

That fantasies of unlimited vulnerability (being subject, for example, to genocide and torture) explain some part of the capacity of collectivities both to struggle and make peace is undeniable. This can be true when the fantasies reflect a fear of being victimized again and also when they reflect a fear of being punished by one's former victims. The element of projective identification in all such fantasies supports the approach of the TRC in treating white and black fears equally. This splitting of the victim of systemic injustice into an object to be loved and an object to be feared is a way of ensuring that guilt and loss are not directly experienced by the beneficiaries of past evil, because they never recognize the objects of that guilt as having been damaged by themselves.

Thus described, the model that I have called "justice-as-reconciliation" is not a path to justice at all. It is, rather, a form of what some psychoanalysts call "mock" or "manic" reparation, which is also based on a splitting-off of truth and justice. In psychoanalytic theory, mock reparation is a manic response to anxiety that one's aggression will destroy a damaged object on which one also depends. In the words of one psychoanalyst:

> manic reparation is a defense in that its aim is to repair the object in such a way that guilt and loss are never experienced. . . . [T]he object in relation to which the reparation is done must never be experienced as having been damaged by oneself [and] must be felt as inferior, dependent, and, at depth contemptible. . . . Manic reparation can never be complete, because, if it were complete, the object fully restored would again become . . . free of the manic person's omnipotent control and contempt.[73]

In the United States, as in South Africa, the transitional devices for splitting questions of historical truth from questions of distributive justice are manic responses of this kind—fantasies of forgiving our victims for the guilt that we would otherwise feel. This is one way to relieve our anxiety about the self-destructive aspects of continuing to hate, but it does not address the victim as anything more than an internalized accuser, a part of the self. In effect, we cope with our fantasies of eliminating or controlling the victim we fear by internalizing a "good" victim who has recognized and coped with his (justifiable) hatred of us. In this way we continue to deny that the good victim and the bad victim are one and the same, and that reparative justice is necessary to reintegrate our experience of them.

Freud was first to describe the roles that identification, ambivalence, and fantasy play in our emotional responses to traumatic loss, a process that he called "the work of mourning." He understood that the immediate experience of survivorship is often accompanied by a sense of elation and triumph (which is what we do with our feeling of hatred and aggression toward the lost or injured object) and that these manic feelings are often followed by depressive bouts of intense self-criticism that are oddly unaccompanied by shame or remorse. What explains this pattern, he said, is that in our inner experience (fantasy), being a victim and having a victim are the same; that is, we understand what it means to be victimized by imagining ourselves to be the objects of our own aggressive fantasies about others. For this reason, victims of loss must always forgive themselves for the crimes that they did *not* commit as part of the work of mourning and recovery.[74] This is the kernel of moral truth on which justice-as-reconciliation rests—the pathological guilt of victimhood, which stands in the way of recovery.[75]

The moral error of justice-as-reconciliation, however, is to suggest that those who inflicted injury or benefited from it must also focus on recovery and self-forgiveness. The problem here is not only to understand the respects in which they were *like* victims because they too were driven by fantasies of being punished and thus projected the inner sources of their anxiety onto those whom they consequently feared. If this were enough, then beneficiaries and perpetrators would merely need to recover from their own inner pathologies to be reconciled with former victims. The problem, however, is that to some degree their guilt is not pathological but appropriate;[76] and as a result, the real work of mourning is not merely recovery but authentic *reparation*. For reparation to occur, the guilty mourner must overcome his sense of euphoric triumphalism in which anything is possible because he no longer needs an enemy. This manic fantasy of omnipotence is, indeed, the other face of depression and not a form of reparation at all. Neither is the phenomenon described by later Freudians as a "refusal to mourn"—a way of "swallowing loss" by incorporating and entombing the lost object within ourselves where we can punish it interminably without addressing our own feelings of guilt and aggression.[77] This occurs, for example, when German youth become the bearers of a missing *Yiddishkeit*, or American Boy Scouts act out the role of "the Vanished Indian." Consumption, however, is not a form of reparation.

We can, moreover, question whether either the "undamaged" or the "unreconciled" victim really exists in present-day South Africa, except as a projection of the moral anxieties of the rescued beneficiaries of deeply unjust regimes. As things turned out, many former combatants did not have to choose between moral victory and material reward—they rose to power in the new regime (Thabo Mbeki, Frank Chikane) or in the new economy (Moletsi Mbeki, Cyril Ramaphosa). This process has created in a very brief period a racially integrated South African ruling class. It does not, however, correspond to the picture of undamaged victims whose moral victory is to demand nothing more. In the new South Africa, there is also the widespread perception that the morally damaged victims have benefited the most from apartheid's demise.[78] This does not fit the model of justice-as-reconciliation, especially at a time when the degree of inequality between rich and poor is greater than it was when apartheid still seemed invulnerable.[79]

We have seen that the justice-as-reconciliation model has a moral logic that makes sense as a critique of justice-as-struggle, but we have not yet seen that it provides anything more than a form of mock-reparation, like playing Indian. The question we must now address is whether the moral strategies through which beneficiaries come to identify with their victims depoliticize the sense of injustice to a degree that blocks the possibility of large-scale societal change.

Pain and Pastness

For an answer, we must return again to the work of the TRC. To its credit, the TRC does not put forward either struggle or reconciliation as a model of justice. It employs, instead, the term "restorative justice," which is its English translation of *ubuntu*.[80] The *Report's* long list of examples of "reconciliation through truth"[81] are all intended to illustrate "restorative justice," which involves in each case a moral triumph over pain. From the standpoint of many moral views, the very notion of moral triumph is an oxymoron—no true morality can present itself as a way of winning. For this reason many moral philosophers, including Rawls, make a sharp distinction between retributive justice, which is based on historically given identities, and distributive justice, which must abstract from those very identities so that no one can be said to have "won." The work of the TRC, however, is of a different register than Rawlsian liberalism. Like previous truth commissions, the TRC reasons morally in the genre of melodrama. According to the literary scholar Peter Brooks: "The connotations of the word [melodrama] . . . include: the indulgence of strong emotionalism; moral polarization and schematization; extreme states of being, situations, actions; overt villainy, persecution of the good, and final reward of virtue; inflated extravagant expression; dark plotting, suspense, breathtaking peripety."[82] The written accounts of the ANC's work—whether in its own five-volume *Report,* or in the personal accounts of Antjie Krog[83] and Archbishop Tutu himself—are all powerful examples of "the melodramatic imagination," as described by Brooks. Their focus is overwhelmingly on intense confrontations, acts of torture, bodies in pain; their dramatic project is to equate pain with truth and cruelty with evil. In revealing the truth about pain, they thus achieve a partial victory over evil. Suffering is redeemed, and the victim is vindicated in the end.

It is hard to write about the reporting on truth commissions as a literary genre without seeming insensitive to the real human pain described. That, however, is part of the point. The work of truth commissions (and the vast literature about them) is *supposed* to make atrocities unthinkable by constructing moral evil as itself an insensitivity to the pain of others—a personal moral failing brought about by the individual's commitment to an ideal or to a group. The liberal theorist George Kateb makes this claim precisely:

It may be that evils on the greatest scale come about when governments and political groups persuade people to believe that there is evil greater than moral evil, or good greater than moral goodness. . . . [W]hen morality is dislodged from its supremacy, terrible evils result. . . . On the other hand, the production of evil on behalf of fighting moral evil or trying to achieve a positive moral good has also been enormous. . . . [P]olitical evil on a large scale is instigated when the normal abstract mentality of power holders is inflamed by an ideology that simultaneously inflames group identity . . . and ties that identity to a moral or transmoral purpose. Inflamed identity pursues its purposes without regard to moral limits: I mean respect for individual human beings, for what we now call human rights.[84]

For Kateb, evil itself is the result of the human temptation to struggle *against* evil in pursuit of some seemingly higher goal. To overcome evil, thus conceived, is to become more sensitive to the pain of individuals. The moral victory of the victims of torture and atrocity is to make the intentional infliction of human pain literally unthinkable by making readable their bodies in pain. It is a victory produced by the telling of their story.

This latter point, however, should give us pause. Bodily pain is not directly expressible in words: what makes it "readable" are the political conventions we have for representing its significance. These conventions are at work when the secret infliction of pain as "torture" is objectified as a social humiliation and defeat, and, again, when the public revelation of past torture is objectified as a melodramatic reversal that restores the victim's dignity in the world.[85] Were it not for these political conventions, the victim's moral experience of pain might be otherwise: pain's disclosure might be humiliating, in which case dignity might be best preserved by keeping suffering to oneself.[86]

What, then, are these political conventions? The most salient, perhaps, is that "pain is universally intelligible . . . trauma stands as truth," as Laura Berlant, a cultural critic, puts its. She describes this as the foundational assumption of an identity politics in which "pain is the only sign readable across the hierarchies of social life."[87] The notion that the true self is the self in pain, she argues, promotes the illusion that a nation can be built (or repaired) through "channels of affective identification and empathy . . . when the pain of intimate others burns into the conscience of classically privileged national subjects" (p. 53). According to Berlant, "this tactical use of trauma to describe the effect of social inequality . . . overidentifies the eradication of pain with the achievement of social justice" (p. 54). She concludes:

> The desire to use trauma as the model of the pain of subordination that gets congealed into identities forgets the difference between trauma and adversity: trauma takes you out of your life shockingly and places you into another one, whereas structural subordination is not a surprise to the subjects who experience it, and the pain of subordination is ordinary life. . . . The reparation of pain does not bring into being a just life. (pp. 76, 78)

Berlant's striking argument could be read as a partial critique of the concept of moral victory embodied in the TRC. For her, "pain is merely banal, a story always already told" (p. 77). By focusing on this story, the TRC identified a mere 20,000 "victims" of the revolutionary struggle to defeat apartheid (mostly combatants). There are, of course, millions more nontraumatized victims of apartheid and the systems of racialized exploitation that preceded it—victims whose suffering is not directly described in the TRC *Report*.[88]

As social realist melodrama, however, the TRC's *Report,* and the nationally broadcast hearings that preceded it, was in fact an effort to mediate public perceptions of these unmentioned victims of everyday life under apartheid. The Commission's stated purpose in this melodrama was to make continuing beneficiaries of apartheid more sympathetic to the needs of the poor when future redistributive measures are considered.[89] Its effect, however, was to give these beneficiaries hope that large numbers of nontraumatized victims would be inspired and humbled by the public example of victims who suffered *real pain,* and yet escaped moral damage. In the TRC's version of the truth, those who were traumatized and later reconciled became the official heroes of past struggle. Its proceedings would allow all who suffered to share their triumph by identifying with this retrospectively produced form of heroism.

Berlant might have been criticizing this conception of moral victory when she describes "a logic of fantasy reparation involved in the conversion of the scene of pain and its eradication to the scene of the political itself" (p. 57). The fantasy here is largely in the mind of the anxious beneficiary, still haunted by the specter of revolutionary politics.[90] It is a public form of the "mock reparation" described above.

There is, however, another way in which the reduction of injustice to bodily pain diminishes the evil of apartheid. As Elaine Scarry has said, "The most crucial fact about pain is its presentness."[91] Pain is thus our paradigm case of adversity that can be put in the past. When we speak of a pain that exists, we complain that it does not end; yet when it ends, it ceases to exist except in memory. This is not the way we speak of the social injuries that are the ordinary subject of demands for justice. These injuries are not so easily put in the past because they have effects outside us, and because to remember nonbodily injury is often to re-experience it. Here there can be no moral victory over the past that does not involve material changes in the present. As a foundation for forward-looking justice, the moral victory over past pain is hollow.

The introduction to this essay asks whether the cost of achieving a consensus that the past is evil is to agree also that the evil is past. The TRC clearly attempted to do both in its model of justice-as-reconciliation. But by reducing the scope of social injustice to pain, and the scope of political evil to cruelty, it largely failed to confront the forms of structural injustice produced by apartheid that continue after majority rule. Quite possibly, the TRC succeeded in persuading the beneficiaries and perpetrators of apartheid that the past was evil. Banal stories of pain and acknowledgment, always already told, will often serve this purpose for a time. But that consensus will not last unless the beneficiaries also believe that the time of evil is now past in the lives of those who suffered under apartheid. For many South Africans, however, the pastness of apartheid is not a fact, but rather an ideological construction that rationalizes their continuing subordination in a postrevolutionary age.

Notes

This essay was prepared for the Sawyer Seminar, Columbia University, 1 April 2000, and the "Forgiveness: Traditions and Implications" Conference organized by the Obert C. and Grace A. Tanner Humanities Center at the University of Utah, 13–15 April 2000. Earlier versions were presented at the University of Seattle, 31 January 2000; the University of Arizona School of Law, November 1998; and the University of Cape Town, August 1998. I am grateful for comments from Professors André Du Toit, Mahmood Mamdani, Sampie Terreblanche, Jeffrie Murphy, and Ronald Slye.

1. See, e.g., Kader Asmal et al., *Reconciliation through Truth: A Reckoning of Apartheid's Criminal Governance*, 2nd ed. (Cape Town: David Philip, 1997). Cf. Aryeh Neier, *War Crimes: Brutality, Genocide, Terror, and the Struggle for Justice* (New York: New York Times Books, 1998), pp. 104–5.

2. Dullah Omar, Minister of Justice, "Introduction," *Justice in Transition* (1995). (http://www.doj.gov.za/trc/legal/justice.htm).

3. See, e.g., Asmal et al., *Reconciliation.*

4. George M. Fredrickson, *The Comparative Imagination: On the History of Racism, Nationalism, and Social Movements* (Berkeley: University of California Press, 1997), pp. 147–48. See also Jakes Gerwel, "National Reconciliation: Holy Grail or Secular Pact?" in *Looking Back, Reaching Forward: Reflections on the Truth and Reconciliation Commission of South Africa*, ed. Charles Villa-Vicencio and Wilhelm Vervoerd (Cape Town: University of Cape Town Press, 2000), pp. 277–86.

5. The Promotion of National Unity and Reconciliation Act No. 34 of 1995, amended in 1997 and 1998 (http://www.doj.gov.za/trc/legal/index. htm#miscellaneous). The original eighteen-month term of the TRC was extended to two years through amendment.

6. See, e.g., Robert Meister, "Forgiving and Forgetting," in *Human Rights in Political Transitions: Gettysburg to Bosnia*, ed. Carla Hesse and Robert Post (New York: Zone Books, 1999), pp. 135–76.

7. Charles Villa-Vicencio, "Getting On with Life: A Move toward Reconciliation," in *Looking Back, Reaching Forward*, pp. 199–209.

8. Classical Marxism, for example, provides a theory that allows those who suffer under capitalism to identify the beneficiaries, and a practice intended to provoke those beneficiaries into identifying *themselves* as would-be perpetrators when their benefits are threatened by political action on behalf of the victims.

9. William Hinton, *Fanshen: A Documentary of Revolution in a Chinese Village* (New York: Vintage Books, 1966); see, e.g., pp. vii, 400–16, 473–75, 495–508, 548–66, 601–13.

10. Hannah Arendt, *Eichmann in Jerusalem: A Report on the Banality of Evil* (New York: Viking Press, 1963).

11. Primo Levi, *The Drowned and the Saved* (New York: Summit Books, 1988), pp. 70–73.

12. See, e.g. Frank Stern, *The Whitewashing of the Yellow Badge: Antisemitism and Philosemitism in Postwar Germany* (New York: Oxford University Press, 1992); idem, "German-Jewish Relations in the Postwar Period: The Ambiguities of Antisemitic and Philosemitic Discourse," in *Jews, Germans, Memory: Reconstructions of Jewish Life in Germany,* ed. Y. Michal Bodemann (Ann Arbor: University of Michigan Press, 1996), pp. 77–98; Philip Gourevitch, "The Return: With a Million Exiles Coming Home, Killers and Genocide Survivors Are Being Forced to Live Together (Letter From Rwanda)," *New Yorker,* 20 January 1997: 44–51. See also Gourevitch, *We Wish to Inform You That Tomorrow We Will Be Killed with Our Families: Stories from Rwanda* (New York: Farrar, Straus, Giroux, 1998).

13. Hanna Segal, *Introduction to the Work of Melanie Klein* (London: Hogarth Press [for] the Institute of Psycho-Analysis, 1975). See also Melanie Klein, "Love, Guilt, and Reparation (1937)," in *Love, Guilt, and Reparation, and Other Works, 1921–1945* (London: Virago Press, 1988), pp. 306–43.

14. Postamble to the Interim Constitution of the Republic of South Africa; Preamble of the Promotion of National Unity and Reconciliation Acts No 34 of 1995 (http://www.doj.gov.za/trc/legal/index.htm#miscellaneous).

15. Alok Rai, "Afterword," in Premchand, *Nirmala* (New Delhi: Oxford University Press, 1999).

16. Cf. C. Fred Alford, *Melanie Klein and Critical Social Theory: An Account of Politics, Art, and Reason Based on Her Psychoanalytic Theory* (New Haven, Conn.: Yale University Press, 1989). See also Robert Meister, "Two Concepts of Victimhood in Transitional Regimes," paper submitted to "Commissioning the Past," University of the Witwatersrand, Johannesburg, South Africa, 7–9 June 1999 (http://www.trcresearch.org.za/papers99/meister.pdf).

17. *Truth and Reconciliation Commission Report* (Cape Town: Juta, 1998), vol. 2, ch. 6; vol. 5 §138; Desmond Tutu, *No Future Without Forgiveness* (New York: Doubleday, 1999), pp. 167–75; Martin Meredith and Tina Rosenberg, *Coming to Terms: South Africa's Search for Truth* (New York: Public Affairs, 1999,) ch. 14; Alex Boraine, *A Country Unmasked: Inside South Africa's Truth and Reconciliation Commission* (Oxford: Oxford University Press, 2000), ch. 7. On the Mandela United Football Club Hearings, see *Report,* vol. 2, ch. 6; vol. 5, ch. 6 §138. For full transcripts, see http://www.truth.org.za/hrvtrans/event%5Fhearings.htm.

18. Mandela made this view explicit in his description of the TRC's charge: "All of us, as a nation that has newly found itself, share in the shame at the capacity of human beings of any race or language group to be inhumane to other human beings. We should all share in the commitment to a South Africa in which this will never recur" (Speech in National Assembly, 15 April 1997: http://www.doj.gov.za/trc/media/1997/9704/s970415e.htm).

19. I originally encountered this idea in Gandhi's *Hind Swaraj,* which explains why responding violently to past oppression is not the only alternative to cowardice. Imagine, Gandhi suggests, that you are awakened by a thief entering your bedroom and that in turning on the light you discover that the thief is in fact your own father. Would you not be embarrassed for his shame?

Gandhi is not here making the case for forgiveness, as we generally understand it. His moral point is rather about *winning.* The parable describes the moral attitude appropriate to someone who has *already won,* not the attitude of someone who is afraid that the moment he stops struggling he will lose. In developing this point, Gandhi goes on to suggest that this kind of moral victory converts the guilt of a defeated enemy into shame, and that embarrassment for this shame is a kind of empathy that can exist between the morally victorious and the morally defeated. He thus urged his fellow Indians to claim their moral victory over the British and to act accordingly. See Mohandas K. Gandhi, *Hind Swaraj or Indian Home Rule* (Ahmedabad: Navajivan Trust, reprinted 1946), pp. 72–75.

20. See, e.g., S. J. Terreblanche, "Production of the Past: Some Relevant Historical Truths Distorted and Ignored by the Truth and Reconciliation Commission," paper read at Sawyer Seminar, Institute of African Studies, Columbia University, New York, 1 April 2000; Sampie Terreblanche, "Dealing with Systematic Economic Injustice," in *Looking Back, Reaching Forward,* pp. 265–76; Bob Myers, *Is This Really What We Fought For? White Rule Ends, Black Poverty Goes On* (London: Index Books, 1997).

21. Alford, *Melanie Klein,* pp. 80–87.

22. For an authors' perspective on the *Report,* see Charles Villa-Vicencio and Wilhelm Vervoerd, "Constructing a Report: Writing up the 'Truth,'" in *Truth v. Justice: The Morality of Truth Commissions,* ed. Robert I. Rotberg and Dennis Thompson (Princeton, N.J.: Princeton University Press, 2000), pp. 279–94.

23. *Report,* vol. 1, ch. 1, §71–72.

24. Desmond Tutu, *The Rainbow People of God* (New York: Doubleday, 1994), p. 254.

25. *Report,* vol. 1, ch. 1 ("Chairperson's Foreword").

26. *Report,* vol. 5, "Minority Position Submitted by Commissioner Wynand Malan," pp. 436–56.

27. See, e.g., David Beresford, "TRC Slams ANC, PAC and Winnie," *Electronic Mail and Guardian,* 27 October 1998); Stephen Laufer et al., "ANC in Court Bid to Block Truth Report," *Business Day,* 29 October 1998; Suzanne Daley, "South African Panel's Report Arrives in Swirl of Bitterness," *New York Times,* 30 October 1998; Maureen Isaacson and Jean le May, "Human-Rights Group Slams ANC," *Sunday Independent* (SA) 1 November 1998. These events are recounted in Meredith and Rosenberg, *Coming to Terms,* pp. 103–7.

28. *Report,* vol. 1, ch. 2, §64–81 and Appendix. In his "Minority Position," Commissioner Malan suggests that this is inconsistent with the spirit of amnesty insofar as it could subject both leaders and minor functionaries of the apartheid system with prosecution under international law in the courts of any country. See also André Pretorius, "What the House of Lords' Ruling Means for SA's Rogues," *Sunday Independent* (SA) 29 November 1998; Robert Brand, "Truth, Yes, but Not Much Justice," *Sunday Independent* (SA) 1 November 1998.

29. For specific "findings" on "violations" committed by liberation movements engaged in "just war," see, e.g., *Report,* vol. 5, ch. 7, §130–50; vol. 2, ch. 4.

30. "The sense of powerlessness experienced by communities was increased by

the culture of impunity within which the police and security forces operated" (*Report,* vol. 5, ch. 4 §145). See, generally, *Report,* vol. 1, ch. 4, §64–81; vol. 5, ch. 6, §65–77.

31. "We know that we may, in the present crime rate, be reaping the harvest of the campaigns to make the country ungovernable. We know that the immorality of apartheid has helped to create the climate where moral standards have fallen disastrously" (vol. 1, ch. 1 §70). Most discussions of the ANC's "ungovernability" campaign (begun in 1984) touch on a similar theme. Nevertheless, the TRC concludes (in the chapter "Causes, Motivations, of the Perpetrators") that "violence of the powerful, the South African state, was not necessarily equivalent with violence of the powerless, the disenfranchised, oppressed and relatively voiceless black majority" (vol. 5, ch. 7, §60).

32. "[I]t can never be forgotten that the system itself was evil, inhumane and degrading for the many millions who became its second and third class citizens. Amongst its many crimes, perhaps the greatest was its power to humiliate, to denigrate and to remove the self-confidence, self-esteem and dignity of its millions of victims" (*Report,* vol. 1, ch. 4, §51).

33. The theoretical basis for this conclusion is illuminating: "The primary cancer . . . will always be the apartheid oppression, but the secondary infection has touched many of apartheid's opponents and eroded their knowledge of good and evil" (vol. 5, ch. 7 §56, quoting testimony by Bishop Peter Storey as an illustration of the theory of Frantz Fanon).

34. Charles Villa-Vicencio, "Restorative Justice: Dealing with the Past Differently," in *Looking Back, Reaching Forward,* pp. 68–76; André du Toit, "The Moral Foundations of the South African TRC: Truth as Acknowledgment and Justice as Recognition," in *Truth v. Justice,* pp. 122–40.

35. Judith N. Shklar, *The Faces of Injustice* (New Haven, Conn.: Yale University Press, 1990), p. 101.

36. See, e.g., Neil J. Kritz, ed., *Transitional Justice: How Emerging Democracies Reckon with Former Regimes* (Washington, D.C.: United States Institute of Peace Press, 1995), 3 vols.; Ruti Teitel, "Transitional Jurisprudence: The Role of Law in Political Transformation," *Yale Law Journal* 106 (May 1997): 2009–80; idem, *Transitional Justice* (New York: Oxford University Press, 2000); Jose Zalaquett, "Balancing Ethical Imperatives and Political Constraints: The Dilemma of New Democracies Confronting Past Human Rights Abuses," *Hastings Law Journal* (August 1992): 1425–38; Naomi Roht-Arriaza, *Impunity and Human Rights in International Law and Practice* (New York: Oxford University Press, 1995); Jaime E. Malamud-Goti, *Game Without End: State Terror and the Politics of Justice* (Norman: University of Oklahoma Press, 1996; Mark Osiel, *Mass Atrocity, Collective Memory, and the Law* (New Brunswick, N.J.: Transaction Publishers, 1997); Neier, *War Crimes;* and Fareed Zakaria, *The Future of Freedom: Illiberal Democracy at Home and Abroad* (New York: Norton, 2003).

37. Judith N. Shklar, "The Liberalism of Fear," in *Liberalism and the Moral Life,* ed. Nancy Rosenblum (Cambridge, Mass.: Harvard University Press, 1989), pp. 21–38. See also George Kateb, "On Political Evil," in *The Inner Ocean: Individualism and Democratic Culture* (Ithaca, N.Y.: Cornell University Press, 1992), pp. 199–221.

38. See Robert Meister, "Forgiving and Forgetting" and "Sojourners and Survi-

vors: Two Logics of Non-Discrimination," *The University of Chicago Law School Roundtable* 3, no. 1 (1996): 121–84.

39.	For a description of the lessons learned from past truth commissions, see *Report*, vol. 1, §§24–30; See Timothy Garton Ash, "The Truth About Dictatorship," *New York Review of Books* 45, no. 3 (1998): 35–40; idem, "True Confessions: On Past Human Rights Violations in South Africa," *New York Review of Books* 44, no. 12 (1997): 33–37; Tina Rosenberg, "Afterword: Confronting the Painful Past," in Meredith and Rosenberg, *Coming to Terms*, pp. 325–70. See also Ruti Teitel, "From Dictatorship to Democracy: The Role of Transitional Justice," in *Deliberative Democracy*, ed. Harold Hongju Koh and Ronald Slye (New Haven, Conn.: Yale University Press, 1999), pp. 272–90; and idem, "Bringing the Messiah Through Law," in *Human Rights in Political Transitions*, ed. Hesse and Post. For a comprehensive selection of the theoretical literature through 1995, see Kritz, ed. *Transitional Justice*, vol. 1.

40.	See Terreblanche, "Production of the Past," Part III; Mahmood Mamdani, "Reconciliation without Justice," *Southern African Review of Books*, no. 46 (November 1996–December 31, 1996); idem, "When Does Reconciliation Turn into a Denial of Justice," (unpublished talk, 18 February 1998); Truth and Reconciliation Commission, Public Discussion: "Transforming Society Through Reconciliation: Myth or Reality" (12 March 1998). For a discussion of the impact of these interventions on the Commission, see Antjie Krog, *Country of My Skull* (Johannesburg: Random House, 1998), ch. 10.

41.	See, e.g., *Report*, vol. 2, ch. 3, §42–45 on the increase in police shootings during the mid-1980s.

42.	Priscilla Hayner, "Same Species, Different Animal: How South Africa Compares to Truth Commissions Worldwide," in *Looking Back, Reaching Forward*, pp. 32–41; idem, *Unspeakable Truths: Confronting State Terror and Atrocity* (New York: Routledge, 2001), chs. 4, 6–8. See also idem, "Fifteen Truth Commissions, Impunity, and the Inter-American Human Rights System," *Boston University International Law Journal* 12 (Fall 1994): 321–70.

43.	See, e.g., *Report*, vol. 5, ch. 7, §61–85.

44.	Jeremy Cronin, "Á Luta Dis-Continua: The TRC Final Report and the Nation Building Project," paper delivered at the TRC: Commissioning the Past Conference, University of the Witwatersrand, 11–14 June 1999 (www.trcresearch.org.za/papers99/cronin.pdf).

45.	DeKlerk's initial decision to abandon apartheid was a direct result of the loss of Thatcher's support after the Cold War ended in 1989. Lack of Soviet support may also have influenced the ANC to seek peace (Sampie Terreblanche, personal communication).

46.	See, e.g., Osiel, *Mass Atrocity*.

47.	See, e.g., Hesse and Post, ed., *Human Rights in Political Transitions;* Kritz, *Transitional Justice*, vol. 1.

48.	While carefully labeling apartheid a "crime against humanity," the TRC *Report* generally treats it as the "context" for the "gross abuses of human rights" (killing, torture, etc.) that were committed to defend (and sometimes to oppose) it (Mahmood Mamdani at The Politics and Political Uses of Human Rights Discourse Conference, Columbia University, 8–9 November 2001). See also *Report*, vol. 1, ch. 4, and vol. 5, chs. 1–2.

49.	See, e.g., Kritz, ed., *Transitional Justice;* Neier, *War Crimes;* and the contributions by Post and Hesse, Neier, and Teitel in Hesse and Post, ed., *Human Rights in Political Transitions.*

50. See, e.g., Kateb, "On Political Evil," pp. 206–12; Carlos Santiago Nino, *Radical Evil on Trial* (New Haven, Conn.: Yale University Press, 1996), chs. 1–4. See also Koh and Slye, eds., *Deliberative Democracy and Human Rights,* pt. V.

51. See, e.g., "Statement by Mr. Wynand Malan, Deputy Chair of the Human Rights Violations Committee of the Truth and Reconciliation Commission, 16 May 1997" (http://www.doj.gov.za/trc/media/prindex.htm).

52. Rian Malan, *My Traitor's Heart: A South African Exile Returns to Face His Country, His Tribe, and His Conscience* (New York: Atlantic Monthly Press, 1990).

53. Shklar, "The Liberalism of Fear," p. 29. See also Shklar, "Putting Cruelty First," in *Ordinary Vices* (Cambridge, Mass.: Harvard University Press, 1984), ch. 1. For a further discussion of Shklar's liberalism, see Robert Meister, "The Liberalism of Fear and the Counterrevolutionary Project," *Ethics and International Affairs* 16, no. 2 (2002): 118–23.

54. See the works cited in notes 37, 40, and 43; also Martha Minow, *Between Justice and Forgiveness: Facing History after Genocide and Mass Violence* (Boston: Beacon, 1998); idem, *Breaking the Cycles of Hatred: Memory, Law, and Repair* (Princeton, N.J.: Princeton University Press, 2002).

55. For a further elaboration of these arguments, see Robert Meister, "Human Rights and the Politics of Victimhood," *Ethics and International Affairs* 16, no. 2 (2002): 91–108.

56. The TRC *Report* addresses this issue as follows: "A pertinent question is the extent to which individual South Africans can be regarded as responsible for the premises and presuppositions which gave rise to apartheid. The kindest answer consists of a reminder that history suggests that most citizens are inclined to lemming-like behavior—thoughtless submission rather than thoughtful accountability. This is a tendency that needs to be addressed in ensuring that the future is different from the past and serves as a reminder that the most penetrating enquiry into the past involves more than a witch-hunt. It involves, rather, laying a foundation against which the present and all future governments will be judged" (vol. 1, ch. 4, §105). The TRC's "findings" on the responsibility of civil society for the crimes of apartheid appear in vol. 5, ch. 6, §§151–58.

57. Why should inaction be more blameworthy for citizens whose interests were served by the evil they condoned than for those who were relatively unaffected? Moral philosophers have frequently noted how difficult it is to make principled moral distinctions among the passively unjust. See Shklar, *The Faces of Injustice,* pp. 40–50; Herbert Morris, "Shared Guilt," in *On Guilt and Innocence* (Berkeley: University of California Press, 1976), ch. 4. The essential point is that opposing injustice is always costly and that unwillingness to pay that cost is blameworthy for bystanders and beneficiaries alike: both are likely to be better off than they would have been had they actively resisted. This means that (from the standpoint of post-traumatic politics) bystanders are beneficiaries who are yet to be blamed, and beneficiaries are bystanders who are yet to be absolved. The fluidity of these categories can persist over many generations.

58. The TRC *Report,* for example, concludes by displacing onto "other structures"

the redistributive project that might have been implied by its findings: "The primary task of the Commission was to address the moral, political and legal consequences of the apartheid years. The socio-economic implications are left to other structures. . . . Ultimately, however, because the work of the Commission includes reconciliation, it needs to unleash a process that contributes to economic developments that redress past wrongs as a basis for promoting lasting reconciliation. This requires *all those who benefitted* from apartheid, not only those whom the Act defines as perpetrators, to commit themselves to the reconciliation process" (vol. 5, ch. 6, §165).

59. There are significant analogies here with the Pauline conception of messianic time *(kairos)* as something distinct from both the historical time *(chronos)* that it "realizes" and the final moment *(parousia)* at which justice can be done.

60. Meister, "Forgiving and Forgetting," and "Justice as Afterlife" (unpublished paper delivered at the University of Cape Town, August 1998).

61. See Meister, "Human Rights and the Politics of Victimhood," pp. 99–100.

62. See, e.g., Osiel, *Mass Atrocity;* Avishai Margalit, *The Decent Society* (Cambridge, Mass.: Harvard University Press, 1996).

63. See, e.g., Kateb, "On Political Evil," pp. 212–14, 220.

64. See Meister, "Sojourners and Survivors."

65. This conception of victimhood is characteristic of postmodern identity politics, which on the one hand idealizes victims, but on the other refuses to ascribe responsibility to perpetrators or beneficiaries. In this respect, postmodernism fits the model of justice-as-reconciliation more closely than the model of revolutionary justice. See Meister, "Two Conceptions of Victimhood." For a related argument, see Wendy Brown, *States of Injury: Power and Freedom in Late Modernity* (Princeton, N.J.: Princeton University Press, 1995).

66. In Rawlsian liberalism, all social good is regarded as a collective product—the product of a moral consensus on the principles of justice itself. See Robert Nozick, *Anarchy, State, and Utopia* (New York: Basic Books, 1974), p. 198. Achieving that consensus would require that individuals abstract from their present and past social positions in order to debate the degree of inequality that would be justified in the *future*. Like Rawlsian liberalism, transitional liberalism also regards all social good as the product of a hard-won political consensus, but here the consensus will be on the illegitimate inequality of the *past* rather than on principles of redistribution for the future.

67. For a discussion of how class might be reconceptualized along these lines, see Robert Meister, *Political Identity* (Cambridge: Blackwell, 1991), pt. II.

68. "We that come from the old order—or the majority of us—are horrified by the stories that victims of gross human rights violations have told over the past year. We are horrified and feel betrayed. We feel done in. We feel our dignity impaired. That things like these were possible, right under our noses. How could this have happened? We are victims of the cruelest fraud committed against us! . . . But the experience of those who come from the struggle, those who were on the receiving end of these things, the things that horrify us . . . this pain can help us soften in our own indignity at the betrayal" (Statement by Mr. Wynand Malan, Deputy Chair of the Human Rights Violations Committee of the Truth and Reconciliation Commission, 16 May 1997).

69. *Report,* vol. 5, ch. 9, "Reconciliation." See also Krog, *Country of my Skull,* passim.

70. Malan, *My Traitor's Heart,* p. 189.

71. Philip Joseph Deloria, *Playing Indian* (New Haven, Conn.: Yale University Press, 1998).

72. See Meister, "Forgiving and Forgetting," pp. 155–64.

73. Segal, *Introduction to the Work of Melanie Klein,* pp. 95–6.

74. Sigmund Freud, "Mourning and Melancholia," in *The Standard Edition of the Complete Psychological Works of Sigmund Freud,* ed. James Strachey (London: Hogarth Press and the Institute of Psychoanalysis, 1957), vol. 14, pp. 237–58. See also Melanie Klein, "Mourning and its Relation to Manic-Depressive States," in *Love, Guilt, and Reparation and Other Works 1921–1945,* pp. 344–69.

75. John Bowlby, "Pathological Mourning and Childhood Mourning," *JAPA* 11 (1963): 500–41.

76. See, e.g., Morris, "Shared Guilt," *On Guilt and Innocence,* ch. 4; Bernard Williams, *Shame and Necessity* (Berkeley: University of California Press, 1993), esp. pp. 88–94. For a discussion of the replacement of guilt with shame, see Meister, "Forgiving and Forgetting": 155–64.

77. Nicolas Abraham and Maria Torok, "Mourning or Melancholia: Introjection vs. Incorporation," in *The Shell and the Kernel: Renewals of Psychoanalysis* (Chicago: University of Chicago Press, 1994), pp. 125–38.

78. See, e.g., Heribert Adam et al., *Comrades in Business: Post-Liberation Politics in South Africa* (Cape Town: Tafelberg, 1997); Mahmood Mamdani, "Now Who Will Bell the Fat Black Cat?" *Electronic Mail and Guardian,* 17 October 1997.

79. S. J. Terreblanche, "The Production of the Past"; and "Testimony Before the TRC during the Special Hearing on the Rule of the Business Sector" (11 November 1997), Carlton Hotel, Johannesburg; see, more generally, Terreblanche, *A History of Inequality in South Africa, 1652–2002* (Scottsville: University of Natal Press, 2003); Pule Molebeledi, "SA Still Needs Economic Liberation," *Business Day,* 12 February 2003; John Battersby, "Academic Slams Mbeki for Neglecting the Poor," *Sunday Independent,* 12 December 2002; idem, "The ANC is Not a Socialist Movement," *The Mercury,* 12 December 2002.

80. *Report,* vol. 1, §80–100.

81. *Report,* vol. 5, ch. 9, esp. §62–152.

82. Peter Brooks, *The Melodramatic Imagination: Balzac, Henry James, Melodrama, and the Modes of Excess* (New Haven, Conn.: Yale University Press, 1976), pp. 11–12.

83. Krog, *Country of My Skull,* esp. chs. 1–8, 13–17; Tutu, *No Future Without Forgiveness,* chs. 5–8.

84. Kateb, "On Political Evil," pp. 212–13.

85. Elaine Scarry, *The Body in Pain: The Making and Unmaking of the World* (New York: Oxford University Press, 1985), Introduction, ch. 1.

86. In some cultural contexts, the experience of intense pain is itself a spiritual exercise with positive connotations. See, e.g. Talal Asad, "Thinking About Agency and Pain" and "Reflections on Cruelty and Torture," in *Formations of the Secular* (Stanford, Calif.: Stanford University Press, 2003), chs. 2–3. For an earlier version of this argument, see Asad, "On Torture, or Cruel, Inhuman, and Degrading Treatment," in *Social Suffering,* ed. Arthur Kleinman et al. (Berkeley: University of California Press, 1997), pp. 285–308.

87. Lauren Berlant, "The Subject of True Feeling: Pain, Privacy, and Politics," in *Cultural Pluralism, Identity Politics and the Law,* ed. Austin Sarat and Thomas R.

Kearns (Ann Arbor: University of Michigan Press, 1999), pp. 72–73. Page numbers in the text are to this volume.

88.   For a comprehensive account, see S. J. Terreblanche, *Labour Patterns and Power Relations in South African History (1652–2000)* (Cape Town: African Institute of Policy Analysis and Economic Integration, 2000). He criticizes the *Report* in "Production of the Past." The *Report* addresses the issue of its limited mandate with respect to the history of racialized oppression in vol. 1, chs. 2, 4–5.

89.   "[T]hose who have benefitted and are still benefitting from a range of unearned privileges under apartheid have a crucial role to play. Although this was not part of the Commission's mandate, it was recognized as a vital dimension of national reconciliation. This means that a great deal of attention must be given to an altered sense of responsibility; namely the duty or obligation of those who have benefitted so much (through racially privileged education, unfair access to land, business opportunities and so on) to contribute to the present and future reconstruction of our society" (*Report*, vol. 1, ch. 5, §111).

90.   Jacques Derrida, *Specters of Marx: The State of the Debt, the Work of Mourning, & the New International,* trans. Peggy Kamuf (New York: Routledge, 1994).

91.   Scarry, *The Body in Pain,* p. 9.

8 Abjection and Film: Displacing the Fetishistic, Racist Rhetoric of Political Projection

Tina Chanter

Abjection happens when individuals; peoples; political, religious, or ethnic groups; nations; or states attempt to set themselves up as pure and good by requiring others to occupy a place of impurity, a place of evil. It is not always—perhaps only rarely—that people consciously try to make others represent all that is bad in order to prove themselves as good, righteous, holy, morally rigorous, unimpeachable. As often as not, it happens outside the circuit of conscious, deliberate intentions or voluntary, well-conceived, well-controlled actions. As often as not, it happens out of feelings of insecurity or anxiety, defensiveness or inadequacy, weakness, and fear of contamination. In order to rid myself of my guilt, my feelings of unworthiness, I deny my fear or cowardice and project it onto others, who then come to represent it for me. I cannot be dirty and disgusting, so another must be it for me. I must purify myself. It is a dynamic that is set into motion despite our best intentions.

When a nation sets itself up as benevolent and powerful, and in order to sustain its mythical narcissism requires that other nations occupy the symbolic place of an axis of evil, it appeals to an imaginary that fosters an image of itself as only good and pure. The often unstated rhetoric that underlies this abjection of the other as evil and impure appeals to a mythical Edenic prehistory, a time of absolute innocence. The mythical status of such ostensible innocence needs to be interrogated. September 11th is constructed as if it appeared as a full-blown monstrosity, preceded by an untheorized time of innocence—as if this event consisted of a victimized nation, which both prior to the castration of the twin towers, and in its aftermath, can lay claim to purity, remaining invulnerable to critique. So long as we accept this mythically innocent origin that covers over a history of atrocities—including US support of the Taliban regime—while occluding the economic interests of the United States in securing the rights to Iraqi oil, we can avoid confronting the moral question of how the war with Iraq abjects Arab identities by refusing to acknowledge their humanity. To accept the ostensible threat posed by Iraq is to acquiesce to its mythological status, as if it stood for all that is evil, pernicious, and inhuman. By remaining in thrall to this threat, we avoid asking ourselves about the morality of killing thousands of Iraqi citizens, which was always the undoubted outcome of the projected war. At the same time, we can gloss over the fetishistic logic of substitution at work in the representation of Saddam Hussein as a stand-in for Osama bin Laden.

A racialized discourse is already in play that not only fails to acknowledge the true humanity of those who do not fit the paradigm of an inculpable American ideal but that easily substitutes one racialized subject for another—despite the lack of any causal or logical connection beyond the marking of certain subjects as raced others. The implicit standard of whiteness against which these raced others are judged remains unthematized. To render it explicit would also render it available for interrogation, which in turn would render it patently mythological. The citizenry of America is of course far from a homogenous mass of whites. The hidden standard of whiteness must remain hidden. Its effective operation depends on its veiling, its secrecy. To expose the myth would be to undermine its validity. So long as the myth remains intact, the death of racially marked others, the citizens of Iraq, is not envisaged as an outrage. The paradox that surfaces once the myth is debunked is allowed to remain unchallenged: certain lives, it would seem, are not worth as much as others. Certain bodies are dispensable, the waste products of a system that continues to parade itself as benevolent even as it threatens the peace, security, and lives of the very people it advertises itself as wanting to save.

Not only must women's bodies be rethought as not always already subject to a mythical castration that marks them as having emanated from a masculine imaginary; the question must also be raised as to why some bodies are considered indispensable to a Western economy, while others are deemed to be all too readily dispensable. How does race function within this discourse, how do certain bodies come to constitute the waste products of Western civilization, and what discourse of substitution governs their ejection from a system that can figure one racialized people for another, as if there were no meaningful symbolic difference between them? And what do we make of the fact that the more American lives are lost in Iraq after a presidential declaration that the war is over, the less sanguine Americans are about it? On the one hand, the percentage of people who believe that there is a connection between Al-Qaida and Saddam Hussein increases (despite the fact that even President George Bush has repudiated, finally, a direct connection), and on the other hand, as the death toll of Americans increases on a daily basis, public opinion is less happy with the way the war is being conducted. What can this mean, except that the loss of *some* lives is acceptable, as long as those lives are not American (read white, Christian, of the "free world")? The loss of those who are already deemed unworthy by dint of their race is figured as a necessary price for the freedom of others. This mandated sacrifice is written off as the cost of war until it impacts Americans, whose freedoms apparently include the freedom not to die, the freedom to kill others while safeguarding Americans, who embody the ideal of freedom that is being exported to other, less fortunate countries who have not had the benefit of enlightened leadership. There is no letup in the belief of the freedom for which America is taken to stand, even as civil rights are systematically eroded.

How can Saddam Hussein stand in for Osama bin Laden in a way that allows Iraqi citizens to become just as dispensable as members of the Taliban regime? What law governs an economy that claims to liberate the people of Iraq and the people of Afghanistan, as if there were no difference between them—an economy whose mode of liberation consists of a preemptive so-called war on terror, in which the liberation of some comes at the expense of others? What discourse is in place such that those subjects who are supposedly liberated become symbolic equivalents of other subjects who supposedly liberate them? What does liberation mean here? Insofar as it means to become like us—where "us" means by default the white, entrepreneurial, masculine subject who is taken to represent the West—the mimetic system in play has not begun to address the sexual and racial assumptions on which it relies. Insofar as the very freedoms for which we are told we are fighting—as the ground shifts conveniently from the imaginary and never-existent threat of weapons of mass destruction to the benign desire to free Iraqis from their aggressor, Saddam Hussein—are no longer secure even "for us," the mythical status of what America stands for is exempted from interrogation. By fiat, America is free. America is free because Republican rhetoric insists that it is so; and if Americans notice that they are less free than before, that is a price that Americans are encouraged to accept. At least Americans are freer than those who are presented as being freed, as lacking freedom, as in need of freedom. We must be—otherwise we could not "free" the others. Right?

I suggest that a pervasive fetishistic discourse permeates not only academic discourse that has been influenced by a Freudian-Lacanian standpoint but also the political rhetoric underlying recent political events. Such a discourse is in need of demystification. To that end, I mobilize the notion of abjection, which I think can provide a more adequate framework for thinking about a situation that transcends the particular limitations that the discourse of fetishism imposes on theory and that theory replicates in different guises.

It might seem surprising, but even feminist theorists whose work is deeply political seem unable to shed a recalcitrant commitment to the logic of fetishism. Teresa Brennan argues that "the split between affect and signifier has deepened over the past few centuries . . . in a way that means it is hard even to recognize that the split exists, and that affect has effects. It has become the norm to assume that only signification is at issue."[1] She focuses on "how the escalating split between thought and affect plays itself out in the masquerade of 'political correctness,' political correctness as it is presented by the right," suggesting that "the right's use of a fantasy of what political correctness is meant to be about parallels the left's arguments on signification" (p. 99). In addition to containing the delicious line that "as a rule, people on the left are simply more intelligent than those on the right" (p. 101), Brennan argues that the right appropriated the term "political correctness" from its self-consciously satirical and self-critical usage, which Alice Jardine, whom Brennan quotes, points to when she says, "Ten years ago one feminist might have said to another 'I know it is not politically correct, but I really love my red nail polish.' Or one Marxist might say to another, 'We have to try this expensive restaurant in the Village. It's not politically correct, but the food's fabulous'" (p. 100). Brennan seeks, then, not to defend the term political correctness, but to expose, following Richard Feldstein, how "the right's pronouncements on political correctness . . . represent a projection" (p. 101). Taking up a Freudian/Lacanian notion of projection, Feldstein analyses propaganda by Rush Limbaugh and Dinesh D'Souza, showing "how the right seeks to obliterate the memory of the past" (p. 100). As Brennan says, the point to affirmative action is lost if one forgets that those it is meant to advantage are in fact coming from behind. "They have been historically disadvantaged at the same time and because they have effectively advanced the lives of others. . . . The right can insist that the basic claims of African Americans are claims for special treatment only while it forgets that thirty years ago they had no claims to desegregated education, among other things" (p. 101).

By appropriating the language of the left, as the right does when it uses terms like "the Republican Revolution" to describe welfare cutbacks, the right takes the affective power of a word like "revolution" and applies it to its own conservative agenda. In doing so, the right deprives the left of its language, leaving it, at least temporarily, without any language of resistance, so that "depression, inertia, and lack of conviction" become symptomatic of this loss which has no verbal means of expressing itself. The transferal of the "affective meaning" of the word "revolution" to the right hijacks the emotional connotation of this signifier, which retains its "power to mobilize certain emotions" until or unless "another signifier becomes the site of investment for the same historical affective meaning" (p. 104). "Because the left's language still conjures the affects that it does, it is the case that those affects can be captured, at least for a time, by causes that embody their antithesis in action" (p. 104).

In the light of Brennan's argument, I want to suggest that the accumulation of affect behind the signifier of the phallus requires an accounting. If Brennan is right that the affective charge of a particular signifier—in this case the phallus—will be retained until "another signifier becomes the site of investment for the same historical affective meaning," this suggests that we need to work on developing such signifiers.[2] Irigaray's reading of two lips that speak together might be read as one example of such signification, but one that, rather than foreclosing new meanings, invites the creation of new signifiers. Read synecdochically and catachrestically, as Jane Gallop suggests, and as Judith Butler reads her, the symbolic figure of the lips invites new imaginaries.[3] Here then, I'd like to suggest that the signifier of maternal identification—a site of identification that only figures as impossible for both Freud and Lacan, a site that only operates in their texts as foreclosed—might be read as a signifier that could have taken up, and might still take up, the affective charge of the phallus.

I argue that a reworked notion of the abject can provide a viable alternative to the model of fetishism that has dominated so much theory and political rhetoric of late. I suggest that Freud's famous enigma of femininity founders on the rock of "primitivism" at strategically predictable points, so that the impasses of sexual difference turn out to be structurally bound up with a racialized discourse. This racialized discourse that subtends Freud's ideas is buried under his more overt—although still highly problematic—discourse about sexual difference, supporting it, shoring it up, and facilitating it at key points in ways similar to (but also different from) the manner in which the feminine enables masculine assumptions to proceed at the expense of women as feminine.

There is a symptomatic avoidance in Freud's texts of maternal identification, one that can be mapped out by tracking Freud's "discovery" (invention?) of the phallic phase in "Infantile Genital Sexuality" (1923), an essay that revisits and reworks the account Freud had given in "The Three Essays on Sexuality" (1905). Due to Freud's unquestioned Oedipal commitments, he is wedded to a theory of the superego that privileges identification with the father over any significance the object-choice of the mother could have. In fact, this insistent privileging, coupled with his blind spot about the potential of maternal identification, produces a tension in his works, seen perhaps most clearly in the essays "On Narcissism," "Mourning and Melancholia," and "Group Psychology." On the one hand, Freud makes maternal identification all but incomprehensible by aligning the mother with object-choice and separating object-choice from paternal identification; but on the other hand, he needs infantile sexuality to be capable of privileging the penis as a site of excitation, even though genital organization will not have occurred until much later. He therefore introduces the phallic phase as a way of solving this problem. It allows him to account for the boy's "narcissistic" attachment to the pleasure of masturbation—a term rife with conflict, however, once Freud has distinguished between the anaclitic (attachment) mode of object-choice and the narcissistic mode of object-choice.[4]

At the same time, in his account of melancholia, Freud describes the process of incorporation as one in which the subject internalizes the loss of an other as a way of continuing to identify with that other or refusing to let this lost other go. This account compromises the rigorous distinction that he wants to maintain elsewhere in his account between object-choice and identification. It therefore also compromises his ability to distinguish between the love of the mother and the authority of the father, and thus his claims that the institution of the superego is unequivocally associated with paternal authority. Freud recognizes this, if only for a moment, in a footnote to *The Ego and the Id*,[5] where he acknowledges in his concept of the father of individual prehistory the impossibility of distinguishing between mother and father. It is worthy of note, first, that Freud has recourse to a phylogenetic language, the full import of which is then eclipsed by a move that is all too familiar in Freud, namely, a refusal to entertain the significance of his concession. Just as most of his texts rely on cases that concern boys, so here he excises the complications that the sexual ambiguity of the father of pre-individual history presents for his argument, by focusing only on the father. Kristeva has taken up the importance of the father of individual prehistory (the imaginary or archaic father) in her work but has not followed through as radically as she might have the departure from Freudian discourse that I think it could signal.[6] In my view, it can open up not only the import of the superego but also larger questions about the possibility of sublimation with regard to both the sexual and (implicitly) racial distribution of social roles Freud assumes.

It is, of course, because women ostensibly have weaker superegos that, according to Freud, we are incapable of sublimating as well as men. Once Freud's account is challenged in a way that doesn't leave unquestioned the phallic, fetishistic logic that governs his arguments and assumptions—including the ideologically driven priority he accords to paternal identification over maternal identification—it becomes possible to open psychoanalysis to its blind spots, and thereby to provide a more adequate treatment of its reliance on racial and sexual tropes—and the way in which they constitute one another—than has been done to date.

Freud's attachment to the phallic mother and his refusal to question the metaphorics governing the horror of the no-thing that informs his discourse on uncanniness proceed, I suggest, from an unrelentingly fetishistic belief. As threatening, women are figured as the site of imaginary loss (castration) and at the same time as bearers of a mythical penis, one that derives from a masculine imaginary that cannot contemplate a radically different morphology. An imaginary penis is replaced by a fetishistic substitute to cover over the "knowledge" that women "are castrated," thus also serving to cover up the fact that women never in fact had the penis ascribed to them by boys/Freud/a masculine imaginary. The extent to which castration theory is orchestrated by the logic of fetishism needs to be uncovered and confronted, since it infects psychoanalytic and political (and, by extension, film, race, cultural, and feminist) discourse at every level. The notion of abjection, I suggest, can help to do this work.

Once abjection is used as a lever to open up Freud's texts and the assumptions of the cultural imaginary in which they are embedded, we can begin to map out the ways in which various terms—race, sex, class, sexuality—function in place of, or in tandem with, the name of the father. That is, they produce symbolic systems that operate, as often as not, at the level of the imaginary; they allow us to make distinctions that function as mechanisms of exclusion. I am suggesting that the role of the third—typically usurped by Freud and Lacan by the symbolic position of the patriarchal father—needs to be seen as circulating between the discourses of racism, sexism, heterosexism, and classism, to mention only a few of the more salient discourses of oppression. The dichotomous and vastly oversimplified oppositions between black and white, female and male, homosexual and heterosexual, and upper or middle class and working class, produce a symbolic and imaginary scene that comes to inform our social and political landscape in ways that often function invisibly. These oppositions are naturalized and reified and are rendered inaccessible to interrogation.

By oscillating between the point of view of the little boy who attributes to the mother a phallus, and the point of view of Freud the theorist, who is also Freud the adult, Freud develops in effect a fetishistic attitude to women that he then reifies, conceptualizing it into his discovery of the phallus. But if the reign of the phallus is in fact underwritten, at least in part, by its affective connotation—that is, by a culturally specific masculinized aggression of the death drive—its ideological weight rests upon a repudiation of other affects, not the least of which are those associated with maternal care and idealized as love. What interests me in returning to this affective site of maternal identification is not only the possibility it offers for rethinking the maternal figure as such— though I think that this is one thing that must be done. Just as pressing, in my view, is the need to think about how certain others, other than the mother— racialized and classed figures, for example—have been pushed into positions of maternal care.

Sam, in *Casablanca*, might be read as such a figure. He does not quite fit into the array of stereotypical African-American figures readily available to filmic representation: he is not a coon or a buck or a sambo, but rather, I suggest, a mammy figure. His piano-playing, as Robert Gooding-Williams suggests, carries the erotic baggage of Rick Blaine (Humphrey Bogart) and Ilsa Lund Laszlo (Ingrid Bergmann), the white, heterosexual couple whose love Sam (Dooley Wilson)—the still marginalized, still minstrel figure—reluctantly facilitates.[7] Sam's musical role as Cupid summons up the mythical idyllic past of the imaginary perfection of Paris—mythic and illusory because Victor Laszlo (Paul Henreid), unbeknownst to Ilsa, is still alive. The Nazi invasion of Paris is about to interrupt the false harmony of Rick and Ilsa's love, which only flourishes because of the war in the first place. Laszlo's absence in the war and presumed death has facilitated Rick and Ilsa's romance.[8]

By reading Sam as a mammy figure, my intention is not to subordinate his position as a raced subject to his position as feminized subject—as if sexual difference were a more fundamental trope than racial difference—but rather to think about the ways in which the discourses of sexual difference and racial difference operate as substitutes for one another. These discourses become interchangeable, but not in a way containable by fetishistic logic. I want to challenge the discourse of fetishism in terms of which Sam is liable to be read. When race theorists take up the discourse of fetishism, certain psychoanalytic assumptions about sexual difference are imported into race theory in a way that renders them unavailable for interrogation. Since sexual difference is itself played out in the texts of Freud in a way that implicates a discourse of primitivism that is unmarked as such, one might even say that the question of race is also foreclosed in a certain sense—in the sense that it opens onto sexual difference, rather than closing it off.

By developing the notion of abjection rather than the trope of fetishism, I want to displace not only the priority of fetishism but also the Oedipal myth with which it is bound up, allocating to maternal identification a role that Freud's fetishistic proclivities preempt. To think of Sam as a mammy figure—as someone who takes care of Rick, the one who mops up the messes he makes of his romantic life, the one who metaphorically dries his tears when Ilsa abandons him, but also the one who is violently ejected from the love triangle between

Ilsa, Rick, and Sam when his care/love becomes too explicit, too eroticized—is to think about the way in which African-Americans have been required to occupy subordinate social positions in white American society.[9] Caretakers, caregivers, cleaners, bus-boys, nannies, shoe-cleaners, service workers, musical entertainers—these positions are occupied in the white American imaginary by those who are raced as other. These others are occupied in various ways with the affects that white, middle-class American men have such trouble dealing with. Sam becomes a repository of the poetic, the musical, the romantic, which his music channels. An empty vessel, he permits the circulation of desire between Ilsa and Rick, while himself being excluded from the circuit of meaningful or acknowledged desire. He thus facilitates an economy of white, heterosexual desire in which he himself does not participate. He lends Rick his allure, and thus functions ambiguously as castrated and uncastrated. He is deprived of his masculinity inasmuch as he yields it to another—to Rick, the white male protagonist. He is thus not seen as a subject in his own right, yet as Rick's sidekick he is at the same time invested with a hypermasculinity, a hypersexuality that is underwritten by the hyperbolic oversexing of black folks. The seedy side of Rick's café is lined with the attraction of Sam's piano-playing, which lends cachet to the café that is transferable to Rick as owner.

The dynamics of this exchange are not reducible to commodity fetishism, since part of Sam's contribution consists in the invisible status of his own desiring subjectivity, and the transferability of his erotic allure to Rick. Sam is thus both invisible in his own subjectivity and hypervisible in Rick's sexuality, which Sam's always subordinate presence makes possible. Sam's hypersexuality as a black man is only permissible at the level of representation when it is camouflaged as white, grafted onto the body of Rick, his boss, who controls more than Sam's wages.

Frantz Fanon has followed out this dynamic but has not questioned the underlying assumptions about fetishism that make it possible. Racist myths of the negro as rapist inform the white child's imaginary, as he points to Fanon, "Look, a negro! . . . I'm frightened," myths that Fanon's black skin comes to represent. The corporeal schema is interpreted through a reduction of the historico-racial schema, fabricated by the myth of the negro, to the "racial epidermal schema"[10] so that the body becomes a sign for racist myths that become reified. The problem with this narrative is that it leaves intact the sexist discourse that facilitates it, as becomes all too evident when Fanon affirms the pernicious sexist myth that women want to be raped.

Let me step back a moment in order to comment more generally on the legacy of fetishism inherited by film theory and passed on to race theory, an inheritance that has occluded the intimate relationship and interdependence between sexual and racial myths. The maternal body was effectively written out of the picture, even by feminist film theorists, while Lacanian film theory, almost ad nauseam, and often oversimplistically—as Parveen Adams, Joan Copjec, and Jacqueline Rose, among others, have pointed out—took up the mirror stage and ran with it.[11] While the oversimplistic interpretation of Lacan by film theorists has been addressed by Lacanian-inclined theorists, very little attention has been paid to the relative neglect of another aspect of early psychoanalytic film theory, namely, its reference to the maternal body. Perhaps this is because of Laura Mulvey's highly influential "Visual Pleasure, and Narrative Cinema,"[12] which, aside from a brief mention of "maternal plenitude," which plays no role in her main argument, concentrates more or less exclusively on the analogy between the Lacanian mirror stage and the experience of the cinematic viewer. Not only the mother's body but also the suggestive remarks Jean-Louis Baudry makes about metapsychology, dreams, sleep, and hallucination are left out of account.

The canonical role that Mulvey's essay played in feminist film theory cannot be overstated. It became almost obligatory to cite it, if only to register one's disagreement with it. The strength of Mulvey's account lies not only in its vivid portrait of the striking similarity between Lacan's mirror stage and the experience of the cinematic viewer but also in its harnessing of psychoanalytic theory to a feminist agenda. She conceded the patriarchal nature of psychoanalytic theory but found it useful nonetheless as a tool that helped to unpack the patriarchal nature of cinema. This, however, left unaddressed a number of important questions: how could Mulvey's theory accommodate the attempts of progressive cinema that resisted the white, middle-class, heterosexual paradigm that Mulvey (and psychoanalysis) assumed? If Mulvey adapted psychoanalysis in order to "destroy" the pleasure of the (male) spectator, wasn't there a sense in which she confirmed, rather than brought into question, the status of women as passive, victimized subjects and men as active, scopophilic subjects that she seemed to want to challenge at another level?

What would it mean, then, to return to the references in Baudry that suggest the importance of the breast and to take up the metapsychological references he makes there? What would it mean, in other words, to rethink the imaginary that stages the cinematographic scenography, the imaginary writing of the filmic stage, not in terms of a phallic, fetishistic economy, but in terms of the feminine coding that facilitates it? Let me recall, with Baudry, that while in the *Interpretation of Dreams* the optical model of psychical apparatus prevails, Freud will "later abandon the optical model in favor of a writing instrument, the 'mystic writing pad.'"[13] Baudry is well aware of Derrida's essay "Freud on the Scene of Writing," in which the mystic writing pad plays such a pivotal role.[14] The analysis Derrida provides in that essay, along with Baudry's neglected references to dream, sleep, and the mother's breast, point in the direction that I want to pursue here, one that is informed both by Irigaray and Kristeva, whose account of abjection is more indebted to Melanie Klein than is often acknowledged.

In a short but important essay that, like those of Baudry and Mulvey was also anthologized in a standard film theory text but that unlike them has received little attention, Kristeva addresses the idea of the "thought specular" in relation to fantasy, and specifically in relation to film.[15] Like Irigaray's essay on Plato in *Speculum*, it is clearly indebted to Derrida's essay "Freud and the Scene of

Writing." While this essay has found little airplay, film critics have turned to Kristeva's notion of the abject, albeit in a limited way, largely restricting their attention to horror film.[16] My own view is that, especially if one is concerned, as I am, to develop more conscientiously than Kristeva the pertinence of abjection for political discourse, narrative film provides a more productive forum for developing a discourse of abjection. In doing so, however, I think it is imperative to bear in mind the masculine imaginary to which Irigaray has drawn attention. Otherwise we risk repeating, with Freud, not only the marginalization of women, the denigration of femininity, and the assumption of a male perspective, but also Freud's unthinking use of a discourse of primitivism. Moreover, any recasting of the discourse of abjection—which is the larger project at stake here—is liable to fall back into the assumptions of fetishism, replete with its reliance on a dichotomous, hierarchical, and exclusionary model of sexual difference, which is then transposed all too easily, via film theory, onto fetishistic accounts of race. Fetishistic theories of race thereby themselves replay in an unacknowledged way a phallic, hierarchical presupposition about sexual difference, which remains inarticulate and therefore incapable of interrogation, just as feminist accounts of gendered subjectivity still too often rely on unexamined presuppositions about race and thereby perpetuate an unthematized priority of whiteness.[17]

Irigaray's work, even as it is blind to the question of primitivism, provides some help. Inasmuch as Irigaray provides a serious interrogation of the imaginary scene that enables the metaphorics of the phallic system while itself being excluded from that system, she provides a clue as to how to open up that system to multiple levels of questioning. That her own work displays a blind spot when it comes to race, that she is caught up in a white imaginary in which whiteness is invisible in ways that echo, repeat, and are implicated in the ways that femaleness is rendered invisible by metaphysics, is something that needs to be confronted. In order to confront it, the cultural imaginary not only of psychoanalysis and metaphysics but also of feminist theory itself—which has taken over in some instances some of the problems it should be interrogating—needs to be challenged.

Engaging in a mimetic, hyperbolic reading that exacerbates the tensions in Plato's cave allegory, Irigaray describes the prisoners trapped in its illusory world in phallic terms, "Heads forward, eyes front, genitals aligned, fixed in a straight direction and always straining forward, in a straight line. A phallic direction, a phallic line, a phallic time, backs turned on origin."[18] Capitalizing on the phallogocentrism that she sees as permeating Plato's scenography, she goes on to point out the fetishistic status of the objects whose shadows are projected onto the wall of the cave/womb, the objects that the prisoners/cinema spectators take for reality:

Shadows of statues, of fetish-objects, these and one other would henceforth be named truth—*to aléthes*—by the men in chains. Projections of symbols for men's bodies, raised high enough so that they show over the top of the little wall so as to dominate and sublimate it—though the wall has been raised in the cave artificially—would, theoretically be the only possible representation of the truth for the prisoners because they provide, in addition, the echo of the words pronounced by the same men. The echo is possible because of the reflecting property, the so-called virginity and muteness of that back of the matrix/womb which a man, an obstetrician, turned round, backward and upside down in order to make it into the stage, the chamber, the stronghold of representation.[19]

By reading the figures that are paraded along the parapet of Plato's cave as fetishes, and by reading the little wall, *teikhion*, behind which the men parade, as diminutive—a low wall, a wallette, a veil, a curtain,[20] a hymen—as having been sublimated; by reading the cave as hystera, womb, speculum, as the mother's body, Irigaray challenges the discourses of fetishism that have dominated psychoanalytic film theory, along with the prevailing phallic metaphorics of disavowal that accompany it. The logic of disavowal has been appropriated by film theory because it seems to fit so exactly not only that which is represented on-screen but also the cinematic experience.

The *femme fatale*, for example, who according to Freud's fetishistic theory threatens castration, is punished, often killed, for her status as threatening. The phallic mother must be destroyed. A fetish is of course a substitute for the missing penis of the mother. It thereby covers over what the masculine subject (although not marked as such) nevertheless knows (the ostensible horror of women's genitals, the gaping hole, the lack, the abyss). The double logic of disavowal—I know that the woman lacks a penis, but I attribute one to her all the same—is reiterated at the level of the cinematic apparatus. I know that the film is a fantasy, but I take it for reality all the same. What enables me not merely to follow the film diegetically, but even to identify with its characters, to cathect on to them, to cry with them and for them, to commiserate with and in their sorrow, or to laugh, to rejoice at their good fortune, is that even though I know the film is not real, I still allow myself to take it for reality. As Octave Mannoni puts it, "*Je sais bien, mais quand même* . . . [I know very well, but all the same . . .]."[21]

The Hollywood system of continuity editing, and all the machinery, or apparatus, that enables this system to function so smoothly, is complicitous with the logic of fetishism, partakes of it, perpetuates it—covering over, in a move that echoes the veiling of *aletheia*, all those objects that in fact create the image, not to mention the invisible hand of the director. Like Plato's prisoners, we gaze, fascinated and absorbed by the film's image; and like Lacan's infant in the mirror stage, we are captivated by what we see, our stable, instantaneous body-image both facilitating and alienating us. We are not the characters with whom we are fascinated and with whom we empathize—but we could be. It is not until we are suddenly jolted out of our state of fascination by some director's ploy, or else by the other, the third, who watches the film along with us, that this alienation comes to the fore. Someone drops popcorn, dispelling our illusion of communion with or in the film, or the hand-held camera distances us from our acceptance of the illusion. Instead of the reverse shot sequence that sutures us into the visual field of the protagonist in Lars von Trier's *Breaking the Waves*, we are out of breath, jolted along by the rhythm of the hand-held camera, as Bess (Emily Watson) is almost out of life, as she knocks hopelessly on the door of her mother's house, an outcast of the church, and now cast out of her own home. The scenes of sacrifice and abjection that pull us into her demise are broken up by musical interludes, by Elton John singing "Yellow Brick Road," and rural stills that are not quite stills because the river that is supposed to be still, still runs. We are not quite allowed to sink with Bess into the sacrifice of abjection. These musical interludes act as bookmarks, dividing the film into chapters but also giving us a respite from its inexorable culmination in Bess's death, the ultimate sacrifice that allows a dying Jan to get up and walk, to take up his bed and walk, as Jesus said—and there is an explicit transposition of the sacrifice of Christ onto Bess's sacrifice as a woman. We are thus encouraged to reflect on our complicity in the symbolic order that banishes Bess, as a woman from the church that forbids her to speak and would bury her as a sinner, had Jan (Stellan Skorsgård) and his friends not stolen her body to bury it at sea, where, as it breaks the waves, bells chime inexplicably. The bells that one of Jan's friends remarked as absent in the austere Protestant church in which Bess and Jan were married now magically appear, in a shot that can only be described as kitsch. The chimes ring out to confirm the miraculous nature of Jan's recovery, borne of Bess's sacrifice, while at the same time, Lars von Trier underscores the irony of the bells. At whose expense the irony is employed remains in question. However ironic the gesture is intended to be, Bess is still dead; she has still sacrificed her life for Jan in the belief that she is saving him—a belief that turns out not to be as misguided as her doctor and best friend would have her believe. She dies so that Jan might live. Like Antigone's role in Hegel's dialectic, she proves to be dispensable, and the last laugh is not hers but that of the system that ejects her. No longer the eternal irony of the community, she is simply dead. And her death breathes life into an economy that goes on without her.

In Thomas Vinterberg's *The Celebration*, another Dogme 95 film, Christian (Ulrich Thomsen) is physically ejected from the house, an outcast because he has disrupted his aristocratic father's 60th birthday party by revealing his father's incest. The camera's unsteady focus follows Christian outside to a sylvan glen where all should be calm and gentle according to the song sung by the patriarch's mother, but again we are jolted along as the cinematographer runs behind Christian. Christian's brother, Michael (Thomas Bo Larsen), and Michael's friends drag him outside and tie him to a tree in order not to allow the civilized proceedings to be interrupted any further by Christian's unwanted outbreaks. Assigned to nature like the animal he must be, given the wild and extravagant stories he is said to have invented, Christian must be expelled from the celebration of his father's life, excluded from the paternal home in which his sister Helene (Paprika Steen) remains, along with the rest of the family. When Helene's boyfriend (Gbatokai Dakinah) arrives, Michael assumes, because of the color of his skin, that he has come to the wrong place. He thinks he is a musician, tells him to leave, and calls him a monkey. He thereby falls into the stereotypical imaginary that has been pointed out by Michael Omi and Howard Winant, and by Richard Dyer, among others, of assuming that non-whites must be in service, that their skin color automatically marks them—in the contours of a move that Fanon had already mapped out in terms of the corporeal, the racial-historical, and epidermal schema—as inferior.[22]

Given that he too is made to feel his status as outsider, it is significant that a black man, who, precisely because of his status as one who is outside this white, privileged family, shows solidarity with Christian. Michael leads the guests in a raucous racist song—in which once again semiotic energies come to the fore—in the presence of "Gonzales" (as Christian's mother, Birthe Neumann, insists on calling him, despite the fact that it is not his name)—in a deliberate attempt to humiliate him. The song, which begins with the words, "I've seen a real Black Sambo/His face was black as pitch/He spoke all funny/And he had a ring in his nose," provokes Helene, who has up until this point denounced her apparently renegade brother, to show solidarity toward him. Thus, child abuse and racism are aligned with one another as capable of marking certain others as victims who must be represented as savages and excluded from the realm of humanity that their perpetrators are perversely represented as constituting.

A similar dynamic, selected out of the many examples supplied by the white racial imaginary, is played out in Mike Leigh's *Secrets and Lies.* When Hortense (Marianne Jean-Baptiste) arrives at the door of a house to which she has been invited for a party, because of the color of her skin, Monica (Phyllis Logan) assumes that she has come to the wrong place. The fact that it simply does not occur to Monica that this racially marked woman—who also happens to be urbane, genteel, and middle class—might be the "friend" from work whom Cynthia (Brenda Blethyn) has invited, prefigures the shock registered on the faces around the dining table when Cynthia reveals that Hortense is, in fact, not just a "mate" from the factory in which Cynthia works, but the daughter she gave up for adoption. Hortense's black skin renders this an impossibility, since its acceptance would require the unthinkable: that Cynthia has had sexual relations with a black man. In *Secrets and Lies,* we are privy to a series of stills, photographs taken by Maurice (Timothy Spall), Monica's husband and a photographer by profession. He takes pictures of weddings, or people with their dogs, or women who used to be beautiful and who worked as models but whose faces, after serious car crashes, bear terrible, ugly scars. The pictures are for the insurance, and Maurice draws the pain out of his clients as he talks to them in order to get them to reveal their truth in pictorial form. The pain becomes inscribed on their faces and etched into the photographic image. Leigh wants us to reflect on the look of the camera, and on the manipulation he subjects us to, as he inserts these photographic stills into the moving picture. He wants to stop us in our tracks, to interrupt our fascination. But he also wants us to think about the fact that, when Hortense arrives on the doorstep, her black skin freezes her into an other in Monica's gaze, just as the camera catches us unawares in our grimaces.

In *Hollow Reed* (Angela Pope, 1996), when Frank Donally (Jason Flemyng) is discovered by his live-in girlfriend, Hannah Wyatt (Joely Richardson), beating her former husband, Martyn Wyatt (Martin Donovan), just as he had abused their son, Oliver (Sam Bould), the camera swivels 360 degrees, round and round, dizzying the audience, as Frank realizes that he is trapped. Hannah, for her part, realizes that she can no longer pretend that Frank can give up his child abuse of her son, a pretense she has been desperately clinging to, in order not to be left alone again. Abusing or terrifying Oliver is a way for Frank to establish control in a world in which he feels inadequate, a way of making him seem to himself a whole person, a way of venting his feelings of rage at his own abuse without confronting them directly. He deflects these feelings onto Oliver, continuing a chain of abjection. The social text of homophobia presents itself as available to him, and he draws upon this socially sanctioned form of prejudice in order to facilitate his own denial of his own child abuse. Frank channels the violence he suffered from his father onto Oliver, alleging that he doesn't know how to get close to him. By instilling in Oliver a fear of contamination, that he might somehow be infected by his father's homosexuality, Frank attempts to consolidate the boundaries of his fragile family unit by exposing the "unnaturalness" of Oliver's real father. At the same time, he disguises his true motives from himself and displaces his own abjection of Oliver onto Martin's homosexuality.

The dynamic of abjection played out in *Hollow Reed* can help put into perspective the trauma of September 11th. An important distinction, of which *Hollow Reed* reminds us, has recently become obscured. The distinction is between understanding and justifying evil. One can understand what makes a victim of child abuse turn others into victims of child abuse—indeed, it is imperative to do so in order to try to intervene in the cycle of violence that is otherwise perpetuated. To understand this cycle is far from justifying it. Yet attempts by those on the left of the political spectrum to understand what might have led the terrorists responsible for September 11th to act have been typically condemned by the right as if they were attempts to justify the attack. How could such an apparently elementary distinction be obfuscated? Perhaps because the distinction between facts and feelings, between knowledge and affect, is not as clear as those who herald objectivity and universality as impeachable standards would have us believe. Perhaps because trauma operates in a way that tends to obliterate distinctions that we sometimes want to take for granted—distinctions between self and other, good and bad, me and you. To project our own feelings of inadequacy, rejection, or worthlessness onto others is to attempt to defend ourselves against these feelings. We separate ourselves off from affects that are hard to integrate into the image of ourselves that we want, and we ask or demand that others take care of those affects for us, thereby alleviating ourselves of the burden of responsibility. We turn moments of vulnerability that others display into opportunities to attack them. We experience the vulnerability of others, their lack, as a threat to our own integrity, and then we ward off the threat that they have come to represent for us with death threats. We provide them with alibis, in a fetishistic logic, with imaginary weapons that we take to be real, and then we punish them for having objects that we have given them.

In the films I have mentioned, the stills, musical interludes, playing with colors, the questioning of stereotypes, feminine and masculine, homosexual and heterosexual, black and white, are meant to disrupt our processes of identification at the level of the individual psyche. To the extent that they succeed, they not only partake in a Brechtian distanciation, which can still be read in terms of the trope of disavowal that I am arguing needs to be brought into question, but they also function as an interrogation of the social and political assumptions that create the fabric of our lives and provide the codes in terms of which we interpret film. This background scenery, like the maternal womb of Irigaray's cave, is populated by shadowy, racialized, classed, and variously othered figures who provide the backdrop for the white, middle-class, heterosexual, masculinized characters whose lives get depicted in the "real" diegetic world of cinema, with which "we" are meant to identify. So long as we allow the play to remain at the level of aesthetic invention, or even at the level of the individual psyche, without parsing out its implication at the socio-symbolic level, we refuse to ask the more fundamental questions about the scene of representation, its scenography. We thereby refuse to question the background imaginary informing our social and political assumptions.

I want to suggest that these raced, sexed, gendered, or classed scenarios—these imaginary, cultural scripts that privilege whiteness, heterosexuality, maleness, and middle- or upper-class existence—function as the third. That is, they perform a mediating discourse, that which Lacan restricts to the function of the father, who governs over the symbolic in a way that forecloses any meaningful challenge to the Oedipal scenario, which is itself a legacy of patriarchy. In different moments, a racialized or sexualized imaginary informs events, such that the imaginary performs the function of the third—that which allows us to exchange signs among ourselves and in doing so to rely on, and constitute and recreate, a system whereby certain others are marginalized on the basis of what we take to be their racial otherness, or sexual deviance, or class inappropriateness.

As is clear from the following quotation from "The Three Essays on Sexuality," there is another insistent question at the heart of the question of fetishism, other than the alleged need for protection against mythical female castration, one that is often bypassed. Freud says, in a famous passage: "What is substituted for the sexual object is some part of the body (such as the foot or hair) which is in general very inappropriate for sexual purposes, or some inanimate object which bears an assignable relation to the person whom it replaces and preferably to that person's sexuality (e.g., a piece of clothing or underlinen). Such substitutes are with some justice likened to the fetishes in which savages believe that their gods are embodied."[23] The standard response to such passages used to be to simply read over the reference to the savage, clearly a racial reference, or to use ellipses to erase it.[24] Instead of reading over it, I want to stay with it, and thereby follow up the ways in which racialization of certain subjects benefits other subjects, who assume their subjectivity without it being marked as raced.

Since the work of Fanon has been taken more seriously by Bhabha and others, it is harder for psychoanalytic theorists to simply elide this question by assuming that questions about race can be adequately dealt with either by ignoring them or by resolutely subordinating them to the question of sexual difference.[25] The problem, in my view, is that a good deal of race theory, like film theory and feminist theory, remains dominated not only by the metaphorics of deferral and delay but also by its underlying dynamic. Notwithstanding the fertility of their readings, what remains unproblematized is the governing discourse of fetishism.[26] The mechanics of disavowal gets displaced into racialized scenarios, without its dependence on the abjection of the feminine that castration theory relies upon ever being brought into question. By raising the question of affect—not as something that can only ever be approached once its energies are already signified by an idea that owes its existence to a phallic signifying system, but in returning to the staging of the scene of representation that affect both makes possible and helps to produce—we can begin to address the senses in which racial and sexual identity are implicated in one another. Racist and sexist representations are shored up by one another in a phallic system that relies on, and draws its energies from, both the feminine other and the racialized other, while at the same time disavowing those marked by their race and wounded by their femininity.

In Freud's own anxiety about confronting the horror of women's genitals, the enigma or riddle of femininity, we confront the irreducible impact of the stamp of patriarchy, which has always already decided in favor of the dominance and superiority of masculinity over femininity. As I indicated earlier, the Oedipal stipulations of Freud's theories are inextricably interwoven with the privilege of masculinity that society has enshrined in its institutions and upheld by an unthematized reliance upon a racialized discourse. Elsewhere I develop at greater length the argument that Freud's discourse exempts women from the norm, understood as masculine, by having recourse to the exclusion of those other others, those racialized others.[27] Suffice it to say for the moment that not only does Freud tend to problematically equate the feminine with the pathological and also with the primitive, but that, predictably, he has recourse to a discourse of primitivism at precisely the points at which the enigma of femininity defeats him.

The perceived threat of terrorism seems to replay this logic. In the last two years, it seems to me, the right has accelerated the theft from the left that Brennan points to, to the extent that now, not content to merely steal its language, it systematically pillages its ideas, which it feeds to the American public as if there were no contradiction. Before September 11th, Bush ran for office on a fairly conventional, conservative, anti-interventionist platform. The rhetoric supporting this standard Republican fare follows the same contours as the individualist, competitive logic of the so-called free market. Live and let live. It's not our job to interfere with the way other countries do their business. Now, having declared "a war on terror"—and "war" is a good example of a term whose affective connotation has not changed but whose signifying function has altered dramatically—apparently it is part of the conservative agenda not only to interfere in the way others run their countries, but to do it for them.

We are bigger than you.

We've got more weapons than you could ever hope to have, let alone hide, or smuggle out of the country.

And yet you are a threat.

What is the imaginary that fuels this threat? And where have we heard this logic before? The fact that you are powerless renders you a threat to our power because it represents the possibility that, at some future point, we too might become powerless. Your lack of power can only be read as a loss of power (by projecting some mythical past in which you were once threatening, which myth then takes on a life of its own and proves that you might still be threatening, or be capable of becoming so). While the unconscious "knows no time, psychical reality needs a delay," Brennan reminds us. She adds, "And there can be no experience of delay without some experience or concept of time."[28] The past, in this case, is the trauma of September 11th, the symbolic castration represented by the felling of the twin towers, from which we are still recuperating and which apparently set up a logic by which any preemptive aggressive act we commit without provocation is justified in that it might prevent another unlikely but remotely possible act of aggression. The logic is not only alarmingly phallic but also, of course, racialized. We can act with impunity because the defensive aggression with which we act out is directed toward those whose lives, in the grand scheme of things, do not really matter anyway, those whose lives are already marked as being essentially dispensable because of the way in which we have raced them.

What is happening here? In a world where defense means attack, where threat means that there could be a minuscule possibility that someone in some faraway country might begin to think about amassing the resources for creating a bomb (for which the United States would have supplied the materials in the first place), and where war is justified by nothing more than "just because we can," it does not seem to be the language of the left that is appropriated so much as the ostensible slippage of meaning that poststructuralism has been (wrongly) accused of for so long.

I have focused here on the work that projection does, and the ways in which it can manipulate affects by producing abjects, because I think it speaks to the manipulation that is currently making itself felt throughout American and British politics. I have focused on the question of maternal identification as a question that is foreclosed by the phallic logic of Freud and Lacan because I think that opening up this question within the corpus of Freud might enable us to think through the affective charge still carried by the phallus and thereby to reflect more adequately on its logic and continue to develop alternatives.

While Kristeva herself is not necessarily inclined to explore the social and political ramifications of abjection in the way that I have indicated, she has illuminated the sense in which abjection is profoundly ambiguous, and the extent to which religious discourses make use of this ambiguity in the process of designating the sacred and the holy. This can be most readily seen in the procedures by which what is set up as pure is constituted as such by means of a taboo or prohibition. In this sense, what is profane, impure, unclean, is required by religion, even as it is required only to maintain its status as outside, as irreligious.

By imposing rigorous boundaries, religions maintain and endorse moral and political codes. While some separation between the unclean and improper, and the clean and proper is probably necessary in any society, it is legitimate to ask questions about the systematic designation of certain identities as outsiders, and the tendency for the moral purity of privileged groups to be propped up by the alleged moral impurity of others. It seems to me especially important to think about such dynamics when nations such as the United States, backed by Britain but without the sanction of the UN, rely on a fictitious and fetishistic rhetoric that sanctifies as innocent the actions of Western governments at the expense of dehumanizing and demonizing others as evil and impure. In the words of one of the generals entrusted with fighting against Iraq on our behalf, where "we" are subjects construed as Christians/Americans/whites, the enemy we are fighting is "Satan," where Satan is embodied by Muslims/Arabs/racially marked others.

Notes

1. Teresa Brennan, "Projecting Political Correctness: The Divorce of Affect and Signifier," *Southern Journal of Philosophy* 34, Supplement (1996): 99. Page numbers in the text are from this article.
2. Luce Irigaray, "When Our Lips Speak Together," in *This Sex Which Is Not One,* trans. Catherine Porter (Ithaca, N.Y.: Cornell University Press, 1985), pp. 205–18; "Quand nos lèvres se parlent," in *Ce Sexe qui n'en est pas un* (Paris: Editions de Minuit, 1977), pp. 203–17.
3. See Jane Gallop, *Thinking Through the Body* (New York: Columbia University Press, 1990), and Judith Butler, *Bodies that Matter: The Discursive Limits of "Sex"* (New York: Routledge, 1993).
4. Sigmund Freud, *The Standard Edition of the Complete Psychological Works,* trans. James Strachey (London: Hogarth Press, 1953): "Infantile Genital Organization" (1923), vol. 9, pp. 141–45; "The Three Essays on Sexuality" (1905), vol. 7, pp. 125–243; "On Narcissism: An Introduction" (1914), vol. 14, pp. 73–102; "Mourning and Melancholia" (1917 [1915]), vol. 14, pp. 239–58; "Group Psychology" (1921), vol. 18, pp. 69–143.
5. Sigmund Freud, "The Ego and the Id" (1923), in *The Standard Edition,* vol. 19, p. 31, n. 1.
6. Julia Kristeva, *Tales of Love,* trans. Leon Roudiez (New York: Columbia University Press, 1987); *Histoires d'amour* (Paris: Éditions Denoël, 1983).
7. Robert Gooding-Williams, "Black Cupids, White Desires: Reading the Representation of Racial Difference in *Casablanca* and *Ghost,*" in *Philosophy and Film,* ed. Cynthia A. Freeland and Thomas E. Wartenberg (London: Routledge, 1995), pp. 143–60.

8. Ilsa's assumption of Laszlo's death is, of course, not without significance. It is probably impossible to separate completely such an assumption from wishful thinking.

9. Robert Ray comments on the multiple triangular relationships that are played out in *Casablanca*; see Ray, *A Certain Tendency of the Hollywood Cinema 1930–1980* (Princeton, N.J.: Princeton University Press, 1985), p. 92.

10. Frantz Fanon, *Black Skin, White Masks*, trans. Charles Lam Markmann (New York: Grove Press, 1967), pp. 112, 110.

11. See Parveen Adams, *The Emptiness of the Signifier: Psychoanalysis and Sexual Differences* (New York: Routledge, 1996); Joan Copjec, "The Orthopsychic Subject: Film Theory and the Reception of Lacan," in *Feminism and Film: Oxford Readings in Feminism*, ed. E. Ann Kaplan (Oxford: Oxford University Press, 2000), pp. 287–306; Jacqueline Rose, *Sexuality in the Field of Vision* (London: Verso, 1986).

12. Laura Mulvey, "Visual Pleasure and Narrative Cinema," in *Issues in Feminist Film Criticism*, ed. Patricia Erens (Bloomington: Indiana University Press, 1990), pp. 28–40.

13. Jean-Louis Baudry, "Ideological Effects of the Basic Cinematographic Apparatus," in *Film Theory and Criticism*, 5th edition, ed. Leo Braudy and Marshall Cohen (New York: Oxford University Press, 1999), pp. 345–55.

14. Jacques Derrida, "Freud and the Scene of Writing," in *Writing and Difference*, trans. Alan Bass (Chicago: University of Chicago Press, 1978), pp. 196–231.

15. Julia Kristeva, *Intimate Revolt: The Powers and Limits of Psychoanalysis*, vol. 2, trans. Jeanine Herman (New York: Columbia University Press, 2002). In the chapter on fantasy and cinema, Kristeva develops some ideas she had already introduced in an earlier essay, "Ellipses on Dread and the Specular Seduction," in *Narrative, Apparatus, Ideology: A Film Theory Reader*, ed. Philip Rosen (New York: Columbia University Press, 1986).

16. See Barbara Creed, *The Monstrous Feminine: Film, Feminism, Psychoanalysis* (New York: Routledge, 1993), and Carol J. Clover, *Men, Women, and Chain Saws: Gender in the Modern Horror Film* (Princeton, N.J.: Princeton University Press, 1992).

17. So, for example, Henry Krips, Homi Bhabha, Robert Gooding-Williams, and Frantz Fanon all fall prey to this in different ways. Hazel Carby and bell hooks, among others, have persuasively exposed the senses in which feminism, despite its best intentions, often remains prey to racism. See Hazel Carby, "White Woman Listen!" in *Theories of Race and Racism*, ed. Les Back and John Solomos (New York: Routledge, 2000), pp. 389–403; and bell hooks, "The Oppositional Gaze: Black Female Spectators," in *Reel to Real: Race, Sex, and Class at the Movies* (New York: Routledge, 1996), pp. 197–213.

18. Luce Irigaray, *Speculum of the Other Woman*, trans. Gillian C. Gill (Ithaca, N.Y.: Cornell University Press, 1985), p. 245.

19. Ibid., p. 263.

20. Ibid., p. 249.

21. Octave Mannoni, *Clefs pour l'imaginaire òu l'autre scène* (Paris: Éditions du Seuil, 1969), pp. 11–12.

22. Richard Dyer, "The Matter of Whiteness," in *Theories of Race and Racism*, ed. Les Back and John Solomos (New York: Routledge, 2000), pp. 539–48; Michael Omi and Howard Winant, "Racial Formation in the United States,"

in *The Idea of Race,* ed. Robert Bernasconi and Tommy Lott (Indianapolis: Hackett, 2000), pp. 181–212.

23.   Freud, "The Three Essays on Sexuality," p. 153.

24.   Elizabeth Cowie, "Fantasia," in *The Woman in Question: m/f,* ed. Parveen Adams and Elizabeth Cowie (Cambridge, Mass.: MIT Press, 1990), pp. 149–96.

25.   See Homi K. Bhabha, *The Location of Culture* (London: Routledge, 1994).

26.   Brennan, for example, sees the way in which deferral and delay marks the boy's development but not the girl's, in Freud's account, yet remains committed to the discourse of fetishism that underlies this symptomatic deferral. See *The Interpretation of the Flesh: Freud and Femininity* (New York: Routledge, 1992). Gooding-Williams also provides a wonderfully productive interpretation of Sam in *Casablanca,* one that I have drawn on freely here, but one that ultimately remains tied to a logic of fetishism, which prevents him from taking his analysis as far as he might. Specifically, it prevents him from questioning the reliance of the discourse of fetishism on a sexualized discourse that privileges the phallus.

27.   Tina Chanter, *Abjection: Film and the Constitutive Nature of Difference* (Bloomington: Indiana University Press, forthcoming).

28.   Brennan, *Interpretation of the Flesh,* p. 27. It is worth noting in passing that the structure that Brennan alludes to here echoes Heidegger's discovery of the horizonal structure of temporality, or the "within-time-ness" of time—the fact that we already have an operative understanding of temporality, which is given to us by our understanding of our own mortality or finitude, within which we can then make sense of the future, past, and present. Brennan refers to Derrida's essay "Freud and the Scene of Writing," which is of course also informed by Heidegger's understanding of temporality.

Filmography

Breaking the Waves (Denmark, 1996). Lars von Trier. 159 min. October Films.

Casablanca (U.S., 1942). Michael Curtiz. 102 min. Warner Brothers.

The Celebration (Denmark, 1998). Thomas Vinterberg. 106 min. October Film, Nimbus Film.

Hollow Reed (England, 1995). Angela Pope. 105 min. Scala Ltd./Senator Film Production/Channel Four Television Company.

Secrets and Lies (England, 1996). Mike Leigh. 142 min. October Films.

9   Faith, Territory, and Evil

William E. Connolly

The Experience of Evil

I heard about the first plane attack on 9/11 from a colleague. We did not immediately appreciate the scale of the attack. Shortly after the second plane crashed into the other tower, a staff member announced that the university was closed for the day. I felt a crushing need to go home. Riding there on a bike, the horror of it overwhelmed me. I stopped a couple of times to steady myself and to wipe my glasses clean of the tears that kept fogging them. By the time I reached home, images of the first tower collapsing were playing and replaying on CNN. Images of the second collapse soon followed. As the images sank into the visceral register of my being, feelings of desolation and uncertainty sank in with them.

Something roughly akin to this had happened before, during the Cuban Missile Crisis of 1962, the assassination of President John F. Kennedy, and the killings of Martin Luther King and Bobby Kennedy. The experiences, I say, were comparable, though they varied in severity. My mind wandered to those earlier events a day later, triggered no doubt by the trauma the tower attacks had spawned.

I note public events close to home not because they embody the most horrific instances. The holocausts against Amerindians in the New World; against Jews, homosexuals, and Romana in Europe; and, more recently, against the people of Kosovo took more devastating tolls. I focus on this set to bring home the link between public recourse to the language of evil and shared experiences of surprise, devastation, fear, and uncertainty.

During the Cuban Missile Crisis no one died, but there was a palpable sense that it might issue in a nuclear conflagration, bringing human life on earth to a close. That anxiety was not tied to the conviction that one agent was alone responsible for the danger. The language of evil was thus muted, despite the awesome stakes. The danger flowed from an arms race between two highly armed nuclear states that had spiraled out of control. So the experience of tragic possibility overwhelmed the idea of unilateral evil. The three assassinations, while traumatic, were not accompanied by that sense of the tragic. Those killings were officially absorbed into the category of crime, though many suspected that such a resolution did not exhaust them. Who are the guilty parties? How can they be brought to justice? Those were the overriding questions.

The experience of 9/11 was linked both to the shock accompanying violence against a country that tended to think itself exempt from attack and uncertainty as to how to characterize the act. A categorical uncertainty filtered into the heart of the matter, an uncertainty both disclosed and muted by the language of "terrorism." The terrorists were not states; they were unannounced; they did not use traditional military weapons; they did not attack military targets; and they did not declare traditional territorial objectives. Yet the event produced a large number of casualties; it was tied to a struggle of civilizational proportions; and the non-state perpetrators defined themselves as enemies of America. The term "terrorism" fills a zone of indiscernibility between criminal acts within a state and acts of war between states. Terrorism is bonded to evil because of the surprise it engenders, because its victims are not military agents, because its perpetrators are not recognized as state agents in a world of legitimate states, and because it points to the insufficiency of the categories of territorial state, war, crime, and justice through which people ordinarily seek to come to terms with violence.

A world with terrorism is more dangerous than many Americans had allowed themselves to believe; it harbors actors and events that unsettle established concepts of territory, faith, morality, order, and war. Should the perpetrators be brought to justice or treated as military opponents? Should we tie them to the states in which they are based? If so, how many states are to be put on the list? Does it include Saudi Arabia, Pakistan, Palestine, Israel, and the United States, if and when secret operatives from the latter state engage in assassination plots or overthrow attempts overseas without declaring war? Should states now be treated as unstable nodes of power traversed by a perverse anti-cosmopolitan network that subverts and disrupts a world of territorial states?

Terrorism issues in the lived experience of evil. Evil surprises; it liquidates sedimented habits of moral trust; it foments categorical uncertainty; it issues in a fervent desire to restore closure to a dirempted world; and it generates imperious demands to take revenge on the guilty parties. When you experience evil, the bottom falls out of your stomach because it has fallen out of your world. If you have experienced other such traumas, they help to color the experience of this one. The accumulation of such events becomes layered into the soft tissues of personal and cultural life, finding expression in both modes of explicit recollection and embodied dispositions to judgment and action subsisting below the threshold of recollection.

In thinking about evil, it is wise to attend to its phenomenology. For the regime that takes charge of the experience of evil will find itself free to mobilize energies of response in a variety of possible directions, and the response mobilized sometimes engender new evils. If the most compelling task is to forestall evil, it becomes pertinent to work upon ourselves so that we respond firmly to it without extending the phenomenon we seek to expel.

The Augustinian Story of Evil

A story of evil defines the character, sources, and appropriate mode of response to such experiences of devastation, suffering, and moral shock. A familiar story becomes bonded to the new experience, providing the cultural script through which to respond. There are, however, several such stories. They compete within us as well as between us. The Augustinian story is the most familiar to those growing up within the orbit of Christendom. I focus on that part of the story dealing with responsibility for evil, for that is the script many return to when the bottom falls out of their world. Through this story, Augustine seeks not only to identify responsible agents of evil but to ensure that the omnipotent, omniscient, salvational God he confesses is not tainted with responsibility for it. If the infection were to spread to God, the Augustinian story would incline toward the tragic vision he resists.

The first act by Adam was an act of evil freely chosen. The brand new man, upon receiving an order from his God, was tempted by the new woman to disobey; she, in turn, had been tempted to do so by the serpent, who had posed a simple question to her. Adam nonetheless chose freely when he consented to eat of the tree of good and evil, drawing evil into the world through a free, rebellious act. As Augustine says:

> The injunction . . . was so easy to observe, so brief to remember; above all, it was given at a time when desire was not yet in opposition to the will . . . Therefore the unrighteousness of violating the prohibition was so much greater, in proportion to the ease with which it could have been observed and fulfilled.[1]

The first act of free will was an act of disobedience. It ushers evil into being; it elicits just and severe punishment by the Creator; and it ensures that human beings shall be plagued henceforth by a will divided against itself. The accusation by Jerry Falwell that Americans brought the destruction of 9/11 upon themselves through their secularism and support for homosexuality echoes this story. For Adam and Eve deserved the consequences—the suffering as punishment—visited upon them after that fateful act. Humans, after Adam's act, are divided against themselves; they can henceforth move closer to freedom, virtue, and salvation only by receiving the unfathomable gift of God's grace. If the first rebellion was an act of pure will, it was also so inexplicable as to be gratuitous. Indeed, evil, on this reading, is gratuitous disobedience to the commands of God (even as Augustine articulates a corollary story in which acts of apparent evil contribute to a better world in the future). Evil is freely undertaken; it deserves punishment in proportion to its severity; and human beings, after the fall, are incapable of eliminating it by their own actions alone.

But which *acts* of rebellion are most evil? When people worship a false God or fill the true God with false content, they participate in radical evil. When this occurs, they themselves are appropriately defined as evil, even though there are limits to the action that other human beings—as opposed to God—can take against them. Consider what Augustine says about the Manichaeans, a sect within Christianity to which he once belonged and which he now defines as a heresy. The problem with the Manichaeans, he says, is that they translate the two wills contending for hegemony within the human soul into two contending forces in the world, representing two contending deities, one good and the other evil. The dangerous implication of this translation is that the good God lacks omnipotence, perhaps even the capacity to deliver on the hope of salvation. Augustine found such a sacrilege unsettling enough to call it evil. Although he himself recognized Lucifer as a real being, he defined him to be a divine creation who fell away from God by his own free will, thus enabling him to avoid positing Lucifer as a primordial force in cosmic competition with the God he worships. Augustine could not find it in himself to treat Manichaeism as a contending faith within Christianity with which to enter into a relation of agonistic respect:

> Let them perish from before your faith, O God, even as vain talkers and seducers of men's minds perish who detect in the act of deliberation two wills at work; and then assert that in us there are two natures of two minds, one good, the other evil. They themselves are truly evil, when they think such evil things.[2]

There are sore spots in Augustine's story. They include, first, the question of how the initial act by a divinely created human *could* be untainted by the will of the God who had created it, and second, the question of how an omnipotent, omniscient God could be both offended by such actions and know in advance that they must occur.[3] We focus here, however, on a related issue. Against the probable views of Jesus, Augustine helped to consolidate a tradition in which the Universal Church defines what counts as official doctrine and which views are to be constituted as heresies to be excluded or punished. While he counseled Christians to obey "Caesar" in regimes that did not profess Christianity, he pursued a future in which all of civilization would profess the truth of Christianity as he did. Here is what he says in a letter to a pagan who had protested gratuitous Christian violence against his people and their sacred places:

> You plainly see the Jewish people torn from their abode and dispersed and scattered throughout the whole world . . . , everything has happened just as it was foretold. . . . You plainly see some of the temples of [pagan] idols fallen into ruin and not restored, some cast down, some closed, some converted to other uses . . . ; and you see how the powers of this world, who at one time for the sake of their idols persecuted the Christian people, are vanquished and subdued by Christians who did not take up arms but laid down their lives.[4]

"Torn from their abode," "cast down," "idols fallen into ruin." Augustine does not explicitly condone violence against these inferior faiths, and he elsewhere sets limits to the actions Christians can take against heretics and pagans. But in adopting the passive voice with respect to these acts of violence, and in refusing to counsel corrective action against such actions, he does sound as though the pagans and the Jews have brought these tribulations upon themselves.

For me, Augustine's doctrine of divinity, will, grace, universal authority, and evil is too close for comfort to the doctrine of Sayyid Qutb, the cleric whose extreme version of Islam inspires Osama bin Laden. Augustine and Qutb disagree on the role and status of Jesus; they diverge in their presentations of the obligations to God or Allah. But Qutb, as Roxanne Euben presents his doctrine in *Enemy in the Mirror,* parallels things Augustine says in the *City of God: Against the Pagans.* Each thinks that only *his* God is salvational and that salvation is a key to religion as such; each thinks the one true God must eventually be worshiped by all; each claims that the secular world is filled with corruption; each claims that there are clear and undeniable truths of revelation applicable to all humans; each calls those who deviate from the true faith heathen and pagans; and each uses these claims and admonitions to bolster the authority of the church he embraces. For Augustine the heathen were Greeks and Romans who denied the Christian God; in the middle ages they become the Islamists; and in America, the new pagans. For Qutb, they are, first, Western Christians, secularists, and rationalists who forsake the true God, and second, those within Islam who deviate from pure Islamic faith. Here are a couple of formulations from Qutb:

> The purpose of the righteous guidance is the good and prosperity of humanity: the good that springs from the return of mankind to its Creator; the prosperity that emanates from the congruence between the movement of humanity and . . . the noble stature that God intends, freed from the dominance of desires.

> When the highest authority is God alone—and is expressed in the dominance of divine law—this sovereignty is the only kind in which humans are truly liberated from slavery to men. Only this is "human civilization," because human civilization requires that the basis of rule be the true and perfect freedom of man.[5]

Let me be clear about the scope and limits of the parallels cited here. I do not say that Augustine and Qutb are the same, or even that Augustinianism takes the first step on a road that *necessarily* leads to Qutbism. Augustine acknowledged more limits than Qutb does—in limiting the degree of repression against those defined as pagans or heretics. Moreover, just as Augustine is not reducible to Slobodan Milosevic in the latter's war against Islamists in Kosovo, Qutb is not reducible to Osama bin Laden. I do suggest, however, that something that might be called the Augustinian temptation circulates within both of these confessions of faith, namely, the tendency to define one's faith as absolutely authoritative for others and to consider it to be under severe assault unless and until it is confessed by everyone with whom you interact. The Augustinian/Qutb temptation is to find it all too easy to define those outside one's respective faith to be evil. To do so is to take one fateful step toward either enacting or tolerating violence against them when they do not otherwise threaten your existence.

The Augustinian problem of evil revolves around how to locate responsible human agents of evil in a world created by an omnipotent, benevolent, salvational God who is innocent of it. Another problem of evil, entangled in the experience of faith itself, however, is *how to embrace your faith ardently without acting forcefully to punish, correct, exclude, or terrorize those who interact with you and contest it.* The problem of evil within faith, as I will call it, is not confined to Augustinianism and Qutbism. It operates within practices of faith more generally, in a world where the domain of faith is never empty. It does not flow from any particular *doctrine of faith alone*. The *sensibility* with which bearers of a faith are infused exerts an independent effect upon the degree to which they feel besieged by unbelievers who do not threaten their lives or stop them from expressing their faiths. In this respect, Augustine is more moderate than Qutb, and the Islamic moderate, rationalist, and mystic, Muhammed ʾAbduh, is more moderate than either of them.[6] All three tower above Osama bin Laden and Milosevic.

The Spinoza Story

An alternative story finds its spiritual anchor in Baruch de Espinoza, the young man expelled from Judaism by the Elders of Amsterdam in the seventeenth century and yet labeled a "Jewish philosopher" by Christian philosophers who encountered his work. Benedict Spinoza, as he renamed himself, thus experienced the ugly side of the passions of faith firsthand. But he did not thereby seek to expunge faith from his soul. He also knew Hebrew, the language in which the book of Genesis was written. He concluded, before it was established more closely by modern scholars, that the book was patched together from several sources. He seemed drawn to what is now called the "J version," the earliest version, written in sparse and sweeping prose.[7]

While Augustine reads most of Genesis literally, with only those passages inconsonant with the salvational doctrine of his church read allegorically, and Qutb seeks to follow the divine words of Al-Qurʾan exactly, Spinoza asserts that the Bible is best read allegorically. It is taken literally only by children and simple people inducted into the lower levels of ethical life. "I say," says Spinoza, "that Scripture, being particularly adapted to the needs of the common people, continually speaks in merely human fashion, for the common people are incapable of understanding higher things."[8] If the allegory is taken literally, it readily contributes to evil, that is, to quick attributions of pure evil against those who diverge from the details of your faith and to violent energies of revenge against them disguised as just punishment.

Read allegorically, however, Genesis helps people to climb above the crude morality of law, will, and punishment of difference toward a higher ethic of cultivation grounded in intellectual love of the complexity of being and oriented to presumptive tolerance of a variety of faiths. It encourages us to recraft the simple model of morality into a complex ethic of cultivation. Here is how Spinoza interprets the oldest version of Genesis at a critical juncture:

> Therefore the command given to Adam consisted solely in this, that God revealed to Adam that eating of that tree brought about death, in the same way that he also reveals to us through our natural understanding that poison is deadly. If you ask to what end he made this revelation, I answer that his purpose was to make Adam that much more perfect in knowledge.[9]

It was necessary to eat from the tree of knowledge to learn that humans are mortal, but the experience is like eating poison. Upon eating the fruit, the simple couple began to hallucinate, and the bottom fell out of Eden. Under the effects of this hallucination, they *retrospectively* interpreted their action to be an act of free disobedience to divine law and the consequences issuing from it to be just punishment of Yahweh. While Augustine interprets death to be a just punishment visited on humanity after Adam's sin, Spinoza construes it to predate the act. While Augustine holds Adam to be primordially responsible for disobedience to a divine command, Spinoza denies primordial responsibility and says that idea emerges as a secondary formation treated as if it were primary. The Augustinian and Qutb stories would be read by Spinoza as reversals of the human condition recited under the experience of suffering and duress. They are retrospective reversals in something like the way we experience ourselves after the fact to have jumped away from a hot stove because we felt pain, when in fact it is demonstrable that we responded to a rapid infra-percept formed below consciousness before the feeling of pain arrived.

That is why it is important to keep the phenomenology of evil before us. For on Spinoza's reading, when the bottom falls out of your world, you become predisposed to bond that experience to agents of pure evil; you become sorely tempted to ignore the question of how to avoid the recurrence of such experiences in the future. You are tempted to become another carrier of the very thing you resist.

Spinoza eschews the language of evil because he finds it tied too closely to ideas of a commanding God, free will, and primordial guilt. But it may be possible to retain the senses of suffering and despair attached to the word, while pulling it away from *necessary* attachment to these ideas. I am drawn to such a combination. It responds to the trauma of evil. It supports action to forestall evil in the future, while challenging what I will call the problem of evil inside faith itself. It maintains ample space for faith in life. And it encourages creative exploration of how multiple faiths can coexist on the "same strip of territory," to use a favorite phrase of Spinoza's.

Still, this story contains difficulties of its own. How certain can we be of the philosophy of univocal substance that expresses Spinoza's own existential faith? What is to be done with or to those who insist upon correcting or punishing others based upon their ("literal") readings of Scripture, even when the others do not threaten their lives or the possibility of expressing their faiths? How and when does a Spinozist attribute responsibility for violent acts? These difficulties, in my view, correlate with a corresponding set in the stories Spinoza contends against: How stable and steady, anyway, is the Augustinian notion of responsibility through free will, particularly after the human will is said by him to have become divided against itself, humans are said to be plagued by original sin, and freedom and salvation are said to depend more upon the grace of God than self-caused actions by the faithful? How much evil has been ushered into the world by those who confess such a faith?

Is it possible that the struggle against evil is better pursued in a world where these stories compete actively within and between us?

Existential Faith and Evil

By existential faith I mean an affect-imbued experience of the ultimate character of being deeply inscribed in you. It is shared with others, albeit often incompletely and imperfectly. It typically finds expression in organized institutions. It often—but not always—revolves around belief in a personal God. And it is not entirely defined by the pile of beliefs its adherents profess. An existential faith does find expression in the field of doctrine and belief, but its intensities extend below that field. It thus has a *horizontal dimension,* in that its beliefs about such issues as divinity, morality, and salvation are professed and refined through comparison to alternative beliefs advanced by others on the cultural field. And it has a *vertical dimension,* in that the doctrinal element is confessed and enacted in ways that express investments sedimented into embodied habits of judgment and conduct, typically reinforced by entrenched institutional practice. When your faith is disturbed, you feel a bodily reaction to the disturbance expressed in the roiling of your gut, the hunching of your shoulders, and the tightening of your skin. The vertical dimension of faith bubbles up into the field of belief, affecting the way you respond to debates about the existence of God and the variety of faiths to be tolerated. The relation moves the other way too: a crisis of belief might lead you to adopt exercises to consolidate or modify the visceral register of faith. There is a fugitive *circuit* in play between visceral faith and explicit belief, in which neither can be said to be the cause and the other the effect.

To be human is to be inhabited by existential faith. There is no vacuum in this domain, though there might very well be ambivalence, uncertainty, and internal plurality. On this reading there are a variety of faiths, but no constituency who is faithless. Faithlessness is a name that proponents of some faiths give to others of different faiths. A faith, moreover, is not entirely reducible to that fugitive experience of the oblivion of being, or remainders beyond meaning, invaluably explored by Heidegger, Levinas, and Derrida.[10] The oblivion of being may subsist as a disruptive dimension within faith. But a faith will inflect this experience in a specific way. It makes a difference whether you confess that Jesus is the Savior; or that God grants eternal salvation to some through his unfathomable grace; or that the Unnameable forbids idolatry in any form; or that morality takes the form of laws we are obligated to obey; or that it is imperative to pray every day while facing Mecca; or that mystical experience helps to release you from the power of the grasping ego; or that the gods do not worry about affairs of this world; or that nontheistic gratitude for the abundance of being nourishes an ethos of presumptive receptivity and generosity in this world.

One sign of the stubborn facticity of faith is how some intellectuals who honor the oblivion of being attach the name "God" to the experience, while others speak at that precise point of a "swarm" of virtual differences without divinity. Faith, on my reading, is ubiquitous, even as it is punctuated by that which may exceed its doctrinal form. Moses, Buddha, Jesus, Paul, Augustine, Muhammad, Spinoza, Qutb, ʾAbduh, Nietzsche, Emmanuel Levinas, Jon Elster, and John Rawls are inhabited by existential faiths; and each investment makes a difference to both the public doctrines enunciated and how life is lived. That's why I do not make the sharp distinction between religious faith and secular reason, or between theology and philosophy, that many secular philosophers and theologians make (though not Nietzsche, Kierkegaard, Derrida, James, Deleuze, or Levinas).

The problem of evil *within* faith flows from the dissonant conjunction between the layering of faith into the bodies of the faithful and its relational character in a world marked by a plurality of faiths. A specific faith, indeed, *requires* difference in order to be; that is, it requires an array of differences to provide it with contrasts through which to demarcate itself. But the publication of alternative faiths can also threaten the self-confidence that one's faith hooks onto the essence of being. I suspect, then, that every faith is stalked by a potential for madness; that potential might be tapped when its visceral trust in being is challenged by acts by those outside the faith that strike it as blasphemous or sacrilege.

The tendency to evil within faith is this: The instances in which the faith of others incites you to anathematize it as inferior or evil can usher into being the demand to take revenge against them for the disturbance they have sowed, even when they have not otherwise limited your ability to express your faith. Again, the potential for madness in faith is activated not only in response to threats other faiths pose to our lives or the possibility of expression. It can also arise when their ardent confessions challenge our demand to dominate public space, or destabilize confidence in our faith, or honor a source of morality at odds with the one we treat as universal. Augustine, Qutb, Milosevic, and Osama bin Laden all display this problem of evil within faith, if to different degrees. The more relentless the drive to purify and universalize an existential faith, the more its supporters experience otherwise tolerable differences to be forms of blasphemy or persecution demanding reprisal.

Faith is ubiquitous, relational, and layered, for good and ill. It provides us with sustenance, and it can foment energies of revenge against those whose mode of being assaults its self-confidence. This double logic constitutes the temptation to evil within it. The logic is not sufficiently transcended through the practice of secularism, in which diverse faiths are shuffled into the private realm so that a matrix of public reason free of faith can prevail in the public realm. Secularism constituted a noble attempt to respond to the problem of evil in faith. But secularists too often deny the significance of faith to public life, including their own images of public life. They also have inordinate faith in the autonomy of the public procedures they endorse. In thinking that faith can be left at home when you enter the public arena, they underplay the role of ritual and technique in shaping the visceral register of culture and faith. Euro-American secularists typically overplay the autonomy of public reason (or whatever surrogate for it is adopted), underplay the layering of faith into our bodies and institutions, and discount the extent to which the public concepts of will, punishment, and morality they deploy express the history of Christendom in which they participate.[11]

Territorial Monism and Evil

In an age when the acceleration of speed in several domains compresses distance—extending the plurality of faiths within politically organized territories and intensifying interaction between them—one tempting way to resolve the paradox of faith is to pursue correspondence between the constitution of a territorial state and the institutional organization of faith. Hobbes, Rousseau, and Tocqueville pursued such a solution in different ways, with Tocqueville saying that the unity of Christianity provided the first political institution of America. Several Christian evangelists, Islamic clerics, and supporters of Israel as a Jewish state do too. But such a strategy exacerbates the potential for evil within faith because it cannot be successfully generalized. Even if it promotes its objective in a particular regime, it will not achieve its putative end. It issues in new minorities on that space to be marginalized, punished, or excluded.

A key fact of the late-modern time is that there is not enough contiguous land for every religious "people" (broadly or narrowly defined) to secure a politically organized strip of territory. The most fundamental objection, not to the territorial state, but to a world of territorial, *nation*-states composed of religiously unified peoples, is this: *the religiously unified territorial nation is no longer a universalizable form, if it ever was.* For every "people" to "own" a land, and consolidate a state, you would have to erect huge multilevel garages on the face of the earth, stacking territories so there would be enough bounded land for each people. Many would not receive much sun. Then you would have to organize massive migrations, seeking a new place for each minority on a globe without unoccupied areas. Perhaps the attraction of the *Star Wars* films is the fantasy of finding such virgin territory somewhere. Even hybrid-faiths, of innumerable sorts, would require separate garage space. And these multifarious migrations would then have to be ratified by limitations upon intermarriage, travel, tourism, international communications, and economic intersection so that new forces of connection, hybridization, and becoming would not emerge. To install such a world order, it would be necessary to slow the flow of time to a snail's pace, which perhaps helps to explain why so many devotees of the territorial *nation*-state are captured by the utopian fantasy of slowing the world down.

The religiously unified nation-state—organized around generic categories such as Christianity, Judaism, Buddhism, Islam, or Hinduism—or more specific categories within these generic forms—is simply not a universalizable form. The relentless pursuit of territorial monism, therefore, spawns persecution, forced conversions, refugees, boat people, terrorism, ethnic cleansing, and worse. So the fantasy of territorial monism intensifies rather than resolves the potential for evil within faith. This fact, challenging classic secular theories of democratic politics as well as theocratic visions, either makes the pursuit of deep pluralism an ethical necessity within politically organized territories or sets up future violence on behalf of territorial monism that will make the American holocaust against Amerindians seem like an early shot in an endless series of civil wars.

A Double-Entry Orientation to Faith

We need models of deep pluralism that do not eternalize the wish either to universalize the territorial monism or to multiply minor nations within large territorial states. For those smaller units house minorities too. I do not deny that specific historical conditions present a compelling case for constituting spaces of territorial sovereignty within an established state; the conquest of aboriginal peoples by the settler societies of the United States, Australia, Canada, and New Zealand provide such instances.[12] Nor do I deny that other historical circumstances mean that the quest for pluralism must be deferred or pursued cautiously. My sense, for instance, is that the quest for peace in the Middle East now requires protection of Israel as a predominantly Jewish state joined to the active and rapid support of a state of Palestine. It is if and as such a combination is achieved that the pursuit of pluralism within each territory carries a chance of success over the long term. I do say that such sites of sovereignty will encounter multiple minorities within them, that limits imposed on those minorities are both unwise in themselves and apt to incite their supporters in other states to harden the lines of conflict, and that it is wise to aim, over the long term, at multireligious states eschewing territorial monism.

Some strains within gay/lesbian movements provide valuable pointers here. Many gay/lesbian activists, for instance, press in favor of a positive pluralization of sexual/gender identities on the same territory.[13] The successful enactment of such plurality, however, requires self-modification of the relational identities of straights, pressing them to develop a double-entry orientation to their own sensual practices. You embrace and enact your sexual identity as if it were the natural way of being; but in another gesture, you come to terms, viscerally and reflectively, with the extent to which it is neither the natural nor universal form of sexuality. In the interests of sexual plurality, straights agree to work on themselves tactically until the visceral sense that their sexuality is universal becomes amenable to second-order correction. They take some risks with the self-confidence of their sensual identity to open the door to a culture of multiple sensualities. Indeed, ethical life typically involves acceptance of some risk to the stability of your identity. Such self-work can be aided and abetted by pluralistic films and TV dramatizations that combine image, voice, sound, and rhythm to work on the visceral register of being. For it is through such a synthesis of sensory experience that our sensual orientations were composed in the first place. I would cite *Northern Exposure* and *Six Feet Under* as valuable examples of such a positive micropolitics.

Given the violent, self-defeating character of attempts to universalize territorial monism, the most promising way to negotiate the depth, ubiquity, and diversity of existential faith is to encourage each practice of faith to cultivate a double-entry orientation to itself. This is where the traces inside your faith that exceed its doctrinal dimension can become productive. You cultivate your faith in the company of others in the first instance. You next come to terms receptively with the impossibility of generalizing territorial monism in a world marked by a plurality of faiths. Then you participate, individually and collectively, in artful exercises and rituals to mix an element of self-modesty and presumptive generosity inside your faith. You thus honor the terms of your faith, while acknowledging its contestability in the eyes of others and cultivating a sensibility of presumptive generosity toward them. Finally, you work politically to negotiate a generous ethos of engagement between multiple faiths whose members inevitably bring pieces and chunks of it with them into the public realm.

Such a double-entry orientation to the ubiquity of faith is the best response in a multicultural world to the potential to evil within faith. It is comparable to the double-consciousness achieved when people correct their perceptual sense that the sun rotates around the earth with experimental knowledge that it is the other way around. Or when you correct the recollection that you pulled your hand from a burning stove after it hurt with knowledge that the jerk preceded the feeling thought to initiate it. It is, I say, similar to these more familiar double-entry orientations, but not entirely reducible to either. In the case of faith, as in the other two, you will be touched again by the sense that you just corrected. So the effort will need to be repeated. But in the case of faith, the claim to truth is fundamental to your sense of being in the world, as it once was to those who found the idea of the earth revolving around the sun to be heretical. However, another difference now appears to qualify the significance of this one. It is not necessary that you treat your faith in the second movement to be uncertain to you—though some admirable believers have sought to do just that. You merely need to come to terms viscerally and positively with the extent to which it must appear profoundly contestable to others. The effort is to come to terms positively with how and why your faith is apt to feel strange to others who are immersed in different regimes of ritual, creeds, experiences of awakening, and defining historical events.

Second-order appreciation of the contestability of your faith to others is not confined to the most refined arena of conscious reflection alone. As you cultivate this sense, it begins to sink into the visceral register that promotes conduct on its own and flows into explicit beliefs and judgments. The correction becomes more automatic. This is the dimension of sacrifice inserted into the experience of faith; this second, lighter recoil upon faith is embraced in order to become more ethical in a fast-paced world incongruent with both territorial monism and secular intellectualism.

The double-entry modulation of faith, again, inserts a certain sacrifice or hesitation into collective experience. It receives something in return: You sacrifice the demand for the territorial hegemony of your faith in order to curtail the occasions when its very defense calls upon you to impose suffering on others. You thus respond to another dimension of your faith: its call to tolerance of others unless they make you an object of virulent attack. You do so by curtailing *what counts* as an intolerable provocation to your faith.

Installation of a double-entry orientation to faith is never entirely attained. Nor is it easily approximated by oneself alone, though Spinoza came pretty close. Old flames of anathematization periodically rise up again, and, most pertinently, new movements of relational faith periodically arise or expand to pose the issue in surprising terms. Such a double perspective is fostered by religious work, individual and collective. It involves the juxtaposition of exercises of the self with the ubiquitous micropolitics by which we regularly work on each other.

The most basic problem of public ethics, on this view, is not how to get participants to obey a moral source they already profess in common. That is the issue that haunts Augustine, Rousseau, Kant, Tocqueville, and Qutb in different ways. It is difficult to achieve. But we do not live in a time when most politically organized territories are populated by people of one religious faith and hence when people on the same strip of territory honor the same final source of ethics or morality. Even states said to be Hindu, Buddhist, Jewish, Christian, or Islamic contain significant minorities who do not confess those faiths. And they are also populated by many who are not as pure as the most ardent devotees think they should be. *The basic challenge of territorial ethics, then, is how to negotiate honorable settlements in those persistent settings where interdependent partisans confess different existential faiths and final sources of morality.* When that is acknowledged to be the basic issue, and when the thin secular conception of public culture is seen to provide an insufficient response to it, our attention returns to how to forge a positive ethos of engagement between multiple constituencies on the same strip of territory, and above that, how to infuse such an ethos into relations between territorial states. The most basic questions of morality are ethico-political. And the most basic ethico-political questions touch those circuits flowing between the visceral and reflective dimensions of culture.

I noted earlier that in addressing faith it is wise to pay attention to the continuous circuit flowing between the *creed* professed and the *sensibilities* of those who profess it. For instance, you might resist the doctrines of evil posed by Augustine and Qutb. But then recall that when the bottom drops out of your world these thought-imbued feelings well up in you too. It seems wise to engage these stories as expressions of essentially contestable faiths, even as you strive to make as strong a public case as possible for the story you embrace. Spinoza, for example, defends his reading of Scripture, but he also concludes that, given the difficulty of reaching a single interpretation of such a porous text, it is wise to practice tolerance toward a wide range of readings he does not accept as his own.

The question inevitably arises: What, according to this view, do you do with or to those who militantly refuse the quest to adopt a double-entry orientation to faith? Not much. You seek to inspire them to the importance of the task in the world we inhabit and to identify elements in their traditions that might speak positively to this agenda. But what about those prepared to wage violence against you in the name of their faith? Epicurus, Spinoza, and Nietzsche, in different ways, sought to "pass by" such people and poisonous regimes. That strategy did not suffice in their days, however, and it remains relevant but insufficient today. Here is a supplement to it. If the opponents are indeed violent, that is, if they use violence when you have not sought to colonize or marginalize them, it may well be necessary to take the minimum degree of military action needed to forestall that violence in the future. But if you also acknowledge the potential to evil within your own faith, you will recall that some of its proponents are inclined to exaggerate the danger in order to mobilize its punitive energies, and you will find it incumbent to take another look around. You will explore how to re-engage those who, while not directly engaged in violent attacks against you, provide the attackers with material and spiritual conditions of support. You explore how to reduce their hostility or passive tolerance. Here, war is not the answer.

In addressing the wider culture of Islamic tolerance for terrorism against America, for instance, you attend to the violent history of predominantly Christian states in these areas, you reassess the American military presence in Saudi Arabia, you campaign to reduce American dependence on foreign oil, you seek to engage moderate voices in Islam, you identify tendencies within your state and/or faith that recapitulate themes and dispositions you reject elsewhere, and you push the United States to support much more aggressively a state of Palestine in the territory now occupied by Israel. In these ways, and others too, you work upon your state and your faith to curtail their tendencies to demonization and violence.

Identifying admirable beacons within your faith can be pertinent. Take Bartolemé de Las Casas. This Spanish priest traveled with the conquistadors to the New World in the sixteenth century, armed with a doctrine of universal Christianity and the heartfelt obligation to convert the "heathen." But as he observed and felt the horrendous effects of the project of forced conversion, the doctrine of Christian universalism he confessed eventually gave considerable ground to the reservoir of love that also infused his sensibility. He took another look at these bearers of an alien faith, revising interpretations that had defined them through the lens of idolatry, sacrifice, and sodomy. He showed, for example, how their statues were not idolatrous, but corresponded to how the image of Jesus on the cross *symbolizes* Christ to Christians. This man of faith forestalled the temptation to evil in the Christian-state constellation of his day —expressed through its cultural denigration of Amerindians and conversion imperative—by drawing sustenance from a thought-imbued sensibility of receptive engagement that both infused and overflowed his creed. Stated in another language, his sensibility first disturbed his participation in the official morality of the day and was then drawn upon to modify it.[14]

Most pertinent today, perhaps, are millions upon millions of the faithful in diverse regimes who work upon themselves to curtail the potential for evil within their faith by cultivating the element of presumptive generosity it contains. They periodically find it incumbent to resist the dogmatism of some institutional representatives of their faith and to oppose drives to self-righteous violence by the states that rule them.

Notes

1. Augustine, *Concerning the City of God: Against the Pagans*, trans. Henry Bettenson (Middlesex: Penguin, 1984), Bk. 14, ch. 13, p. 571.
2. Augustine, *The Confessions of St. Augustine*, trans. John K. Ryan (New York: Image Books, 1960), Bk. 9, ch. 1, p. 205.
3. I consider these questions in detail in *The Augustinian Imperative: A Reflection on the Politics of Morality* (1st ed., Newbury Park: Sage Press, 1993; 2nd expanded ed., Lanham, Md.: Rowman and Littlefield, 2002).
4. St. Augustine, *Select Letters*, trans. James H. Baxter (Cambridge, Mass.: Harvard University Press, 1930), Epistle 232, p. 471.
5. Roxanne Euben, *Enemy in the Mirror: Islamic Fundamentalism and the Limits of Modern Rationalism* (Princeton, N.J.: Princeton University Press, 1999), pp. 63–64. Euben explores other Islamic clerics who do not embrace the extreme doctrine of Qutb. Her terms of comparison are between Islamic faith and Western rationalism, arguing that the latter needs to become infused with deep meaning to avoid the alienation that accompanies rationalism. My terms of comparison are between Qutbism and Augustinianism, issuing in a perspective that affirms a deep pluralism of faith in order to counter the problem of evil in faith. The Euben book can profitably be read with and against Talal Asad, *Formations of the Secular: Christianity, Islam, Modernity* (Stanford, Calif.: Stanford University Press, 2003). Among other things, Asad argues that the constitution of modern Europe defines Muslims within it as a special minority, unable to attain the standing of a regular minority.
6. See the discussion of ʾAbduh in Euben, *Enemy in the Mirror*, pp. 105–14. ʾAbduh seems closer to Kant than to Augustine, as long as you treat Kant's "apodictic" recognition that morality takes the form of law to be a mystical experience below the threshold of conceptual experience.
7. See *The Book of J*, trans. David Rosenberg and interpreted by Harold Bloom (New York: Grove Weidenfeld, 1990).
8. *Spinoza: The Letters*, trans. Samuel Shirley (Indianapolis: Hackett Publishing, 1995), Letter 19, p. 135.
9. Ibid.
10. The relation between such traces and the idea of God, particularly as it emerges in the thought of Derrida, is explored closely in Hent De Vries, *Philosophy and the Turn to Religion* (Baltimore, Md.: Johns Hopkins University Press, 1999).
11. I pursue these themes in relation to specific models of secularism in *Why I Am Not a Secularist* (Minneapolis: University of Minnesota Press, 1999).
12. I explore this question in "The Liberal Image of the Nation," in *Political Theory and the Rights of Indigenous Peoples*, ed. Duncan Ivison, Paul Patton, and Will Sanders (Cambridge: Cambridge University Press, 2001), pp. 183–98.

13.   For a thoughtful elaboration of such a perspective, see Judith Butler, *Bodies That Matter: On the Discursive Limits of "Sex"* (New York: Routledge, 1993).
14.   See Tzvetan Todorov, *The Conquest of America: The Question of the Other,* trans. Richard Howard (New York: Harper and Row, 1985), for a superb account of the re-education of Las Casas and other priests in the "New World."

10 Hannah Arendt and the Bourgeois Origins of Totalitarian Evil

Robert B. Pippin

I

In modern philosophy "the problem of evil" has become less and less the theological or theodicy problem, "justifying the ways of God to man." It can appear in that form of course in Leibniz, to some extent in Kant, in a revised form in Hegel, and in Marx. And it can assume analogous but still very similar forms—not as a straightforward question of reconciling God's goodness with the created world in which the innocent suffer, but as a problem about the "meaning" of the world as such. The "Grand Inquisitor" passage in Dostoyevsky's *The Brothers Karamazov* has become a *locus classicus* for this version of the problem: Could I ever be "at home" in a world with so much evil? What does it *mean* that there is such evil, or could one ever make sense of the brutal persistence of such events in human history? What sort of burden is it (if it is) to live a life permanently unreconciled to, or alienated from, such a hostile world, if no such sense can be made? And so forth.

But for the most part, the philosophical problem is now more restricted, and even prior to, such worries. There are two dimensions to "the modern problem of evil," once the question of "natural evil" for the most part has given way to the problem of moral evil, the evil acts human beings commit: (1) Does the concept of evil really pick out anything in the human world? On what authority do we invoke it and condemn by so invoking it? And (2) if there is such authority, can we "account" for such evil, understand why someone would choose to commit an evil deed in indifference to the claims of the good and the right or even in complete acceptance of, embrace of, their perfidious nature?

This latter question obviously requires some guiding assumption about account-giving, explanation, or making sense of the human world. As the traditional story goes, we make sense of someone else's deed by first understanding how it made sense *for* him or her, and that means understanding the reasons they had for doing what they did, and that means understanding in what sense they thought one course of action was more justifiable than another (justifiable even if in a restricted or relativized sense). This account is often supplemented by the realization that at this point we might also need to invoke objective historical, sociological, or anthropological factors to account for why some sort of consideration would be experienced as decisive then and there.[1]

This second set of issues has, especially since the end of the Second World War, come to seem to many mysterious or to raise painfully unresolvable questions, even to lie on the other side of the limits of human sense-making in general. This sentiment is perhaps most associated with Adorno, who, in the last section of *Negative Dialectics* ("Meditations on Metaphysics") suggested several times that the very attempt to comprehend the evil of the Holocaust was close to an act of obscenity, a betrayal of the magnitude and horror of the victims' suffering.[2] (Lyotard's comparison of the Holocaust with an earthquake that destroyed not only lives and buildings but also any instruments with which it might be measured is also apposite.[3]) A more extreme version of such charges: the existence of the death camps demonstrates or proves the failure of the entire modern project itself, a claim somewhat at odds with the claim of utter unintelligibility, even though one can find the two claims uttered by the same author.[4]

Hannah Arendt has no common cause with such "mystifiers" and is in some sense famously on the exact opposite extreme. But her notorious claim about the "banality" of evil in *Eichmann in Jerusalem* (and the all-too-human origins of such evil in "thoughtlessness") must be read together with a much fuller, more historically detailed attempt to make sense of such total or totalitarian evil in her earlier book, *The Origins of Totalitarianism*. In that treatment, there is a two-stage "account" of the sense of such barbarity. On the first level there is a recognizable, straightforward claim about origins. It does not rely on some nomological notion of explanation, but instead on the intentionalist and contextual, commonsense approach we noted above. Once put into the right historical and social context, discussed in terms of the motivations and aversions that would develop in such contexts, the sense of such acts, first "for the agents" and then "for us," why they would have occurred there and then begins to come into focus. There is then another, more ambitious level of explanation as she draws some conclusions about what such an explanation says about the human condition. What turned out to be "missing" in such contexts were, she asserted, aspects of human life essential for any affirmable human existence.

I want, however briefly, to discuss both aspects of her case. Her answer to the first seems to me astonishingly sweeping, but expressive of powerful currents in later modern thought that we have not yet come to terms with well. I disagree with her answer to the second set of questions and want to argue that she introduces a somewhat arbitrary theological dimension into what had been an admirably (as far as I am concerned) secular narrative.

II

Hannah Arendt's *The Origins of Totalitarianism*[5] is one of those books that reads better backward rather than forward. Only when one has come to appreciate her thesis about the nature of totalitarian movements and regimes, advanced in the third part, is one in a position to appreciate what the questions are that the first two parts—on anti-Semitism and imperialism—are trying to answer. It turns out that that question is a very difficult one because her thesis in the third part is so bold and in many ways so unsettling. For she argues, famously and now quite influentially, that twentieth-century totalitarianism is a unique form of political evil, absolutely unprecedented in history and completely unanticipated in any political philosophy. She considers her analysis in this section (rightly, in my view) to be groundbreaking and fundamental at the level of her model, Montesquieu. To his list of republic, monarchy, and despotism, she argues that we must, sadly, add another, a new fundamental type of regime: totalitarianism.

Secondly, once we appreciate why the categories of single-party rule, dictatorship, fascism, and even the most sweeping and most ancient concept of political evil—tyranny—are inadequate, we also have to face the fact that these unique totalitarian movements grew out of, were responses to, social and political experiences in relatively literate, technologically advanced civilizations and that these regimes were nevertheless capable of things never dreamed of by even the most hard-headed and realistic of modern political prophets, even men like Machiavelli (famously referred to by one historian of politics as the "teacher of evil"[6]) and Hobbes. If this is so, and our traditional descriptive and normative categories are inadequate, then a whole set of issues needs to be reframed and rethought if we are to get close to the question of the "origins" of this new type of regime and evil in these unprecedented experiences. She presents an interesting list in describing this distinctive historical situation: the collapse of the nation-state (or the seizure of the state by the nation); the consequent spread of anti-Semitism (the impossibility of either integrating or ignoring culturally and economically important European Jewry into such thoroughly nationalized states); the linking of Europe's economic fate with imperialism; eventually, unavoidably, a race-based imperialism; the creation of large masses of stateless and finally, in her words, "superfluous" peoples as a consequent of ethnic nationalism, and the intra-European imperialism it spawned; the "breakdown of the class system" as a source of social identity in Europe and so the creation of an atomized mass of de-socialized individuals, for the first time addressable and manipulable as a single amorphous "mass."

So for Arendt, as noted already, this historical evil is, while unique and unprecedented, certainly not in some fundamental way mysterious, signaling à la Adorno the limits of intelligibility as such. Indeed, the task she clearly sets herself is precisely to render the phenomenon intelligible, to include it in a historical narrative of the genesis of a new human condition, all without such an explanation rendering the phenomenon too familiar or expectable or unavoidable (it is, after all, new and unprecedented), and certainly without rendering it in some way excusable.

Her most evocative and poetic descriptions of this new human condition portray it as burdened with an intolerable loneliness, as having lost something like the "love of the world," the artificial human world of civilization. (She shares here her teacher Heidegger's epochal warning that human beings can lose, perhaps forever, the characteristic that makes them distinctly human, that these characteristics are not natural species characteristics, but fragile achievements that have to be tended and nurtured.[7]) These unprecedented experiences are also what prompt her urgent call in the 1950 Preface for "a new political principle," a "new law on earth" necessary now because "human dignity needs a new guarantee" (p. ix).

Third, this explanatory task—an explanation that would connect these novel experiences with totalitarian regimes—will be difficult because any sort of historical phenomenology of such "experiences" does not consist of simple (or even complicated) *empirical* questions, and Arendt's claims to account for "origins" is not causal in the sense we might expect from a sociological or economic analysis. It is, as just noted, contextual, and it seems to appeal to something as elusive as it is indispensable—something like the "logic of historical life"—how a certain style of political oratory, a certain appeal to violence, a certain indifference to pragmatic issues, a certain invocation of nature or history or especially race, would come to *mean* what it did to audiences in a certain context at a certain time (ultimately come to provide them with reasons sufficient to account for their actions).

There are thus both methodological and concrete questions that arise immediately in an account like Arendt's. There is no prolegomena about method or goals in the book. We just plunge in and must figure out on the fly just what a question about "origins" is about, given that it is obviously not a causal or even empirical question. (One of her scattered meta-level formulations in a later discussion: the study would be "a historical account of elements which crystallized into totalitarianism."[8]) Moreover, Arendt herself, even in the text itself, seemed to realize that large elements of her analysis fit the case of Nazi Germany much better than the Soviet Union, and there has been voluminous criticism of her on this point. One can almost sense her reminding herself to add a couple of sentences about the Bolsheviks at the end of several paragraphs about the Nazis. To make her thesis work, she has to claim that the Soviet Union was only a totalitarian regime after the early 1930s and until Stalin's death, and that Stalin in effect had to create the conditions of his own origin: "Stalin had first to create artificially that atomized society which had been prepared for the Nazis in Germany by history and circumstances" (p. 318). (To be fair, her analysis of the *nature* of the totalitarian state fits Stalinism quite well, but the etiological account seems off base for, essentially, a coup d'etat in a largely preindustrial society. And it is hard to see how Stalinist totalitarianism could be understood as in any way a *product* of mass society.[9])

III

Given the book's structure and the questions that structure generates, I need first to engage in some brief exposition about the part of Arendt's thesis that I find the most compelling—the claim about the uniqueness of totalitarianism —then attempt to characterize her basic thesis about "origins" and offer some reflections about it. My main point in doing so is to a large extent simply to register a measure of astonishment at the radicality and sweep of that thesis, and then to offer some demurrals. For there is a target coming ever more into view as Arendt wends her way through the Dreyfus affair and the *Protocols of the Elders of Zion* and the Boers and Cecil Rhodes and "intra-European imperialism" and tries to find the culprit in her dramatic and often depressing narrative. And that target is not found in the specific national histories of Germany or Russia, or in the well-documented mass German resentment against the terms of the Versailles treaty; nor is it tied to the evil genius of Hitler or Stalin as individuals or to their charismatic power, or found in the massive economic chaos of post-Weimar Germany. It is, astonishingly, "bourgeois modernity" itself that we find holding the smoking gun. Of course, there is a well-known neo-Marxist thesis that connects fascism with the late stages of capitalism and that thus portrays that distinct sort of evil as due to something like the logic of this degenerating or "contradictory" form of life, almost as if it is a natural pathology. But Arendt shares so few premises with such a mode of analysis that I think we should be astonished that *this* protagonist should shoulder so much of the blame.

Consider first the uniqueness claim and we can then work our way back to the issue of what can only be called Arendt's virulent contempt for the bourgeoisie.[10] According to Arendt, totalitarian regimes are not just more extreme, cold-blooded, or technologically more powerful versions of despotisms, dictatorships, one-party rule, or tyrannies. They differ essentially, in kind. The main qualitative difference, manifested in several different totalitarian phenomena, is a largely negative one—the absence of the usual "utilitarian" logic of strategic action, with its commitment to the most efficient means for the achievement of a definite and desirable end, even if an end or goal that we would regard as immoral or heinous, like the pleasure of the tyrant. For one thing, a totalitarian regime is not a rule by a clique out for its own self-interest, the most obvious sort of goal one might want to attribute to a violent, lawless regime. There *are,* of course, such lawless, tyrannical regimes in modernity, and we know of some in recent history (Duvalier in Haiti, Idi Amin in Uganda, Saddam Hussein in Iraq), and there are clearly also hybrid cases, especially in eastern Europe in the twentieth century (like Ceausescu in Romania), cases where an individual or gang seizes control of the totalitarian apparatus, continues to direct the secret police, and maintains terror, but for the sake of their palaces and dachas, and often with contempt for party philosophy, which they invoke only as a means or screen.

These cases complicate matters because for Arendt they no doubt manifest what she would regard as the end of totalitarian rule and the beginning of one-party or ruling-clique dictatorships. An economic logic and a kind of caution and prudence will have entered the picture, and so a kind of predictability; and with that, we lose the radical *totalization* of efforts, come what may, that characterizes the two regimes in question. Some aspects of appearances to foreign observers begin to matter; leaders do not want to go so far as to kill the goose that is laying their golden eggs, etc. But with Germany after 1938, and in Stalin's Soviet Union from 1930 until his death, since neither profit nor power was the fundamental issue, then, as Arendt writes, "common sense trained in utilitarian thinking is helpless against this ideological supersense, since totalitarian regimes establish a functioning world of no-sense" (p. 458). (One has to assume that this striking appeal to a "supersense" that is in reality a "no-sense" is an intentional paradox and, as discussed below, is meant to differentiate this species of evil from its most familiar relative in the post-Christian world, egoism. The extremity in question in extreme totalitarian evil cannot be accounted for simply by the ruthless indifference to the fate of others in the pursuit of one's interest. Hence the inapplicability of "tyranny.")

Arendt is definitely onto something here, and some of her words, given recent events, sound a chillingly accurate note, especially when she notes "the inability of the non-totalitarian world to grasp a mentality which functions independently of all calculable action in terms of men and material, and is completely indifferent to national interest and the well-being of its people" (p. 419). But there is already that tension in her account between "senselessness" and some "supersense," as in that very sentence just quoted. She can sometimes write as if totalitarian action is simply purposeless, a senseless hurricane swirl of violence, torture, terror, and destruction for their own sake, "an air of mad unreality" (p. 445). But it is also important to remember that she does not doubt that the Nazis were quite serious about their ultimate purposes—the extermination of the Jews and world rule by the Aryan race—and they could be quite efficient about elements of these when they wanted to be. And "achieving a classless society" is not an empty or meaningless goal; it was certainly a goal taken deadly seriously by Stalin and his henchmen. But according to Arendt, as employed by totalitarians, both are not "projects" in the usual sense, with debates possible about efficient means or much concern with what in any detail such end-states would amount to. The language is chiliastic, and the realization of the goal will clearly require several lifetimes. It therefore does not fit into the secular calculation that Hobbes paradigmatically introduced, where the worst calamity for any individual is death, and no good can be a good for me if I am not around to enjoy it. The point of proposing either totalitarian goal is to evoke an ultimate and "total" commitment to whatever the leader says is necessary now, as if the leader were the voice of destiny or fate, not someone proposing a policy justified with reasons consistent with the secularism of bourgeois modernity. (Therein we already have a clue about the origins of such a totalitarian demand: in its sweeping *rejection* of the limitations of bourgeois modernity, and in its assumption that a life without "meaning" might well seem a far worse fate than an early death.)

So the point of totalitarian revolution itself is not simply to replace the leaders of state and civil society and army institutions with true believers who would then put into practice party ideas. The point was to utterly transform every such institution into an instrument of the party, whose ideology had very little to do with policy details and much more to do with world domination based on some iron law of necessity about either nature (racial struggle) or history (class struggle), all as infallibly interpreted by the leader. The specific details of ideological doctrine were nearly irrelevant, given this commitment to what Arendt called this "supersense." If the "total" transformation of society required, say, the arbitrary synthesis of right-wing blood and race nationalism with some sort of communal and worker solidarity, then "national socialism" was as fine a label as any other. If Russia was ludicrously unsuitable for a Marxist revolution, a vanguard theory could be created and implemented. What mattered was honesty about the ultimately unbreakable laws of nature or history and a willingness to throw yourself into a great cause, the success of which has more to do with the perpetuation of the great cause than some ultimate realization of a goal.

Furthermore, the point of totalitarian regimes is not even the power and wealth of the *nation*. Germany itself was surprisingly insignificant to the Nazis, and the German population was even held in some contempt by its own leaders. The point is a vast, generations-long struggle for Aryan supremacy; and with such a goal, strategic planning and careful calculation are irrelevant. Uncompromising commitment and dedication are again what matters, *especially if* some sacrifice is imprudent, unnecessary, or pointless. The more pointless and wasteful a sacrifice for the party, the greater the symbolic glory.

In keeping with this contempt for the give-and-take of strategic debate, the Nazi and Soviet systems were, Arendt writes, non-systems, hardly smooth running machines (p. 395). In her famous word, they were simply "shapeless." They did not even feel bound by their own legal precedent, the laws *they* had passed and had no problem revoking and revising at will as circumstances and their own interpretations changed rapidly.

Now here again, we seem to stray close to traditional categories. The ancient definition of tyranny was rule without law for the sake of the benefit of one man or a clique. But as we have seen, many Nazi policies were hardly designed for the security and well-being of the leaders, and nothing substantive replaced law as an institutional boundary of sorts in human interactions. In tyranny, what replaced law was, to some extent at least, the predictable benefits of the tyrant. Unless he was completely insane, you could figure out where the danger points were and avoid them, could figure out how to advance your own interests while escaping notice. You knew what mattered to the tyrant and knew he would leave you alone if you stayed well clear of any and all danger points. Not so in totalitarian regimes, where *only terror replaces law*.

This last is in many ways the most important point about this qualitative uniqueness claim. What characterizes totalitarian regimes above all is a kind of ultimate non-sense or abandonment of utilitarian thinking—all of which, of course, given the assumptions about intentional psychological explanation noted above, generates quite a task for Arendt in accounting for what such a logic of total commitment could have meant for the participants. With respect to the main methods of governing, this means that terror was employed against one's own citizens—that is, violence, torture, intimidation, the full invasive array of secret police tactics—well *after* such a citizenry has been cowed into absolute, uncompromising compliance, in the absence of any threat to the regime. For the first time in history, people were characterized as enemies of that state with no regard at all to what they did, or might do, or might do with any even microscopic possibility (cf. p. 322). They were tortured and killed simply because of who they were, or even who some distant relation might have been. Jews, gypsies, the disabled and mentally ill, homosexuals, and in Stalin's Soviet Union, intellectuals, teachers, writers, or even loyal party members who had been involved in a policy demanded by Stalin that was now deemed untimely could all, arbitrarily, at any moment, be labeled "objective" enemies of the movement in a way for which there was no defense or recourse since the charge was not based on any claim of "subjective" guilt. These measures cannot be understood as serving the goal of "the security of the regime in power," but rather the goal of "total domination" (p. 422). As she explains, just as totalitarian claims to world rule can look like imperialist expansion but not be, because the regime really recognizes no difference between a home and a foreign country (domination is not desired for the sake of the home country), so the secret police in a despotic and a totalitarian regime can look very similar. But there is a crucial difference. The despot's secret police are searching out the secret thoughts of potential enemies, and they make heavy use of the age-old technique of secret police: provocation. A totalitarian secret police avoids the trouble of trapping someone in a guilty maneuver or presenting evidence of what he said. You are guilty if the state apparatus designates you as objectively guilty. Obviously the secret police have immensely more power in such a regime.

IV

Thus, life under such a regime was a life of complete, constant terror, and the result was exactly what the regime wanted, an internalization of the police's gaze and accusation, a constant internal self-monitoring and self-vigilance, a combination of selfless commitment and ever-anxious uncertainty about whether such commitment was ever "enough."[11] But even this was of no use if you were Jewish, and it is with respect to the camps that Arendt makes her strongest claim to the uniqueness of totalitarian evil. Here she enters the domain of paradox again, both pointing to the gross disutility of the camps, the wasteful irrationality, especially at the end of the war, in spending so many resources and so much rolling stock for the extermination camps, and yet also claiming that "anti-utility is only apparent" (p. 456). Rather, she claims, the camps "are more essential to the preservation of the regime's power than any of its other institutions" (p. 456).[12] This is not so for strategic reasons, as if they really believed that the Jews were potentially enemies in the military sense. (The attempt by the German historian Nolte to claim something like this is what started the bitter *Historikerstreit* in Germany, and one can understand why.) The camps, rather, if one can put it this way, allowed the Nazi regime to fully manifest itself, to express almost without qualification "total domination," their vision of what total rule could be like. (The point of the policy and action is not purposive in the usual strategic sense, but expressive.) It is almost as if, Arendt seems to be suggesting, they needed to manifest *to themselves* their own seriousness about this totality. They wanted to create a fact—a fact that would put the lie to the bourgeois claim that rule like this was "unrealistic," that such a total transformation of oppressor and oppressed was simply impossible, given "human nature." In one of the book's most chilling and compelling conclusions, Arendt argues that in this, at least, they succeeded: "We have learned that the power of man is so great that he can really be what he wishes to be" (p. 456).

These are the elements of her "uniqueness" claim that make the "origins" question so difficult. This abandonment of common sense; the appeal of a risky, dangerous, and especially total commitment; the absence of calculations of self-interest either for oneself or for the nation; the relative indifference to ideological depth or substance or even consistency or plausibility; the appeal instead to an ideology of fatality and necessity, denying not only the usefulness but the possibility of "creative action" by individuals in concert with others; the shapelessness and unsystematic, arbitrary, and unpredictable nature of totalitarian rule; the totality and irrationality of terror as a method of administration (replacing law and the appeal to law); the concomitant use of the secret police and the unchallengeable category of "objective enemy"; and finally, the camps as at once an experiment in total domination and brutal evidence for the seriousness of Nazi faith in its possibility—all these create a very difficult *explicandum*.

And there are controversies aplenty. I have already indicated that Arendt seems to waver on the role actual ideological content played in the realization and self-maintenance of such regimes as well as on the importance of a serious revolutionary goal. A biological racialism must have played a greater positive role in the appeal of Nazism than she discusses, and not just among the mob, but among the masses. One would think that the totality of commitment on the point of a mass society to a single leader, the psychological infatuation with a charismatic personality, might merit some more attention in discussions about uniqueness. And there are some things she mentions but does not develop, such as the unusual role played by hatred, resentment, and paranoia in all modern mass politics (including our own), or the role played by an enormous leap in the technology available for despotic rule. (Sometimes a great quantitative leap in despotic power like this can itself amount to a qualitative difference.)

But many of these issues will lead us quickly into the "origins" side of things, so I turn there now, noting first that there are a number of different emphases and directions in her account, and I'm not sure that they can all be made consistent. At points she describes events like the "breakdown" of class identity, the "destruction" of the nation-state, and the withering away of institutional boundaries as if these events create gaps, breaks in the fence through which an ever-lurking animality (itself rendered more appealing by an ever-growing fatigue with the burdens of civilized humanity, responsibility, sociality) is always ready to leap and is finally unleashed with the gamble of the German bourgeoisie mentioned earlier. At one point she speculates darkly on the possible attractions of totalitarianism, not just to "mass man," but to "normal people around us" who, she muses, experience a "growing incapacity to bear the burdens of modern life," and who might be quite attracted to a program that absolves them of individual responsibility (p. 437). This is all in keeping with the philosophical theme most identified with all of Hannah Arendt's work—her multivalent insistence on the autonomy and centrality of the political, on the priority of *citoyen* over *bourgeois;* her defense of republican virtue and constitutionalism; and her constant warning that this domain, since artificial, fragile, and requiring attentive tending, was at great threat of vanishing under the bourgeois onslaught in modernity. Much of her language in *The Origins of Totalitarianism,* especially her account of the camps, suggests this notion of barriers, fences, limits, and institutional mediations, without which we inevitably become the worst of beasts (without "politics"). This all culminates in one of the best passages in the book, in the "Ideology and Terror" chapter, when she notes what happened when "all human activities have been transformed into laboring," when any "relationship with the world as a human artifice is broken," *homo faber* becomes the *animal laborans* and anything is possible (p. 475).

On the other hand, she often stresses not just the failure of what would otherwise keep such insane attractions of animality at bay, but also the active, historically specific and positive embrace of totalitarian ideology. She writes as if this embrace were a consistent outcome or extension of the bourgeois apolitical world itself, with its creation of "superfluous" because economically useless peoples, and an outcome of the pettiness, venality, and materialism of the bourgeois form of life, all of which prompted an eager (and ever smaller) leap into the Nazi abyss. This "consistent outcome view" is suggested by such amazing claims as "the bourgeois's political philosophy was always 'totalitarian'; it always assumed an identity of politics, economics, and society, in which political institutions served only as the façade for private interests" (p. 336). It is hard to know what she could possibly mean here, since "the bourgeoisie" as a form of life also includes the modern romantic family, with partners chosen on the basis of love, a distinct experience of subjectivity or an "intimacy" with oneself unknown as such in prior eras, the family as a "haven in a heartless world," the refusal to treat children as property or as economic assets, and on and on. The bourgeois creation of a rich private sphere is hardly exhausted by the desire to accumulate property and capital and to subject all of politics to that imperative. The subject of bourgeois literature, more than anything else, by a factor of hundreds, is romantic love, not the totalization of economic life. What can she be talking about? At any rate, this is the repeated claim that I want to focus on, but we also need to explore the general context of her various claims about origins.

V

As we have seen, for the most part, Arendt looks for her origins in the three decades from 1884 to 1914. This period looked like "the golden age of security," but in hindsight we now know that it was then that the storms were forming that would finally amount "to an almost complete break in the continuous flow of western history as we had known it for two thousand years" (p. 123). This is the period when the unsteady balance between nation and state came unbalanced, when anti-Semitism grew and deepened its roots; it was the age of European imperialism, necessary and unavoidable for capitalist expansion, but justified only by race-thinking; and it marked "the political emancipation of the bourgeoisie." And these issues are all linked. While the modern nation-state relied on a common historical experience and tradition of the native speakers of one language, in a common geographical locality with a common sense of place and a linked fate, its claim to rule was based on its claim to be a genuine state, an independent political body, that is, on the universalist aspirations of the French revolution—the protection of the rights of man—and by its claim to rule a class-divided society in a way independent of class interest, above and over such class struggles. Here is Arendt's most concise account of what happened next:

> Only when the nation-state proved unfit to be the framework for the further growth of capitalist economy did the latent fight between state and society become openly a struggle for power. During the imperialist period neither the state nor the bourgeoisie won a decisive victory. Nationalist institutions resisted throughout the brutality and megalomania of imperialist ambitions, and the bourgeois attempts to use the state and its instruments of violence for its own economic purposes were always only half successful. This changed when the German bourgeoisie staked everything on the Hitler movement and aspired to rule with the help of the mob, but then it turned out to be too late. The bourgeoisie succeeded in destroying the nation-state but won a Pyrrhic victory; the mob proved quite capable of taking care of politics by itself and liquidated the bourgeoisie along with all other classes and institutions. (p. 124)

The link with anti-Semitism is made both by reference to the racialism that imperialist expansion required, and especially to the changing social role of European Jews throughout the formation and disintegration of the modern nation-state.[13] This story, with its emphasis on the role of Jewish banking families in the early financing of the nation-state, when rulers could be above class struggle only by being beholden to no class, and then on the later redundancy of the Jews and resentment against them, as the bourgeoisie, which had been content in its indifference to all politics not directly tied to economic policy, came more and more to control (and finance) the modern political elite, is a rich story, but it is not the issue I would like to focus on here. The deepest issue, which Arendt links with anti-Semitism, imperialism, and nationalism all at once, is already visible in the long quotation just cited, with its emphasis on the eagerness of the bourgeoisie to "use the state and its instruments of violence for its economic purposes," and in her giving the bourgeoisie the central role in "destroying the nation-state."

Such claims, and several others that we shall examine shortly, raise the question of the German bourgeoisie's dissatisfaction with the limits of politics as such ("the state") and what accounts for the intensity, almost the insane intensity, of this dissatisfaction, to the point of "staking all" on the Hitler movement. And it is here that Arendt proposes several explanations that recall again an oddly Marxian strain not often prominent in her thinking, as she suggests an *inevitable* dynamic in any bourgeois society: destructive of an independent political community, godless, secular, materialist, and, especially, insatiable in its desire for wealth at any cost (all of which of course Marx, in a provisional way, cheers on rather than laments). Her account slips regularly from any specific attention to the history of the German bourgeoisie (a focus that would help explain the specifically German gamble, as distinct from the British, Northern European, and to some extent French and Italian bourgeoisie, where this dynamic did not spin *so* wildly out of control), to remarks about "the bourgeois world" itself (capitalist, liberal-democratic mass societies) as at bottom the most prominent "origin" of all totalitarianism, the context within which the totalistic appeal of Hitler would look like a welcome escape.

Arendt's underlying attitude toward bourgeois culture suffuses her whole text, not just in her explicit account of origins. Early on, a claim like the following about the deep consistency between the bourgeoisie and imperialism makes that attitude transparent.

> The very fact that the "original sin" of "original accumulation of capital" would need additional sin to keep the system going was far more effective in persuading the bourgeoisie to shake off the restraints of Western tradition than either its philosopher [she means here Thomas Hobbes] or its underworld. It finally induced the German bourgeoisie to throw off the mask of hypocrisy and openly confess its relationship to the mob, calling on it expressly to champion its property interests. (p. 156)

We have already heard about the "totalitarian character" of bourgeois political philosophy; now she anticipates Frances Ford Coppola among many others: capitalism is not *like* the Mafia; capitalism *is* a Mafia—social rule by the elite of a mob.

Later in the section on totalitarianism, she gradually comes to speak more broadly of bourgeois "culture" or "values," and not of just those who own the means of production. This is because she claims that the class system had "broken down." She seems to mean that there was a wide spread of middle-class values without any identification with a social position above or below anybody. Shopkeepers, accountants, truck drivers, dental assistants, mechanics, plumbers, secretaries, teachers, and so forth were neither working class nor bourgeois, even though what the nineteenth century would have identified as bourgeois values were dominant everywhere. The primary characteristic of such a value system was indifference to all politics not affecting them directly. "The competitive and acquisitive society of the bourgeoisie had produced apathy and even hostility toward public life" (p. 313). (Our contemporary view of politics as "interest group" politics counts, for Arendt, as no politics at all. The issue she is raising can be heard in what we mean when we say, "That remark he made was political." We usually mean that it was said in a way designed to appeal to a certain constituency; it was about keeping or acquiring power; it was unprincipled, not about the truth.) And in her narrative, what finally got the bourgeoisie politically active were the irresistible imperialist possibilities opened up by African and Asian adventures and the inability of the traditional nation-state to manage such possibilities.

Arendt is not shy in this anti-bourgeois, anti-liberal role:

> Simply to brand as outbursts of nihilism this violent dissatisfaction with the pre-war age and subsequent attempts at restoring it (from Nietzsche to Sorel to Pareto, from Rimbaud and T. E. Lawrence to Jünger, Brecht and Malraux, from Bakunin and Nechayev to Alexander Blok) is to overlook *how justified disgust can be in a society wholly permeated with the ideological outlook and moral standards of the bourgeoisie.* (p. 328; my emphasis)

To some extent, she goes on to identify herself with this "desire to see the ruin of this whole world of fake security, fake culture, and fake life" (p. 328):

> Since the bourgeoisie claimed to be the guardian of Western traditions and confounded all moral issues by parading publicly virtues which it not only did not possess in private and business life, but actually held in contempt, it seemed revolutionary to admit cruelty, disregard of human values and general amorality, because this at least destroyed the duplicity upon which the existing society seemed to rest. (p. 334)

Her term of art for the bourgeois, with his "single-minded devotion to matters of family and career," with his "belief in the primacy of private interest," is "philistine" (p. 339); and she goes so far as to cite Himmler as the typical example of such a small-minded, prototypically bourgeois philistine.

VI

But all of this poses an obvious problem for her. Why would a selfish, narcissistic, bourgeois philistine become a dedicated fanatic, ready to sacrifice all for the cause? (Arendt makes clear in her Preface to Book 3 that she wants no part of that view of either German or eventually Russian totalitarianism that pictures a cowed and frightened population, tyrannized by a ruling clique. She insists that the evidence is unambiguous for massive, enthusiastic support for both Hitler and Stalin.) Isn't the prudent, ever-calculating, timid, sheep-like, conformist, weak, unheroic bourgeois the *last* person you would expect to make up the core of Nazi sympathizers? The "mob," for sure; the down-and-out, maybe; the resentment-filled unemployed, marginalized, and desperate people, perhaps. But the bourgeoisie? (As Adam Smith reminded us, bourgeois culture tends to be pacific; one doesn't kill one's customers.)

She has, as far as I can see, two answers to such questions. The first is more in the way of a suggestion about the possibility of an explanation. In a typical passage, she notes that "nothing proved easier to destroy than the privacy and private morality of people who thought of nothing but safeguarding their private lives" (p. 338). She means again to highlight the antipolitical attitude and civic vices of the bourgeoisie and to suggest some sort of apt historical irony, that their own obsession with their private well-being is what (by their inattention, willingness to compromise almost anything, and *ressentiment* about inequalities among their own class) made possible a regime completely indifferent to the well-being of its citizens. The bourgeoisie were all too willing to look the other way as the storm clouds grew on the horizon and should not have been surprised at the virulence and fanaticism that they ignored until it was too late.

But this obviously does not yet go to the positive affirmation of the Nazi program that, Arendt maintains, was most characteristic of the German bourgeoisie. To explain the transformation of the sheep-like, apolitical bourgeois to the enthusiastic Nazi, she needs to establish in some way that those most concerned with their own well-being above all else would also come to experience that "range of significance" in their life, let us say, that well-being, as the be all and end all of human existence, as profoundly *unsatisfying,* almost desperately unsatisfying. This is indeed what she suggests in a number of ways. We have already heard her account of the difficulty of bearing the weight of the many hypocrisies of, let us say, "Christian-capitalist" culture; and she now highlights the odd expressions of relief and even enthusiasm among many intellectuals for expressions of (at least) "honest" anti-Semitic hatred. Her chief example is Céline's *Bagatelles pour un massacre,* in which Céline proposed massacring all Jews—a book that was greeted by André Gide with the sort of "delight" at its frankness that she is noting. Her summary remark:

> How irresistible the desire for the unmasking of hypocrisy was among the elite can be gauged by the fact that such delight could not even be spoiled by Hitler's very real persecution of the Jews, which at the time of Céline's writing was already in full swing. *Yet aversion against the philosemitism of the liberals had much more to do with this reaction than hatred of the Jews.* (p. 335; my emphasis)

These remarks are not developed systematically, but they touch on an important point, one made a great deal of by François Furet's magisterial *The Passing of an Illusion.*[14] It has to do with a very unusual aspect of nineteenth- and twentieth-century bourgeois literature especially, the fact that most of the great literary documents of this civilizational epoch (from Balzac to Philip Roth, from Romantic poetry to Larkin and Lowell) continue to express a *deep bourgeois self-hatred*. There are exceptions (I would count among several Jane Austen, Dickens, Henry James—and even Proust, whose tone is comic, not bitterly ironic—as exceptions), but the long melancholic list is well known and might indeed be said to have played a part in the *bourgeois allegiance to totalitarianism* (which allegiance is, again, the most important aspect of Arendt's account of origins). An "inability to bear the burden of modern life," to use her earlier phrase, might indeed amount to an inability to live such a prosaic, small-scale life, filled with some domestic felicity and more security and a better living standard than ever in human history, but filled also with hypocrisy, brutal competition, constant anxiety, a disenchanted, crushingly prosaic existence that can manage to express itself poetically only in an apparently endless melancholic lament and in intensely critical self-consciousness.

This side of Arendt is best given voice in Nietzsche's work, and there are versions of Nietzsche's lament over the bourgeoisie (which he called "the last man") and similar Arendtian calls throughout her work for a more heroic, noble, or beautiful existence. But in this book, she focuses on one aspect of bourgeois existence that must count as the chief unbearable burden of the bourgeoisie, the intolerable aspect that makes most plausible for her the bourgeois gamble spoken of before. This is the account of loneliness in the book's last chapter.

VII

Arendt notes that totalitarian regimes require atomized and disengaged individuals who cannot act in concert; they require this both as a precondition and as the outcome of their policing policies. This sort of disconnect (with respect to action), she calls "isolation," an isolation that she again connects with the totalization of labor, and so an outcome that she attributes to the effect of capitalist or bourgeois culture. "This can happen in a world whose chief values are dictated by labor, that is, where all human activities have been transformed into labor" (p. 475). And again she invokes the word that, I have been suggesting, plays the most important role in her account of origins: when one's capacity to "add something of one's own to a common world is destroyed," then "isolation becomes *altogether unbearable.*"

This situation is even worse in the state of "loneliness," which, she says, concerns "human life as a whole" (p. 475), and it is connected with other phenomena that she has laid such stress on, "uprootedness" and the feeling of being "superfluous." Her descriptions again echo her Heideggerian account of the condition created by the bourgeois or broadly modern form of life: "to have no place in the world, recognized and guaranteed by others," "not to belong to the world at all." In such loneliness, "I am deserted by my own self" and am closed up in my mere—that is, insignificant, even meaningless—brute particularity. This situa-

162 *Robert B. Pippin*

tion, which, she claims, had been a marginal despair—suffered in earlier epochs, say, only in old age—"has become an everyday experience of the ever-growing masses of our century." And again we hear her basic thesis: that totalitarianism represents "a suicidal escape from this reality" (p. 478).[15]

Is this so, or is Arendt, in a bizarre irony, simply assuming the totalitarian premise: that a life without a transcendent, heroic, or noble purpose would be "unbearably" petty, would be to consign ourselves to being the endless butt of the jokes directed at the bourgeoisie by so many nineteenth-century novelists? Put another way, how can Arendt separate out what she admires in bourgeois culture—its constitutionalism; its assertion of fundamental human rights; its equality before the law; its insistence of a private zone in human life, exempt from the political; its religious tolerance—and condemn what she disagrees with—its secularism, its cynical assumption of the pervasiveness of self-interest, the perverting influence of money on human value, its de-politicizing tendencies and the menace it poses for tradition and a sense of place? It suffices to mention the one institution essential for *both* positive and negative tendencies—private property—to suggest that any separation of these intertwined positive and negative elements is facile. Or, while from a traditionalist point of view religious tolerance might just look like a timid unwillingness to assert one's faith against an infidel, from another it might look like the courageously rational refusal to dogmatize in what has become a profoundly uncertain, pluralistic world. (Part of that courage might be the courage to admit that secular modernity comes with frightening risks and that one cannot eliminate the risks, "restore" what was "lost," without abandoning all the aspirations characteristic of modernity itself.)

This sense that the bourgeois world has "lost" something, without which it is so "unbearable" as to make plausible the "suicidal escape" of totalitarian self-assertion (whether what we have lost is an attentiveness to "the meaning of being" as claimed by her teacher, Martin Heidegger, or whether it is the "care for the world" embodied in public life which she espoused), often assumes that such a lost something can be recovered. Hence, the tendentious language of "loss," rather than rejection, almost as if it was hastily misplaced on the way to modernization. But such ambitions might have been set aside for reasons, and the fact that without such a deep, or transcendent or political dimension, the human condition would be unbearable might just amount to showing that it is in fact (now) unbearable.[16] Our need for what was lost establishes nothing at all (sadly enough) about what can be coherently affirmed in the context of all else we are bound to affirm in modernity, and critics of Arendt have complained long and loud that aside from remarks about revolutionary councils in the German revolution and some comments on the American founding, it is not at all clear just what Arendt thinks these common political deliberations will be about, when and if such a common care for the world is restored. She simply concentrates much more on how ignoble life would be, has become, was in Germany, and is becoming now, without such a dimension.

VIII

When Arendt points forward to such a possible restoration in *Origins,* she is not hesitant about adding some conditions to this possibility that are not only, in my view, intrinsically unacceptable, but are arbitrary invocations in this work of secular historical analysis. In the context of a discussion of the dubious status of rights without a community to realize them, and in the midst of her usual attack on the ignoble bourgeois limitation of politics (and thus rights talk) to what is merely beneficial or useful, she makes a revealing claim:

> A conception of law which identifies what is right with the notion of what is good—for the individual, or the family, or the people, or the largest number—becomes inevitable once the absolute and transcendent measurements of religion or the law of nature have lost their authority. (p. 299)

The paragraph ends with an appeal to a quotation from Plato: "Not man, but a god must be the measure of all things." (All this from someone who, presumably, knew her Kant very well, to mention only one alternative to the either-or she gives us here.) And this all echoes her apocalyptic warnings, like that given at the end of Part Two, where she reminds us that we will be "*punished,* so to speak, for having forgotten that man is only the master, not the creator of the world" (p. 302; my emphasis). (All such remarks echo her acknowledgment in one of her letters of her "childish trust in God."[17])

As I've tried to indicate, I don't believe Arendt has made a case that it was something like the utter unbearableness of the bourgeois world that prompted the totalitarian "suicidal escape." But even if it is, her response is still baffling. If we will be saved only "by the measurements of religion or the law of nature," or by a god measuring all things, or by recalling that there is a creator of the world and we are not its masters, or, again in the words of her teacher, that "only a god can save us now," then we are in some serious trouble. We cannot simply conjure up a God because one is needed to save us from this nightmare. Indeed, the whole trajectory of her account works against this swerve in her treatment. Her later account of the banality of evil was not merely a reference to the banality of Eichmann's evil as an individual, but to the banality of demystified crime itself (a secular perspective inevitable in modernity), almost as if she were trying to say: the only "problem of evil" is the continuing obsession with the idea that such evil deeds create some deep problem, as if it signals some rebellion against cosmic order that we fear and are fascinated by. But there is no such "problem." There are conditions, distorted and perverse enough, enough out of tune with what an affirmable human life requires, that, under such conditions, ordinary people just like you and me came to do and accept unspeakably awful things. We need to understand why because it could happen again. Full stop.[18]

Without this rejection of the so-called "problem of evil" (rather than continuing attempts to "solve it," or acceptance in pious humility that "there is no solution"), those of us "philistines" for whom there is no such religion, or god, or creator, will be left out of the moral rearmament Arendt proposes. Either that, or we are headed for totalitarian leaps. And surely those are not the exclusive alternatives.

Notes

1. This familiar "rationalizing" account is given an exceptionally clear treatment in chapter 10 of Bernard Williams, *Truth and Truthfulness* (Princeton, N.J.: Princeton University Press, 2002).
2. There are, of course, many well-known versions of this reticence: that a respectful, horrified silence is the only civilized response to such deeds, that no poetry could be written after Auschwitz, etc. While it can fairly be said that Adorno's main theoretical project was to develop an account of intelligibility itself and its limits that could do justice to this failure to understand (and so to develop a notion of an exclusively "negative dialectic"), the full implications of regarding any human deed as in principle unintelligible (not subject to our conceptual ordering requirements, our disciplining practices, etc., however one wants to put it), were not fully addressed by him.
3. As cited in Susan Neiman's discussion in *Evil in Modern Thought: An Alternative History of Philosophy* (Princeton, N.J.: Princeton University Press, 2002), p. 251.
4. Cf. Neiman's account, pp. 258–67.
5. All page references in the text are to Hannah Arendt, *The Origins of Totalitarianism* (San Diego, Calif.: Harcourt, 1968).
6. See Leo Strauss, *Thoughts on Machiavelli* (Chicago: University of Chicago Press, 1958), p. 9.
7. On Arendt's use of Heideggerian notions like the "loss of the world" or "homelessness" in her *Origins* book, see the discussion in Seyla Benhabib's *Hannah Arendt: Die melancholische Denkerin der Moderne,* trans. Karin Wördemann (Hamburg: Rotbuch, 1998), chapter 3. Also very valuable: Dana Villa, *Arendt and Heidegger: The Fate of the Political* (Princeton, N.J.: Princeton University Press, 1995), especially chapter 4.
8. Hannah Arendt, "Reply to Voeglin," *Review of Politics* 15 (January 1953): 78. Arendt also uses the "crystallization" image in the "Preface to the First Part of *Origins,*" p. xv. In the "Reply to Voeglin," she admits that the book "does not really deal with the 'origins' of totalitarianism—as its title unfortunately claims," and she stresses that "the elementary structure of totalitarianism is the hidden structure of the book."
9. Cf. Arendt, *Origins,* p. 378. It is not easy to connect pan-Slavism with Leninism either.
10. For a good discussion of the differences between Arendt's account and the "traditional" accounts of twentieth-century totalitarianism, see the helpful essay by Margaret Canovan, "Arendt's Theory of Totalitarianism: A Reassessment," in *The Cambridge Companion to Hannah Arendt,* ed. Dana Villa (Cambridge: Cambridge University Press, 2000), pp. 25–43.

11.   Her account anticipates Foucault's famous analysis in *Discipline and Punish*. See Arendt, *Origins*, especially p. 325.

12.   See "Personal Responsibility under Dictatorship," *The Listener* 72 (6 August 1964), where she claims that totalitarianism is genocide, but one undertaken systematically, "within the framework of a legal order" (p. 187), quoted by George Kateb in *Hannah Arendt: Politics, Conscience, Evil* (Totowa, N.J.: Rowman & Allanheld, 1983), p. 76.

13.   Kateb summarizes as well as anyone the relation between the first two parts and the third: "The real continuity between the earlier movements and totalitarianism is found in the readiness of European peoples to think in racist and imperialist categories, to accept the normality of, sympathize with, or embrace ardently such modes of response and half-thought" (*Hannah Arendt*, p. 56).

14.   François Furet, *The Passing of an Illusion*, trans. Deborah Furet (Chicago: University of Chicago Press, 1999). There are a number of similarities with Arendt's account in Furet's (the phenomenon of bourgeois self-hatred links both), but he stresses the complementary relation between fascism and the bourgeoisie on the one hand (a *retreat* of sorts to a premodern and so antibourgeois rhetoric), and communism and the bourgeoisie on the other (an acceleration *beyond* and so post-bourgeoisie).

15.   Perhaps Arendt herself realized some of the difficulties with this appeal to the phenomenon of the masses and its inherent loneliness when she came to write her account of Eichmann a decade later. In that account, published in 1963, the notions of compartmentalization, administrative logic, and the absence of "thinking" play a much more prominent role, and there is little to connect those phenomena to the problem of masses and loneliness. See the excellent discussion in Kateb's chapter on *Origins*, especially pp. 70–74. See also his remarks on her change of mind about "radical evil," p. 79.

16.   Although I don't think it does. See my *Modernism as a Philosophical Problem: On the Dissatisfactions of European High Culture*, 2nd ed. (Oxford: Blackwell, 1999), especially chapter 7.

17.   As quoted in Neiman, *Evil in Modern Thought*, p. 314.

18.   The "devil's banality" theme is given a good treatment by Neiman, *Evil in Modern Thought* (p. 280), but the overall conclusion of her thoughtful book strikes me as puzzling. I think it is fair to say that among all the accounts of the problem of evil that she treats, Arendt's is given the most favorable summary; indeed, she stresses just that secular strain in Arendt highlighted above and evident in a letter to Gershom Scholem: "Evil possesses neither depth nor any demonic dimension. It can overgrow and lay waste the whole world precisely because it spreads like a fungus on the surface" (quoted by Neiman, p. 301). But Neiman characterizes this strain in puzzling ways, at one point calling Arendt's work "the best attempt at theodicy postwar philosophy has produced," as well as (more accurately, I think) saying that throughout her work, "Arendt sought to formulate the task that might replace theodicy" (both on p. 300). The latter seems to me the right Arendtian intuition and the one suggested by the reading of Arendt presented here. Or perhaps one should say, in the spirit of Neiman's dual formulation: the "best" postwar theodicy is a final liberation from theodicean assumptions. Arendt did not achieve this goal, but, I think, she pointed the way.

11 Evil, Evils, and the Question of Ethics

Adi Ophir

In what follows, I propose a Heideggerian approach to the question of Evil that emerges from a critique of his conception of ethics and requires a long detour through some of his scattered reflections on ethics. I start from what in this context is closest and most familiar—that is, closest and familiar to me, a student of philosophy thinking in Hebrew—the word *ettika*, which is a late-modern Hebraized form of "ethics." The inevitable gap between the meaning of the Hebrew *ettika*, the Greek ηθικοσ, and the German *Ethik* helps me ask: What is ethics? in Heidegger and against him. This questioning remains Heideggerian in one important sense: it is faithful to Heidegger's early understanding of ontology as a "hermeneutics of facticity"[1] and insists on seeing Evil as part of Being; hence the "question of Evil" will be presented as an aspect of "the question of Being," and ethics as a branch of ontology.

This moves depends, however, on a certain concept and a certain concern with Evil, which are explicitly distinct from Heidegger's. It will be my contention that Evil, in the way I shall define it here, is the primary object of ethics, "the ethical thing" par excellence, and that its relation to ethics discloses (or allows the formulation of) an important distinction between ethics and the ethical (or the moral).[2] Evil is the primary object of ethics in the same sense that learnable things (of which numbers are the most familiar form) can be described by Heidegger as the primary object of a mathematical concern, "the mathematical" par excellence (MSMM); the act of "enframing" (*Ge-stell*) the primary object of technological concern (QCT); and Being as the primary object of philosophy. In other words, ethics does not "enframe Being," as Heidegger thought (LH)—it enframes Evil, which may be interpreted as being in excess, which is always also an excess of Being.

Editor's note: Although *evil* has been consistently rendered in lower case in the essays in this volume, Ophir uses upper case to avoid confusion between the abstract concept, *Evil*, and a single case of evil, one of many evils. Also, the use of lower and upper case should immediately remind readers of the conventional translation of Heidegger's *Sein* as 'Being' and *Seiendes* as 'beings' or 'entities.'

No Spelling Mistake

Was ist ettika? There is no spelling mistake in the phrase. *Ettika* is the Hebrew cognate of "ethics." Its rather short history is informative for a Heideggerian questioning of ethics and for questioning Heidegger's thinking about ethics. The word has been naturalized in colloquial Hebrew for only a few decades.[3] It designates a philosophical discipline, a theory of morals, but also a system of norms and rules, and a code of behavior. The adjective *ethi* is attributed to things belonging to the moral realm and is used interchangeably with the Hebrew word *musari,* the adjective of the noun *musar.*[4] *Musar* is a biblical word whose semantic field covered practical wisdom, education and upbringing, discipline, and the infliction of pain.[5] In modern Hebrew the word has lost most of its earlier layers of meaning and has been dissociated from most of its ancient synonyms. The association of *musar* with ethics has only helped in emptying *both* words of their ancient connotations. Thus *ettika* has not introduced into Hebrew any traces of the ancient meaning of the Greek ηθοσ and ηθικοσ. It has nothing to do with man's dwelling place, with the near and the familiar, with character and habit, and hardly maintains any link to the customary or the traditional.

The naturalization of the Greek word into Modern Hebrew worked as a kind of filter that screens out ancient layers of both Hebrew and Greek culture. Since *musari* is the standard translation of "moral," and a synonym of *ethi,* there is also no trace in Hebrew of the distinction between the Latin and the Greek word, either in their ancient or in their modern connotations. "Ethics" or "*Ethik*" may contain traces of a forgotten "originary" relation to Being, as Heidegger suggests, but its Modern Hebrew cognate certainly works as a means of forgetfulness. It has also replaced and almost erased another biblical word, *midot,* which literally means "measures," qualitative as well as quantitative, but also traits, and especially moral qualities, both virtue and vice.[6] *Torat Hamidot* (theory of measures) was the common medieval and early modern term for moral philosophy, ethics, or more generally for any moral doctrine.

Ettika makes one forget measures and measurement as well as a variety of genres of medieval Jewish moral literature (*sifrut hamusar*) that placed *midot* at the center of a systematic form of moral reasoning. Unlike *midot,* the Greek *ethos* has never been forgotten, for it has never been remembered in Hebrew, certainly not in the "original" sense that Heidegger ascribes to it. Thus, *ettika* is not only a means of forgetfulness but also as a kind of displacement that blocks the way back to the Greeks. Its naturalization into Hebrew indicates the emergence of something new that had not been articulated in Hebrew before. When questioning that new element, it seems inappropriate to look for recourse to an earlier, more primordial or authentic phase, either Greek or Hebraic. It may even be possible to think about the essence of *ettika* while knowing neither German nor Greek. But precisely because the history of *ettika* is so short, the historicity of "the ethical" (or "the moral," *ha-musari*) becomes rather obvious.

For it is impossible to question *ettika* without distinguishing between this modern, imported word and the ancient words (*musar, midot,* and some of their cognates) that seem to relate to the same domain yet obviously differ in meaning and scope.

However, the historicization of the ethical does not lead one back to any originary point of departure. The genealogy of *ettika* allows no purity of origins; it is a story of contingent, more or less arbitrary substitutions, displacements, and inventions. If there is something in common to *musar* (morality), *midot* (measures), *ettika,* and ethics, to that series of biblical, talmudic, medieval, and modern terms, this commonality should be sought against the grain of the history of any of these terms. Such common ground lies, I would like to propose here provisionally, in a *certain general possibility* of being-with, or of the being of Dasein insofar as it is always already being-with, among, alongside, against, and for others. I will soon come back to the question of what that certain possibility is and how it differs from the general structure of "being-with" as such. In the meantime, I would only like to name it "the ethical."[7] Ethics relates to the ethical as a certain discipline like mathematics relates to the mathematical; as a certain *politea,* constitution, or regime relate to the political; and more generally, as the ontic relates to the ontological. It is a basic, "originary" structure of possibilities (with no specific historical origin, however) of which modern ethics or biblical *musar* are but historical realizations.

Thinking about the Hebrew *ettika,* the distinction between *the ethical,* as a distinct relation to others and a special kind of concern with and for others, and *ethics,* as a modern, quite recent form of the ethical, becomes quite obvious. The modern philosophical discipline and its concern for the "ought" would not be easily mixed with the ancient Greek concern for αρηται, with the medieval Jewish concern for *midot,* or even with the early modern British concern for *moral sentiments.* After all, it is clear that a recent, short-lived notion such as *ettika* cannot capture such a vast domain of possibilities and such a long, complicated series of their problematizations, which is the history of the ethical.

The distinction between ethics and the ethical may seem trivial, and certainly not surprising to any reader of Heidegger. But Heidegger himself failed to make it, and this failure had some consequences. Recourse to Hebrew is certainly not the only way to illustrate that distinction, but it is only natural for a Hebrew-speaking philosopher who is trying to think *à la Heidegger,* not only about him, and therefore starts with the most familiar, with that which is "proximally and for the most part" closest to home. Such recourse may also serve as a reminder of how violent and biased the recourse to the Greeks might be. For Greek, in this case, at least, was laid as an obstacle on Heidegger's path.

The Question of Ethics

As far as I know, Heidegger's path never crossed "the question concerning ethics." He never asked, "*Was ist Ethik?*" The avoidance of this question is not to be confused with the question of Heidegger's own ethics. The question concerning ethics is a pertinent one whether or not a Heideggerian ethics or even a Heideggerian approach to moral questions is possible.[8] Furthermore, the question "What is ethics?" should have preceded and accompanied both Heidegger's critique of ethics and any Heideggerian ethics. Heidegger never opened this question, yet he wrote as if he knew what ethics was. In his scattered remarks on ethics and on particular moral concepts, he did not question ethics in the same concentrated and rigorous way that he questioned other modes of Dasein's relation to Being such as metaphysics, science, mathematics, technology, or art. But his remarks on ethics exhibit a line of reasoning similar to that characteristic of his analyses of technology or, for that matter, mathematics. Speaking very schematically, one may discern a sort of "revisionist critique" that usually consists of two more or less distinguished yet closely related steps. On the one hand, Heidegger analyzes the particular way in which a certain formation of Dasein's relation to Being and entities has reduced Being to one of its aspects: Presence, Idea, Image, or Value. On the other hand, by pushing the particular formation back to its early Greek origin, that is, to its primordial state, Heidegger strives to reopen the question of Being and let Being's essential concealment come into presence. Hence, his approach to ethics (like his approach to other domains of Dasein's existence) is both critical and revisionist. I will present briefly these two moments.

Critique

In *Being and Time*, moral and religious concepts like conscience (*Gewissen*), guilt (*Schuld*), and fall (*Verfallen*) are purged of their moral and religious import and endowed with a peculiar ontological-existential meaning. Morality or ethics are presented as an inferior mode of Dasein's relation to its own being. This relation is dominated by obligation—a special kind of prescription formulated through a universal "ought" (*Sollen*), by an anonymous addresser. The anonymous universality of the moral "ought" is at odds with Dasein's authenticity and detrimental to the opening of the question of Being. Through its "ought," ethics speaks the language of *Das Man*. Through the values that justify this "ought," ethics projects onto Being the full presence of a non-Being and declares it as a lack. The "ought" is conceived, not simply as an aspect of the moral point of view, but as its very essence. The question of ethics, so it seems, has already been closed. But in fact, it has never been opened.

Both the assertion about the essence of ethics and the closure of the question of ethics are reaffirmed in the *Introduction to Metaphysics* (IM 196–99). The "ought" is presented as one of the four "limitations" of Being. The distinction between *is* and *ought*, Heidegger says, was first hinted at by Plato's doctrine of Ideas: "The 'ought' is opposed to being as soon as being defines itself as idea" (IM 197). Kant radicalized the opposition between *is* and *ought* and marginalized other aspects of the ethical not related to obligation. Obligation, which originally was a certain interpretation of being, "needed an extra-being, from which it could emanate, and has found it in values, which now became the foundation of morality" (IM 198). Morality or ethics founded on values is a rather modern offshoot of an old metaphysics of presence (IM 95), and it will come to an end together with it due to "the encounter between global technology and modern man" achieved in and through National Socialism (IM 199).[9]

Heidegger refers to ethics more extensively after the war, in the "Letter on Humanism." First, he explains that in *Being and Time* "humanism is opposed because it does not set the *humanitas* of man high enough" (LH 210). What does set man's *humanitas* high enough and preserves his dignity is a special relation to Being. The dignity of man "consists in being called by Being itself into the preservation of the truth of Being" (LH 221). Dignity consists in the way that, as Dasein, in ek-sisting, man "might guard the truth of Being" as he "takes the *Da*, the lighting of Being, into 'care'" (LH 210, 207). This lighting, that spacing that Dasein guards open as he makes sense of Being is a respect for the immanent difference that inheres in Being, separates it from beings (Being, it is needless to add, is never another, special kind of being), and makes the identity of every being provisory and pending on the mode of its Being and on the sense endowed to it by an always interpreting Dasein.

The example for guarding the truth of Being, and hence for Man's dignity, is set by the ancient poets' and pre-Socratic philosophers' concern for Being. This concern, for Heidegger, is the originary ethical moment. Sophocles' tragedies or Heraclitus's aphorisms articulated the ethical better than Aristotle's *Ethics*. The poet and the thinker had no *ethics*, however; they were concerned with "ethos." In "ethos" lays the primordial meaning of the ethical before it was reified into a distinct discipline of intellectual activity. According to "the basic meaning of the word ηθοσ," ethics means: "ponder[ing] the abode of man," and "original ethics" is "that thinking which thinks the truth of Being" (LH 235). The result of this reading is a conscious fusion of the ethical and the ontological. To think ethically means to think the truth of Being. Hence, "originary ethics" is nothing but concern for/with ontology and for the truth of Being.[10] In its proper, primordial sense, ethics-cum-ontology is not a matter of judgment or directive for proper action, but of a proper relation to the truth of Being, to its mystery or its immanent concealment. At the point where ethics had to be distinguished from the ethical, we find it distinguished from the ontological.

Heidegger extracts this meaning from one of Heraclitus's sayings—"*ēthos anthrōpōi daimōn*" (LH 233)—and from the anecdote Aristotle tells about him. As always, Heidegger offers an idiosyncratic translation and interpretation: "The (familiar) abode is for man the open region for the presencing of god (the unfamiliar one)" (LH 234). In other words, "Man dwells, *insofar as he is man*, in the nearness of god" (LH 233; my emphasis). "Insofar as he is man"—the figure or myth of dignity is implanted into a myth of origin. Poor, shivering Heraclitus warming himself at the stove in his house is an emblem of human dignity. Visitors who come to his house expect to find the splendor they associate with the fame of the most esteemed sage but are surprised and disappointed to find an ordinary man living in poverty. Understanding their disappointment, the sage tells them something about the most basic truth of Being, its concealment in the nearness of the most familiar: "'Even here,' at the stove, at the most ordinary place where everything and every condition . . . is intimate and commonplace, that is familiar . . . 'the gods are present'" (LH 234). Even here, Heidegger probably wished us to continue, in this poor house, under these common, nonheroic conditions, a man could save his dignity if he only let his abode be opened for the presencing of Being. One may be reminded of the time of writing. In the cold nights of autumn 1946, many people tried to save their dignity, or at least to present a dignified posture, in various, and often much less dignified ways.

Man's dignity lies in his vocation to make sense of the Being of beings "in order that beings might appear in the light of Being as the beings they are" (LH 210). Making sense of the Being of beings, that is, not in accordance with any transcendent source of predetermined meanings ("an already established interpretation of nature, history, world, and the ground of the world, that is, of beings as a whole" [LH 202]), but in a way that is entirely immanent, completely engaged with the question of "the truth of Being" (LH 202) and utterly attentive to what is proper *(eigentlich)* to his ek-sistence (LH 204–10). Obviously, Dasein is not responsible for the Being of beings—"man does not decide whether and how beings appear" (LH 210)—but for the sense of their Being. Dasein's task is to preserve that opening or lighting of Being, that spacing through which beings come to be, to guard that opening against pre-given meanings that threaten to close it. It is in this sense that he is called "the shepherd of Being" (LH 210).

Human dignity, it turns out, is a reflection or even a byproduct of the destiny of Being, and it depends on the way one responds to the call of Being: "The advent of beings lies in the destiny of Being. But for man it is ever a question of finding what is fitting in his essence which corresponds to such destiny; for *in accord with this destiny* man as ek-sisting has to guard the truth of Being" (LH 210; my emphasis). Dignity is a mode of taking the addressee's position ("Before he speaks man must first let himself be claimed again by Being" [LH 199]), of acting through withholding. It is the postponement of any pre-given sense in order to make room for the act of making sense. It is due to Dasein's special mode of ek-sistence that Being becomes an object of care and is endowed with the objectivity of sense; at the same time, it is due to Dasein's special way of taking the addressee position that Being can be conceived as an emitter of meaningful signs and thus be ascribed to the addresser's position.[11] Neither an object nor a subject, or rather expropriated for his own objective essence and exiled from his position as a subject, man-cum-Dasein becomes responsible for the projected or simulated "subjectivity" of Being (as an addresser of meaningful signs) as well as for its phenomenal objectivity. This responsibility is the condition of possibility for Dasein's ek-sistence as an ethical being.

Dasein has a mission, which he has not chosen, into which he has been thrown, and the exact meaning of which he is doomed to interpret incessantly. This unchosen mission underlies every human choice, while particular choices articulate a particular way one fulfills or evades one's mission. If ethics concerns the *right* choice, it is this mission that makes ethics possible. There is a primordial form of "concernful existence" that precedes and enables any decision to be concerned about something or another. Furthermore, only through man's special belongingness to Being "can there come from Being itself the assignment *(nomos)* of those directions that must become law and rule for man" (LH 238) and without which "all law remains merely something fabricated by human reason" (LH 239).

But what is that Being that emits calls and requires guardianship? What is it about Being that needs care and response? Whence comes Dasein's responsibility as a shepherd? Jean-Luc Nancy, whose attempt to reconstruct the Heideggerian radical questioning of the possibility of ethics I find the most convincing, gives this text an insightful and favoring interpretation. The shepherd or the guardian, Nancy says, is nothing but the one who keeps the opening open. The opening, which for Heidegger is the difference between Being and beings, is for Nancy always also an opening toward the other, or better: in every opening the other is always also implicated. "Whatever the moral choice, the other is essential to opening—how to 'open' without an 'outside'[12]—which is essential to sense, which is what is essential in the action that makes the essence of Being."[13] Nancy insists on never separating the question of Being from the question of Dasein's mode of being, his conduct as a sense-maker. For him it is Dasein's finitude and the very lack of foundation on which he can establish the act of making sense *(le faire-sens de l'être)*, the complete immanence of his ek-sistence that makes him absolutely responsible for the way difference is introduced into Being (pp. 70–76). Guarding this difference, according to Nancy, is the conduct of making-sense. On its basis, and on it alone, it is possible to articulate the primordial ethical moment. First comes the moment of the ethical subject: "Only a subject that is entirely responsible for sense, and for its own existence as making sense, without prior subjection to any fixed sense, can be a fully fledged ethical subject" (p. 73). And then—the scope of an ethical concern: "The dignity of Dasein [which has now been identified as the ethical subject] consists in needing, in each choice, to engage what can be called, for want of a better term, the objectivity of Being (and consequently humanity and the world)" (p. 73).

This very general description of the "primordial" concern for the sense of being overshadows—and not simply implies, as Nancy would like to have it— the ethical as a very special concern with, and a form of *being-with:* being with oneself and with others. For this reason the ethical is not simply dissolved or fused with the ontological; it is missed altogether. For the ethical, I would like to propose, is not about dwelling in the nearness of Being, not even about the sense of being as such. The ethical is about dwelling and acting in the nearness and distance of one's self and others; it is about the sense of being with others.

But even if one accepts Nancy's favorable reading of Heidegger on this point, it is doubtful whether the critique of humanism developed in the "Letter" may be taken as a radical *questioning of ethics.* A concernful existence in which the sense of Being is always at stake and never assumes as pre-given meaning is indeed a condition of possibility for ethics, but not only for ethics. It is a condition for any other "discipline." These "can only find their place, in fact, as regimes of signification, 'after' making sense as such. This latter is prior to such partitions . . . [f]rom which one ought logically to deduce that all of the discipline orders are 'originally ethical'—the cognitive, the logical, the physical, and the aesthetic just as much as the moral" (p. 78).

Any realm of existence in which choices are made—from science to aesthetics, from politics to economics—presupposes such structures of opening to the "making sense" of Being. In each of these spheres of activity, including the moral, men usually take decisions without waiting for the call of Being but are always capable of suspending their routine course of action and becoming attentive to different possibilities to be and to be otherwise, to act and to act otherwise, to make and to unmake sense. In each of these spheres, the opening of Da-sein, his resolute insistence on exiting "in the nameless" may mean *different concerns for Being*, for making proper sense, and for making sense properly. Whether in accordance with the destiny of Being or with the authenticity of Da-sein, propriety means different things for an aesthetic, ethical, scientific, or political decision. In each case the decision to be taken should be taken in between the two poles—and in light of—a decisive *opposition:* in the sciences, the opposition between the true and the false, the known or the unknown, the certain and the probable; in the moral sphere, the opposition between good and evil, justice and injustice, virtue and vice; in the political sphere, the opposition between sovereign and subject, the authorized and the unauthorized, the legitimate and the illegitimate; and so forth. It may well be the case that what is proper scientifically or aesthetically is morally wrong, and what is morally proper goes against the scientific or aesthetic concern for the Being of beings. By itself the concern for Being is motivated by a *difference*—not an opposition—between Being and beings and can be translated in different ways into different realms of Being, constituted as they are by those various oppositions.

In short, by itself the concern for Being cannot differentiate the ethical from the aesthetic, the scientific, or the political. To call this concern, this structure of openness, *ethical* and to relate it to the entire scope of the horizon opened to the conduct of ek-sistence, or making sense, is to overlook the singularity of the ethical. Moreover, the reflection that places this concern at its center not only fails to differentiate among different types of concern (the scientific, the aesthetic, the moral, etc.), but it also fails to distinguish between ethics as a certain concrete, historically situated regime of signification and the ethical as a general type of concern, care, and interest that this specific regime of signification presupposes and embodies but never exhausts. This is a distinction that Heidegger makes elsewhere between, for example, mathematics and the mathematical, or between a certain technological regime and the technological (to which one may add, by analogy, the distinction between a certain science and the scientific, or between the arts of a certain epoch and the artistic, etc.). By claiming an ethical status to the "originary" and very general concern for Being, Heidegger—

and most of the readers who follow him, trying to reconstruct a Heideggerian ethics—fail to distinguish between ethics and the ethical. A radical questioning of ethics that bypasses this distinction may be radical indeed, but directed at the ontological, not the ethical. In Nancy's words: "If, however, the action of sense is the exercising of the relation with what is nearest but cannot be appropriated as a being, then not only is there an ethics, but ethics is the ontology of ontology itself" (p. 77).[14]

Revision

The ethics about which Nancy speaks here is Heidegger's "originary ethics." His definition—"ethics is the ontology of ontology itself"—is an apt formula for the relation between originary ethics and ontology described in the "Letter," but as stated above, it misses the relation between originary ethics and any particular historically situated ethics. For Heidegger's originary ethics is not only the transcendental condition that makes possible the logos—the saying and the logic—of being; it is also a kind of pre-historical or mythical formation of the care for being, a degree zero of Dasein's responsibility for the sense of being, which any historical ethics presupposes and, at the same time, conceals or makes one forget. Because any historically situated ethics presupposes it, originary ethics is also reproduced, albeit distortedly, through each of its historically situated moments. That the historical differs from the transcendental or the primordial is a condition for its very historicity. This difference, however, remains virtually the same, according to Heidegger, for any kind of ethics throughout the history of the West.

The problem with ethics, for Heidegger, is that it has become a philosophical discipline, and thinking in terms of disciplines has become "untenable" (LH 232). Ethics, Heidegger says, has been a philosophical discipline ever since Plato. It was formed at the time when thinking became philosophy and science, and was differentiated into schools and disciplines like "logic" or "physics" (LH 195–96). This is why Sophocles' tragedies or Heraclitus's aphorisms were better examples of the ethical than Aristotle's *Ethics*, the paradigm for the "disciplinization" of philosophy.

But Heidegger's claim that ethics was a discipline ever since Plato is a dubious assertion. Disciplines, let alone philosophical disciplines, are a modern phenomenon. The career of ethics as a special, distinct domain of philosophical questioning is yet to be told. Here we may consider schematically, very briefly and very quickly, the modern era only. Ethics had not become a distinct philosophical discipline before the second half of the nineteenth century. During the eighteenth and most of the nineteenth century, in the British Isles, ethics was usually considered as a subdiscipline in a cluster of sciences that included metaphysics, logic and rhetoric, philosophy of mind, political philosophy, and political economy, and—in less academic settings—moral statistics and, somewhat later, experimental psychology. In the early part of this period, jurisprudence and history were also included. These sciences or branches of knowledge were usually gathered under the heading of "Moral Philosophy" or "Moral Sciences."[15] On the continent, ethics was a branch of practical philosophy, alongside economy and politics.[16] In the nineteenth century in France, it had become part of the newly institutionalized *sciences morales et politiques*.[17] In Germany it was sometimes related to the "police sciences" *(politzeiwissenchaften)*.[18]

The exact composition of the cluster of sciences to which ethics belonged or related varied in different parts of Europe and changed throughout the nineteenth century, but these differences and modifications were never as dramatic as the gap that later separated ethics from the heir of the moral sciences—the social sciences.[19] Hegel's course on the *Philosophy of Right*, for example, covered much of the same domains covered by a professor of Moral Philosophy like Adam Smith in Scotland. In the middle of the nineteenth century, a somewhat modernized form of this cluster of discourses was introduced into Cambridge, and a few years later it entered Oxford. Even then, ethics was still an integral part of a larger field and was closely related to practical reasoning no less than to metaphysical reflection.[20] Among the German idealists, from Fichte to Schopenhauer, ethics was implicated in metaphysics in a way that may remind one of Plato, yet it was also associated in a completely modern way with theology on the one hand, and with legal philosophy and jurisprudence on the other hand. And what is most important, ethics' claim for autonomy, its unique form of judgment and the special concern with—and the primacy it gave to—a sui generis kind of obligation, which Kant inaugurated, did not become its hallmark before the end of the nineteenth century.

The appearance of ethics as a more or less distinct branch of knowledge was a direct result of the dissolution of the so-called moral sciences during the second half of the nineteenth century and the institutionalization of the social or human sciences as autonomous disciplines. Nietzsche's critique of morals, especially in the *Genealogy of Morals,* which heralded the decline of ethics, actually corresponds (and perhaps contributed) to its demarcation and transformation into a separate domain of knowledge and judgment. Kant came to occupy the central position he currently occupies in the history of ethics—in Germany too, not only in Britain and France—only when the cluster of the moral sciences fell apart, along with the emergence of mathematical economics, experimental psychology, anthropology, and sociology. Ethics' growing indifference to those sciences and its self-understanding as "a science of values" owes less to Kant's radical separation between nature and freedom, between pure and practical reason, than to the attempt of the new social sciences to become value-free intellectual enterprises, purging themselves of any trace of moral reasoning and political interests.

In *Being and Time,* Heidegger seems to be aware of at least part of this story. In section 5, he lists ethics *(Ethik)* with other sciences that presuppose humanistic metaphysics and study Dasein's "ways of behavior, its capacities, [and] powers" (BT 16). Besides ethics, the list includes philosophical psychology, anthropology, "political science," poetry, biography, and "the writing of history"

(Geschichtsschreibung). With the exception of poetry, all these disciplines are modern. If Heidegger had pursued further their historicization, he would have found how modern is the placing of judgment and obligation at the center of ethics and how uncharacteristic of earlier moralists is the radical dissociation of moral questions from other forms of practical knowledge and from the moral sciences. But this path was not pursued. In the "Letter on Humanism," where ethics is presented as a philosophical discipline, a more or less straight, uninterrupted, and homogeneous line is drawn from Plato's dialogue on justice *(Politea)* to Kant's categorical imperative, and on to present-day academic moral theories. Ethics is conceived as a steady aspect of metaphysics, and its essence is said to remain unchanged from its early inception in classical Greece.

This is not a simple historical error on Heidegger's part. It goes straight to the heart of his thinking. Heidegger could project the notions of obligation and judgment on the entire history of ethics and present them as essential to any moral concern only by denying the historicity of ethics. There is a whole history of moral problematizations that Heidegger fails to see because he is interested with one form of problematization only, the problematization of man's relation to Being, and with three major historical moments only: the birth of metaphysics in ancient Greece, the emergence of the modern subject in Descartes, and the closure of metaphysics in Germany in his own time.

According to Heidegger, the history of Being overshadows the history of other domains like mathematics, technology, or art in the same way it overshadows the history of ethics. But with regard to the latter, Heidegger even refrains from drawing that basic distinction, between the historical and the transcendental, so fruitful and so characteristic of some of his other historicized ontological researches. He distinguishes between the ontic and the ontological, or between mathematics and the mathematical, but he never made a clear distinction between ethics and the ethical. Had he asked the question of ethics, this distinction would have been made almost naturally. For this is precisely what the questioning of ethics entails—a distinction between a particular formation of practice and knowledge in a certain domain of being, and the essence or structure of that domain, which any particular historical formation instantiates and no particular formation can exhaust. For us "the question of ethics" should begin with the attempt to free the ethical from the domination of "ethics" as a certain historical formation of the practice and knowledge of morality.

The Question of the Ethical

Forms of Care

Some of Heidegger's readers have emphasized the transcendental argument of *Being and Time* and present one of its key categories—care *(Sorge)*, or resoluteness *(Entschlossenheit)*, or authenticity *(Eigentlichkeit)*, or conscience *(Gewissen)* and its call *(Ruf)*—as a condition for the possibility of ethics, humanistic or otherwise, as well as a condition for the transformation of ethics or its possible overcoming.[21] But *Sorge* is a condition of possibility for any particular concern whatsoever, and there is nothing in it that may serve to distinguish moral from other kinds of concern. Even if one accepts Dastur's claim that "the existential sense of care . . . implies reference to the other,"[22] one still misses the specificity of the ethical. The relation of the technician to her failing instrument, of the businessman to his growing profit, and of the child to her lost doll, are all forms of care that imply others and yet may be conceived as morally indifferent and ethically irrelevant. This may still be the case even when those others are not simply implied but become explicit objects of concern: the technician may try to understand the expert who wrote the instruction to the failing machine; the businessman may try to guess his competitors' reaction to the latest development in the stock market; and the child may find her doll in the nearby public garden. At the same time, any of these may become ethical under certain formations of the ethical—a Protestant ethics of duties for the capitalist businessman, for example, or a Halachic ethics of lost and found objects for the father of the Jewish child. In each of these cases, concern may be a basis for moral as well as purely cognitive or aesthetic judgment and for a playful simulation as well as for a seriously earnest act. Resoluteness, authentic being, and the call of conscience may be involved in each of our three examples, without invoking in any way the specificity of the ethical. The question here is not about the differentiation between good and evil, right and wrong, proper and improper, but between a moral concern and other types of concerns (e.g., political, legal, scientific, or aesthetic), between moral judgment and other forms of judgment. It is a question about specificity of the ethical as a form of intentionality and the demarcation of a corresponding space of objects that initiate or call for a moral concern. It is this demarcation of the ethical that is the proper condition of possibility for any moral distinction. Without it "there would not even be any difference between the opposing poles of being, between the wonder of the without-why sung by Angelus Silesius and the horror of the *kein Warum* evoked by Primo Levi."[23] The question of (the demarcation of) the ethical is formidable. I will postpone my provisional attempt to answer it by saying a few words about the question itself.

Speaking about the mathematical, Heidegger warns us that we should not explain it by mathematics and then goes on to present his method: "In such questions we do well to keep to the word itself" (MSMM 249), which means: let's go back to the very ancient Greeks. And indeed, Heidegger draws from the Greek not only the meaning of the word but also a classification of five kinds of things, of which mathematical things are one class (MSMM 250). We cannot afford this reification of the word and this privilege for the Greeks. We shall not go back to ancient Hebrew either. We must think the ethical in its historicity. Three questions are opened at this point. *A Historical question:* When and under which circumstances was a certain mode of care, with all the particular elements which it entails, designated as "moral" or "ethical," and distinguished from the religious, the political, the juridical, or the economic? *An Ontic-ontological* question: What forms of being-with does this mode of care enframe *(Gestellt)*, make possible, or render impossible? And a *Historical-ontological* question: Is there an essential meaning of care that encompasses all these modes of care, a structure that all the various modes realize and incarnate throughout different epochs and cultures? Or is this "more originary" meaning but an invention or a dream of a certain philosophy that is still stuck in essentialism, even when it calls itself thinking?

In the *Introduction to Metaphysics*, Heidegger says that morality has become "one of the dominant positions of the modern spirit toward the essent *[das Seiende]* in general" (IM 95).[24] One can certainly envision an *ontological* analysis of the being of values, obligations, judgment, and other moral "essents" that foreclose the question of Being. But in line with the above list of questions, one may also opt for an inquiry that would examine the emergence of the concepts of value and moral obligation as the basis of the modern formation of the ethical. Even if it were the case that the history of Being is not at stake here, the modern facticity of Dasein certainly is. Heidegger, for his part, does not dissociate the critique of values from the critique of ideas or metaphysics in general. This is already true in *Being and Time*, where it allows him to maintain the opposition between authentic resolution and moral obligation, to leave the determination of action entirely within the realm of the individual's unfounded decision, and to close in advance the possibility of thinking the ethical in and through various forms of being-with. Later the same structure allows him to think of "the encounter between global technology and modern man" as something that is happening first and foremost to Being, not to people, something that may concern the earth before it concerns its inhabitants.

But when the question of the ethical comes to the fore, the role that moral values and moral judgment play in Dasein's modern facticity must get the same phenomenological attention as instruments get in the context of everyday practice. In the "Letter on Humanism," Heidegger makes some steps in this direction. The moral concern articulated through values and obligations is a fallen form of care that happens "when objectivity takes the form of value. . . . Thinking in values is the greatest blasphemy imaginable against Being" (LH 228). Values must be overcome in order to gain new access to the question of Being. "Thinking overcomes metaphysics by climbing back down into the nearness of the nearest" (LH 231),that is, by turning from the *evaluation* of entities to the *thinking* of Being.

We need not follow Heidegger's quick move from the critique of ethics (conceived as a matter of judgment and evaluation) to the critique of metaphysics; instead we may well dwell for a moment on the former. Values seek to enframe the *meaning* or *sense* of action and of being-with-others in a way not entirely different from the way techniques enframe Being itself and man's relation to it. Values relate action and reaction, suffering and losses, pleasures and gains to an imaginary equilibrium in a system of exchange and distribution. They endow social equipment, that is, different social apparatuses, with imaginary forms and help them relate the "raw material" of social life to imaginary goals. Values enclose the occurrence of violence, suffering, or loss within a system of distribution and give them exchange values; they measure violation of body and property according to those values. Values are quick to congeal bodily experiences and violent events into claims of right, merit, glory, or honor, and to conceal everything in such events that is irreducible to the presence of the valuable—something that value cannot measure, for which value cannot find an equi-valent. Values let one forget violence as an occurrence. They must be deconstructed like any other form of enduring presence, and a close attention should be given to the particular way that the *Ereignis* and the forgetfulness of the ethical—not of Being—come to presence through them.

If Heidegger is right in his claim about the role that moral values have come to play in modernity, then values are the modern form of a particular enframing of the ethical and, more generally, of Dasein's being with others. This form of the ethical can be criticized and even "overcome" without giving up the possibility of distinct ethical concern, interest, and point of view. On the contrary, such a critique may yield a renewal of the ethical, not its destruction. But since for Heidegger the ethical is identified with ethics and understood to be a simple offshoot of metaphysics, a metaphysics applied to practice, the "overcoming" of metaphysics means the end of the ethical.[25] In the "Letter," Heidegger speaks about the overcoming of ethics in terms of turning from *evaluation* and *judgment* as forms of maintaining distance, to thinking as a form of homecoming and "dwelling in." To *overcome* is to come *back*. Back to Being, of course, whose call requires silence, solitude, and a certain indifference to the cries and shouts of everyday language, through which one hears the calls of concrete others, of others who are simply there, near or far away, and for whom it is not the *sense of their Being* (as particular, common, and not very proper or authentic examples of ek-sistence) which is necessarily at stake, but rather their *very existence*.

The outcome is disastrous, as many of Heidegger's critics have made amply clear. But since they too have identified ethics with the ethical and confined it to the foundation of judgment concerning values and obligation, they too were left "without resources" after the "destruction" of ethics. Hence come the reiterated expressions of some deep moral crisis, of which the moral bankruptcy of the man Martin Heidegger is but a symptom. A good example is an emphatic passage from Philippe Lacoue-Labarthe's *Heidegger, Art, and Politics*:

> How and from where could one philosophically get back beyond Heidegger's delimitation of ethics and humanism? . . . *We are entirely without resources.* . . . It is certainly no longer possible to answer the question "from what position can we judge? In the name of what and of whom?" For what are lacking, now and for the foreseeable future, are names, and most immediately "sacred names," which in their various ways governed, and alone governed, the space (public or other) in which ethical life unfolded.[26]

God is one such name, Man another, the Nation ("the Jewish People," "the German Reich," "America," "la France," etc.) yet another. Perhaps reason too is a sacred name. These sacred names were the resources that once made moral judgment possible. Judgment itself—not its ground—is obviously possible, and in the realm of normative judgment, business, so it seems, runs almost as usual. Of course, says Lacoue-Labarthe, "we are . . . forced to live and act according to the norms and prescription of ethics, i.e., norms and prescriptions derived from the old ethical systems,"[27] that is, those that could rely on sacred names. But no name is sacred anymore. Hence, there is no ground, no position, for moral judgment, which presumably means that ethics is no longer possible—or at least that one can presuppose neither its existence nor its possibility when speaking about doing wrong.

John Caputo too accepts this position when he writes in the same vein "against ethics." Heidegger's "originary ethics" simply replaces familiar sacred names with a less familiar one, the name of Being. His originary ethics must be rejected just like the foundationalist attempt to lay the ground of moral judgment: "Though I wait daily by the phone, though I keep my ear close to the ground, I cannot, for the life of me, hear the call of Being. I have been forsaken."[28] Having been forsaken by both kinds of ethics, Caputo proposes to dissociate ethics from obligation, to get rid of the former and become "a clerk" and "scriber" of the latter. He would like to replace ethics with "a poetics of obligation."[29] A plethora of obligations is part of human facticity; it has to be described phenomenologically, analyzed poetically, and thought unsystematically, without lamentation for the lack of foundation, and yet without ever ceasing to think about (and trying to do) the right thing. Ethics is presented like a protective guide that was supposed to lead man through the plethora of conflicting obligations and to provide him with a blueprint for their selection, arrangement, and hierarchization. It has been proven useless and is thrown like a useless shield. The melancholic and witty, courageous yet impotent non-hero of the postmodern age is now ready to wander armless through a jungle of obligations. He looks there for sages, saints, and heroes who have done the same before him and tries to follow them; he writes their eulogies and uses them in order to compose one for himself.

Caputo goes half of the way I am proposing here. By dissociating obligations from ethics, originary or otherwise, he opens the question of the ethical (a questioning implied already in the title of his book, *Against Ethics*). But by limiting his questioning to obligation, he actually reiterates Heidegger's main contention about the historical primacy of obligation for ethics. Thus, *Against Ethics* too presupposes an answer to the question of ethics without dwelling long enough on the question itself. However, this path is not inevitable. Conceived as a form of enframing, ethics is related to technology no less than to metaphysics. It is at this point, when the "technological" aspect of ethics is grasped, that an essential relation between the ethical and the question of Evil may be unfolded.

Evils and Evil

I take my clue from what seems to me to be Heidegger's most fruitful remark in relation to ethics. He presented it in the course of a discussion of Evil in the seminar on Schelling's *Treatise on the Essence of Human Freedom,* which he delivered in Freiburg in 1936 and later summarized at the end of the "Letter on Humanism" (LH 237–38). In his reading of Schelling, Heidegger unfolds a dense metaphysical concept of Evil, presenting his own, not only Schelling's view. What is properly his is the attempt to free Being from the logic of an absolute totality that comes back to itself from its self-differentiation, and to think of Evil in relation to "the essence and the truth of Being" (ScT 146). The task is defined as a fundamental metaphysical one, and ethics is again circumscribed: "The scope of ethics is not sufficient to comprehend [E]vil. Rather, ethics and morality concern only a legislation with respect to behavior toward [E]vil in the sense of its overcoming and rejection or its trivialization" (ScT 146). The interest of ethics in Evil is merely negative: Evil ought not to be. In order to let Evil disappear from the realm of Being, ethics legislates. If human action and behavior would follow the norms ethics prescribes and the laws it legislates, Evil would no longer be. This perspective on Evil trivializes its occurrence and persistence as an inevitable aspect of Being and closes the possibility of putting the being of Evil in question.

But there is certainly more to Evil than ethics allows one to grasp. Ethics, conceived as a specific form of enframing "the meaning or sense of action and of being-with-others" (above, p. 179), does not let Evil appear as what it really is—a tremendous outburst of unlimited rage and fury. In other words, ethics' point of view erases that inexorable excess that belongs to the essence of Evil. Evil is a storm of meaningless, formless violence that precedes ethical values and in fact endows them with their proper task: to let a certain aspect of Evil appear only in order to conceal the overwhelming excess that constitutes it. Ethics may thus be described as an appropriation and forgetfulness of Evil. Ethics does not enframe Being—it enframes Evil. If Evil is conceived as an excess of Being, then ethics enframes Being under one of its particular aspects, its excessiveness. Ethics must be deconstructed in order to let Evil appear in the excessiveness of its being, which is always also the very excessiveness of Being itself, the excess that comes to presence in the eruption of Evil.

I would not follow the rest of Heidegger's discussion of Evil, which, as Nancy has shown convincingly, comes down to another theodicy, or better, onto-dicy.[30] Instead, I venture now to present, very hesitantly, my provisional answer to the question: What is the ethical? thus reformulating the distinction between the ethical and any particular ethics.

First, we have to reformulate the distinction between ethics and the ethical in accordance with our previous discussion. Modern ethics is a *particular* formation of the enframing of Evil. Evil is Being in excess, Being that has lost its measure. However, Being has no measure, except where there is an ethical point of view to delimit it, to endow it with its proper measure, to relate violence and destruction to those who produce and distribute them and to those who undergo them. Violence destroys entities, and through this very destruction produces an excess—of suffering and loss, which have their peculiar, enduring presence in the midst of a growing absence. Evil is superfluous excess that should not have come into being. Evil is the Being of beings stamped by a negated negation. The eruption of Evil is the negation of the "should not have taken place." This double negation is more general and fundamental (primordial?) than the negation implied by the "ought"; it is not opposed to Being but inheres in Being itself, for it is an excess of Being—not its lack—that lies at stake here.

One need not imagine either ideals or values in order to recognize the superfluity of that excess of Being or to understand its nature as a "should not have been." Values (and ideas in general) and obligations are but particular forms of letting that excess appear; there may be others: virtuous dispositions, moral sensibilities, sympathy, and the very experience and display of suffering. Whatever are these forms, they are formations of the ethical, for *the ethical is a certain discourse, point of view, and type of concern*—all the three together—that let Evil appear, or—it comes to the same thing—let a certain excess of Being appear as that which should not have been.

But Evil never appears as such; it is always already enframed by one of these formations. Only evils appear, in the plural, as particular entities, "essents" with certain objective and certain subjective features. The manifold of evils relate to Evil in the same way that the manifold of beings relate to Being: making it present and concealing it at one and the same time, articulating it in and through language (that names and describes this and that particular being or evil), and making one forget the persistence of the yet, or forever inexpressible Being/Evil and the possibility of different kinds of enframing. Kinds of ethics, moral systems, and normative codes see no Evil; they can only designate (refer to, show, put on display, remind and commemorate, predict and warn against) and interpret series of occurrences of suffering and pain, losses, damages, and ruin that should not have taken place.

In conclusion, we may restate the distinction between ethics and the ethical. An ethics is a particular formation of the ethical. Like any such formation, it enframes Evil and lets it appear as a series of evils. The trivialization of Evil by ethics, which Heidegger mentions, is thus the enframing of evils and their reification as objects to be rejected, prevented, and—when unavoidable—justly distributed and compensated for. Thus, there is nothing morally or philosophically wrong about the enframing of Evil. On the contrary, only on the basis of a certain enframing of Evil can one do the right thing—try to get rid of it. At the same time, no ethics can exhaust Evil; at any particular moment it enframes *only some* of the existing evils and lets *only some* of its victims come into presence and assume a voice of their own. Because it is embodied in a structured discourse, a limited point of view, and a particular kind of care, its indifference to other kinds of evils is inherent and structured. The ethical, on the other hand, is an attitude that subsists on the margin of a particular ethics, nurtured from its sources, but that aspires to transcend its limits and always maintains a residual openness to that Evil which escapes articulation within that particular ethics. The ethical is attentive to that Evil which ethics has made one forget; it lets occurrences of Evil come into presence and appear as evils. The ethical is care for the victims to whom a prevailing ethics is blind; it is a willingness to call into question the limit of that ethics and the means it employs in order to objectify evils.

On this aspect of the ethical Heidegger never spent a moment. On his way backward to the primordial and the originary, he rushed from ethics straight to the truth and sense of Being. He finds there, together but unrelated, the immanent possibility of Evil, in fact the impossibility of eradicating it, as well as the dignity of man. In that primordial element, both dignity and Evil have lost their human, all too human face. Dignity, for Heidegger, is a relation to the truth of Being that may be indifferent to the Evil that inheres in it. Evil, for Heidegger, is a relation between Being and entities that is indifferent to the distinction between the dignified and the ignoble. This was Heidegger's standpoint in 1946. It cannot explain the Rectorat address, but it may throw some light on the silence regarding Auschwitz. No dignity is related to Auschwitz; the Evil that inheres in it does not get any special attention. It can be mentioned in the same breath together with the contamination of fresh crops by the motorized food industry.

Whatever we have learned from him, however deeply immersed in his thought we still are, it should be admitted that when it comes to the question of the ethical, only a God could save the dignity of this pious thought.

Notes

Work on this paper was made possible by a research grant from the Israel Science Foundation. An early draft of this paper was presented at the Heidegger Conference in Jerusalem, January 2000.

1.   The title of the last lecture course given by Heidegger in Freiburg in the summer semester of 1923. See Martin Heidegger, *Ontology—The Hermeneutics of Facticity*, trans. John van Buren (Bloomington: Indiana University Press, 1988); the story of the title itself is told by the book's editor, p. 88. Subsequent references to Heidegger's texts are made parenthetically using the following abbreviations:

BT: *Being and Time*, trans. John Macquarrie and Edward Robinson (Oxford: Basil Blackwell, 1962).
IM: *Introduction to Metaphysics*, trans. Ralph Manheim (New Haven, Conn.: Yale University Press, 1961).
LH: "Letter on Humanism," trans. Frank A. Capuzzi in collaboration with J. Glenn Gray, in *Basic Writings*, ed. David Farrell Krell (New York: Harper and Row Publishers, 1977).
MSMM: "Modern Science, Metaphysics and Mathematics," trans. W. B. Barton and Vera Deutsch, in *Basic Writings*, ed. David Farrell Krell (New York: Harper and Row Publishers, 1977).
QCT: "The Question Concerning Technology," trans. William Lovitt, in

Basic Writings, ed. David Farrell Krell (New York: Harper and Row Publishers, 1977).
ScT: *Schelling's 'Treatise on the Essence of Human Freedom,'* trans. Joan Stambaugh (Athens: Ohio University Press, 1985).

2. For reasons that become clear later, I relate to these two terms as synonyms.
3. *Ettika* did not enter colloquial Hebrew before the middle of the twentieth century. Klatzkin's translation of Spinoza's *Ethics,* published in 1924, was titled *Torat Hamidot* (literally, theory of measures). His Hebrew philosophical lexicon that appeared in 1931 did not contain *ettika* among its entries. In 1943 the two first books of Aristotle's *Nicomachean Ethics* were translated under the title *Midot.* In S. H. Bergman's comprehensive *History of Modern Philosophy, ettika* is not indexed at all, and moral theory is indexed under *midot.* In the 1970s, *ettika* had already been naturalized. The complete translation of Aristotle's *Nicomachean Ethics* (1973) was entitled *Ettika Nicomachit* (of Nicomachus).
4. *Ettika* is found, for example, in the name of a special "moral committee" that exists in several Israeli institutions (including the Israeli Parliament); the official role of "the committee of *ettika*" is to deal with misbehavior of members of those institutions.
5. In the Old Testament, *musar* usually means a kind of practical wisdom acquired through education and experience, in a more or less painful process. The root of *musar* is יסר; *le-yaser* means 'to torment; to inflict pain, suffering, or misery.' But nothing of this semantic field is operative in the contemporary use of *musar.*
6. One may "have" or "possesses" both good or noble measures *(midot tovot, naalot)* and bad or lewd measures *(midot raot, megunot).*
7. My choice here is dictated by Heidegger's choice not to give any special attention to the distinction between morality and ethics, and to define ethics as a special form of care, the care for Being.
8. Many of Heidegger's readers have questioned the possibility of a Heideggerian ethics, and some of the more sympathetic among them have tried to reconstruct arguments for a nonhumanistic ethics on the basis of the concepts of *ek-sistence, Sorge, Eigentlichkeit* (which is not quite properly translated as "authenticity"), *Entschlossenheit,* and more generally on his critique of humanism and metaphysics. An impressive collection of essays representing this line of reading has been recently edited by François Raffoul and David Pettigrew in *Heidegger and Practical Philosophy* (Albany: State University of New York Press, 2002). For earlier attempts, see Charles E. Scott, "Nonbelonging/Authenticity," in *Reading Heidegger: Commemorations* (Bloomington: Indiana University Press, 1993), pp. 67–79, and Joanna Hodge, *Heidegger and Ethics* (New York: Routledge, 1995). Other readers of Heidegger have used Heideggerian modes of questioning in moral contexts without necessarily trying to develop a Heideggerian ethics; see e.g., Werner Marx, *Is There a Measure on Earth? Foundations for a Nonmetaphysical Ethics,* trans. Thomas J. Nenon (Chicago: University of Chicago Press, 1987), and Robert Bernasconi, "Justice and the Twilight Zone of Morality," in *Reading Heidegger,* pp. 80–94.
9. Jacob Rogozinski, who gives a similar reading to these passages, concludes:

Evil, Evils, and the Question of Ethics 185

"A single filiation leads from Plato to Kant, and from Kant to the Hitlerian ideologists. In Nazism, as the realm of moral values, the fulfillment of goodness, the ancient victory of the Good over Being, unfolds its most extreme consequences. This rather surprising assertion only develops in all their implication the presupposition of Heideggerian ontology and most of all . . . that Being alone is what 'provides the measures'" ("*Hier ist kein warum:* Heidegger and Kant's Practical Philosophy," in *Heidegger and Practical Philosophy,* ed. Raffoul and Pettigrew, p. 49).

10.   Cf. Jean-Luc Nancy, *La pensée dérobée* (Paris: Galilée, 2001); 2001; John Caputo, *Against Ethics* (Bloomington: Indiana University Press, 1993), p. 2.

11.   Relying on Ricoeur, Françoise Dastur tries to reduce the call of Being to the voice of moral conscience (*die Stimme des Gewissens*) and to interpret the latter as always implying the call of another. She even suggests that *Mitwissen* should replace *Gewissens* ("The Call of Conscience: The Most Intimate Alterity," in *Heidegger and Practical Philosophy,* ed. Raffoul and Pettigrew, p. 92). I don't see any basis for this claim, at least with regard to the "Letter on Humanism," where ethics is explicitly evoked. In *Being and Time,* where Dastur's reading may be valid, Heidegger denies explicitly the ethical connotation.

12.   The English translator omitted this inserted phrase: "*comment 'ouvrir' sans 'dehors'?*" See Nancy, *La pensée dérobée,* p. 96.

13.   Jean-Luc Nancy, "Heidegger's Originary Ethics," in *Heidegger and Practical Philosophy,* ed. Raffoul and Pettigrew, p. 72. Page numbers in the text are to this work.

14.   Jacob Rogozinski speaks in this context about "the ontological reduction of ethics" ("*Hier ist kein warum,*" p. 58).

15.   This is best exemplified by the textbooks of the period. See e.g., Dugald Stewart, *Outline of Moral Philosophy* (Edinburgh: William Creech, 1793); James Beattie, *Elements of Moral Science* (Aberdeen, 1817); Alexander Bain, *Mental and Moral Science: A Compendium of Psychology and Ethics* (London: Longmans, Green and Co., 1869).

16.   See Jürgen Mittelstrass, "Praktische Philosophie," in *Enzyklopädie Philosophie und Wissenschaftstheorie* (Stuttgart: J. B. Metzler Verlag, 1995), Band 3, pp. 214–16; Franco Volpi, "Philosophie Pratique," in *Dictionnaire d'éthique et de philosophie morale,* ed. Monique Canto-Sperber (Paris: PUF, 1996), p. 1133.

17.   See Sophie-Anne Leterrier, *L'Institution des sciences morales: L'Académie des sciences morales et politiques 1795–1850* (Paris: L'Harmattan, 1995).

18.   See Ludwig Elster, Adolf Weber, and Friedrich Wieser, *Handwörterbuch der Staatswissenschaften,* Sechster Band (Jena: Verlag von Gustav Fischer, 1925), pp. 884–93

19.   An early example of this separation may be found in Mill's *System of Logic* (*Collected Works,* vol. 3 [Toronto: University of Toronto Press, 1966]). The last chapter of this voluminous work is entitled "Of the Logic of Practice, or Art, including Morality and Policy." This chapter concludes the book's sixth part: "On the Logic of the *Moral Sciences.*" For Mill, however, the moral sciences were already conceived as social sciences in which laws may be gathered through the use of a logic of inference that fits the nature of the historical and social domain, while morality or ethics was conceived as an art or a nonproductive science, a science that belonged to the Aristotelian realm of praxis (cf. Mill, *Collected Works,* vol. 9 [Toronto: University of Toronto Press, 1968],

p. 349). In England the autonomy of ethics and its dissociation from the "moral *sciences*" that gradually turned into "the *social* sciences" was crystallized in the work of Henry Sidgwick, who gave ethics its special methodologies (*The Methods of Ethics* [London: Macmillan and Co., 1874]), and then its first authoritative history (*Outlines of the History of Ethics for English Readers* [London: Macmillan and Co., 1886]).

20. Despite the many changes and revisions introduced throughout the second half of the nineteenth century, *The Moral Science Tripos* of Cambridge University (ed. James Ward [London: George Bell and Sons, 1891]) still contained Ethics in between Psychology and Political Economy.

21. See the works cited in note 8 above, especially the papers by Dastur, Jean Greisch, and Miguel de Beistegui, in *Heidegger and Practical Philosophy,* ed. Raffoul and Pettigrew.

22. Dastur, "The Call of Conscience," p. 90. This is also Nancy's claim, but it is argued differently, through a reading of Paul Ricoeur's *Soi-même comme un autre* (Paris: Éditions du Seuil, 1990).

23. Rogozinski, "*Hier ist kein warum,*" p. 58. Rogozinski speaks about the absence of any law, but law is only one way to articulate the ethical. I will shortly present another way below.

24. The subject of the quoted phrase is "morality," but as stated above, morality and ethics are used interchangeably by Heidegger, in this context at least, where ethics is said to be dominated by the moral ought.

25. Cf. Bernasconi, "Justice and the Twilight Zone of Morality," pp. 80–94.

26. Philippe Lacoue-Labarthe, *Heidegger, Art, and Politics: The Fiction of the Political,* trans. Chris Turner (Oxford: Blackwell, 1990), p. 31; my emphases. See also Caputo, *Against Ethics,* ch. 2.

27. Lacoue-Labarthe, *Heidegger, Art, and Politics,* p. 31.

28. Caputo, *Against Ethics,* p. 2.

29. Ibid., pp. 20–21.

30. Jean-Luc Nancy, *The Experience of Freedom,* trans. Bridget McDonald (Stanford, Calif.: Stanford University Press, 1993), ch. 12; see also Rogozinski, "*Hier ist kein warum,*" p. 59.

12 Incursions of Evil: The Double Bind of Alterity

Edith Wyschogrod

What, we might ask, could Gregory Bateson's description of the double bind have to do with the question of evil? I hope to show that the double bind, the claim that no matter what one does one cannot win, not only plays a role in determining the development of schizophrenia, as Bateson maintains, but is intrinsic to the emergence of the moral life.[1] I view the double bind as a prior condition for deciding that a contemplated act is evil and for the sense of obligation that enters into the avoidance or pursuit of ends that are deemed to be evil. I argue further that double binds arise not only in individual but also in sociohistorical contexts in which otherness is in conflict with collective rules. The route taken in support of these claims will, of necessity, be circuitous.

I shall begin with Emmanuel Levinas's premise that ethics originates in alterity, in the otherness of the other person whose very existence as it impinges upon the self is experienced as a proscription against exerting violence against that other. But I maintain that the understanding of evil that can be inferred from this account requires expansion. There are not only harms one does to another but harms that one inflicts upon oneself, the evils of physically injurious and psychologically debilitating acts committed against oneself. I examine such acts in light of George Ainslie's discussion of how temporal distance affects the ways in which we make choices, present satisfactions being preferred over remote gains. Next I consider those evils that are inherent in the very modes of rationality that govern contemporary collective life and form the context for evils that can be termed radical: war and widespread poverty. To this end, I discuss Dominique Janicaud's analysis of techno-discourse, a mode of rationality underlying radical evils. These disparate modes of evil are linked by virtue of the double binds that come into play in the self's relation to itself and within a sociocultural whole.

Levinas's Philosophy and the Double Bind of Alterity

Levinas maintains that moral awareness begins when the other person is disclosed in her immediacy, not as another myself, but as absolutely other.

Perceived in this way, the other is grasped, not as a composite of sense data, but as an ethical imperative that is not prescriptive but proscriptive: the other acts upon the self as a directive to refrain from harming or doing violence to that other. That another individual may be given as an object of perception or cognition is not in question in contexts of everyday existence. But when disclosed as an object in the world, otherness disintegrates, and the other enters consciousness as one of its possessions or as part of a totalizing nexus of sociohistorical relations. In thus reducing the other to a content of one's own consciousness, one is always already guilty before the other. On Levinas's radical view of otherness, the face of the other is revealed primordially, not as a phenomenon, but as a command to refrain from doing violence to the other.[2]

It is not hard to see in this account features of the double bind, a situation that, according to Bateson, involves two or more persons, one of whom repeatedly experiences negative injunctions from the other. Such injunctions can either enjoin one to act or to refrain from acting in a given way and may entail punishment if disobeyed. A secondary injunction to undertake or fail to undertake an action may be in direct conflict with a primary prohibition according to which the other (the putatively benevolent parent) is not to be seen as punitive. The pattern of conflicting demands that comes into play in the double bind may enter into all of one's interpersonal situations and, for the recipient, remains inescapable.

It should be noted that the double bind does not go unnoticed in the work of Derrida but that it functions principally in the context of the problem of translation, a problem that he finds instantiated in the biblical account of the tower of Babel. God's resentment at the human effort to create a universal language or, as Derrida would have it, the preemption of the power to name, results in God's dispersion of languages and the imposition of his name, the name of the Father, upon men. At the same time, God demands that humans speak a name they must but dare not translate, the name of God. These conflicting injunctions constitute the double bind that Derrida renders as "translate my name, but whatever you do, do not translate my name."[3] The dilemma for Derrida is one of semiotic permeability, of the simultaneous possibility and impossibility of transporting meaning across linguistic boundaries. By contrast, the double bind of Levinas is expressed in the difficulties generated by an other-regarding ethic, one of repeated negative injunctions issued by the alterity or otherness of the other person. Such an ethic may designate as evil self-regarding claims as well as those imposed by a social field that operates in disregard of the demands of the other. The pain arising from the double bind of these conflicting claims is unmistakable.

The basic question for Levinas can be construed as a weighing of epistemic against moral claims. Is meaning, he asks, derived from what is revealed to one's consciousness, thought as revealing the truth of being? Or is meaning primordially ethical, showing itself in and through one's relation to the other? In his words:

[Is meaning not] the consciousness of that unassimilable strangeness of the other, the bad conscience of my responsibility, the bad conscience of that difference of the non-additive other . . . ? In it there can be heard the demand that keeps me in question and elicits my response or responsibility.[4]

If the proscription against violence is to be effective, it enters into one's relations with another as an ever-present meta-rule that proscribes doing harm to the other. Even more radically, Levinas advocates placing the other before the self so that one is willing to substitute oneself for the other, even when she or he is in a life-threatening situation. It is apparent that this rule is in conflict both with the juridical rules of most societies that allow for at least retaliatory violence and with the desire for self-preservation. When alterity precipitates a conflict of rules, we are caught in the double bind of obligation that inaugurates moral existence.

The Evils of Techno-discourse

In his description of the etiology of schizophrenia, Gregory Bateson attributes this "mental condition" to a double bind understood both epistemically as a confusion of logical types played out against one another and interpersonally as difficulty in communication between self and other. Appealing to the theory of logical types according to which the members of a class and the class of which they are members operate at different levels of abstraction, Bateson concludes that the difficulty in distinguishing these logical levels is reflected in situations of actual communication. Errors are made in the classification of messages, a process determined by contextual cues.[5] Yet for Bateson, the schizophrenic response is somehow experienced as fitting the context of her life, so that the result of repeated primary negative injunctions "enforced by punishment or signals which threaten survival" traps the individual. There is no exit from the field of prohibitory restrictions.[6]

Just such a conflict of rules is inherent at a macrolevel, in the evil of an all-encompassing discourse, the globalization of rule-bound thinking, what Janicaud calls techno-discourse. In a world of rational rules, any violation of these rules is bound to induce psychological dissonance, an inability to function within the ambit of the logical and social constraints of that world. Moreover, if we want to comprehend the constraints themselves, the "rationality of the rational," as Janicaud calls it, the conditions for understanding this meta-rationality already presuppose the rules they are to explain. Must we not move from a formal to a merely operational definition, Janicaud asks, to rules that enable us to distinguish true from false statements or, borrowing Quine's terms, to "an exposition of truth functions"?[7] We are constrained to think of rationality as arising in the process of its determination through the formation of operational rules or, referring to French philosopher Jean Ladrière, through the enactment of constitutive and transformational procedures, "the constitution of a network of mutual connections" (p. 5).

However—and this is Janicaud's point—in successfully realizing predetermined ends within a plurality of specific domains, rationality "runs wild" and becomes the subject of a will to totalize or, as Heidegger had observed, transforms thinking into calculation. In its social, political, economic, and cultural manifestations, rationality is globalized as power. Its language, techno-discourse, transcends the operational practices of specific technical discourses to become the lingua franca of an all-embracing audio-visual information culture that constitutes and disseminates meaning. Thus, says Janicaud:

> Techno-discourse . . . is a parasitic language inextricably woven into technology, contributing to its diffusion . . . making almost impossible any radical analysis or any questioning of contemporary technological phenomena. Every technology has its vocabulary, its codes . . . its operative scenarios. Such is not the case with techno-discourse; it is neither strictly scientific, nor philosophic, [nor] poetic. (p. 65)

Janicaud concludes that "the scientific and technological revolution is only the most recent manifestation of a process that is much older, more fundamental: the *potentialization* of knowledge as power" (p. 75).

Is there any egress from the entrapment in techno-discourse? Can rationality thus understood acknowledge its own limits, an outside that remains refractory to incorporation within a limited whole? Janicaud notes that Nietzsche had already provided some premonitory insights into such rationality when he asserted that "a superior civilization must give man a double brain . . . one to experience science, the other to experience non-science. Lying next to one another without confusion, separable, self-contained: our health demands this."[8] Nietzsche's claim may seem less than helpful in that he offers no account of how the domains are to be segregated, no description of a gatekeeping mechanism. Yet there is in Nietzsche's *aperçu* an implied paradigm of what constitutes health: the parceling out of discourses and the solidification of difference itself.

Continuing along this Nietzschean road of parceling out, Janicaud points to the dilemma posed by rationality. "To think is to enter into relation."[9] But there is a limit within the relational that he calls *partage,* a multivalent term that carries connotations of share, allotment. One need not, as with Heidegger, think an unthought that is other, apart from rationality. Instead, we must recognize rationality as inescapable, as our lot. Difference, then, must be inscribed within the rational itself.

To be sure, when rationality is expressed as the will to objectivity, it must be understood as power, its history as the history of power. Still, we must not, Janicaud contends, effect a break with rationality, but rather we must recognize that the rational can face "its destiny of power" and in so doing need not return to its claims of self-sufficiency. In pondering the enigma of rationality—and this is the crucial point—"there is released the possibility of an 'examination of the *conscience*' of the rational facing its destiny of power" (emphasis mine). It is this reserve of open possibility that challenges the evil of rationality. We can envisage this *partage* or limiting of power because "the possible is held in reserve at the foundation of the power of the rational" (p. 238). What opens this fissure in rationality is its confrontation with its power, with the evil inherent in it. A totally rational, self-enclosed system must implode upon or reverse itself just as, he notes, production and efficiency when maximized may implode and manifest themselves in individual atomization and insecurity.

But how is reversal to be understood? It is not, as Hegel might have thought, a dialectical movement of negation, but rather, reversal is that which "rationalization cannot or does not wish to think" (p. 247). But if one clings both to the reversal of thinking and to thinking, can one renounce the power of the rational non-irrationally? Janicaud's query expresses a classical double bind. When the effects of power become sufficiently great, we are compelled to think about rationality. At the same time, we try to escape rationality by thinking what cannot be formalized, that is, "the constitutive limits of the power of the rational," so that the rational will somehow fall outside itself (p. 249). The demands of rationality thus construed remain consistent with Bateson's principle: whether you do or whether you don't, you will still be punished.

Yet it is at this point that a barrier seems to be broken, releasing one into a freedom that is beyond power:

> [The] purity [of this outside] has the value of a sign transcending all instrumentalizations. It calls the rational to its vocation of freedom and to an absolute autonomy. . . . It connects with a possible that does not seem mortgaged by the will to power; under the starry sky, a mark of the Enigma. (p. 254)

The joyful possibility of an open future unconstrained by the rules of techno-discourse is a gift bestowed by rationality as it undoes itself.

But Janicaud does not consider a crucial question that persists: Does possibility, when presenting itself as the outside of rationality, not dissemble? In Bateson's terms, does this open possibility not aspire to appear otherwise than as the agent of an inescapable rationality? Yet without the evil of the rationality that has expelled it, possibility could not impinge upon rationality, a rationality that is and is not *partage*. May we not infer from Janicaud's account the impossibility of overcoming the aporias of rationality, a double bind that arises within rationality as a pathological process, the pathos (in an etymological sense) of ethics? In sum:

> Operative rationality has passed the point of no return . . . [but it may have] outside itself or within *itself* the resources that would permit it to master the mastery, or better still: to open itself to the reserved but still closed dimensions of language and the Enigma. (p. 25)

How, we may ask, are we to "master the mastery" if rationality is the prerequisite of the move that condemns it? Just as the child in condemning the mother who has caused her to see something that is not there is condemning herself, the painful double bind of alterity arises as the self-condemnation of rationality itself.

Evil as Harming Oneself

I have argued that Levinas's description of an alterity-driven ethics can be expanded to include an account of what drives the rationality of a techno-discourse "run wild" to undo itself. The relation of ethical existence and otherness can also be extended by considering the self as riven by difference. Although conceding that the self is multifunctional—a thinking, feeling, and laboring self—Levinas maintains that it remains at bottom a unitary self and that ethical imperatives arise solely through incursions of another outside the self. But the self often inflicts harms upon itself that do not directly involve others. In self-defeating or self-harming behavior, the agent and the one acted upon are in a relation of internal partition so that the self is always already multiple. The claim of intrapsychic multiplicity has generated widely differing responses: hermeneutical, Paul Ricoeur; historico-political, Jon Elster; economic, George Loewenstein; and psychological, George Ainslie, upon whose work I shall focus in that his account of self-defeating behavior can be read as an illuminating example of a double bind.

Ainslie begins by asking whether doing something of which we later repent can be satisfactorily explained by Aristotle's account of *akrasia,* or weakness of will. Even if, for Aristotle, the self is partitioned into rational and passionate elements, and the passions can get in the way of reason, it is still possible for the rational part to overcome them. But Aristotle fails to explain reason's inability to control self-harming behaviors. What is more, the role of time in decision making is absent from his account.

Utility theorists who consider the maximization of satisfaction as motivating action represent an advance over cognitivist analyses such as that of Aristotle. Hume, an early representative of the utility view, astutely grasps the nature of intrapsychic conflict as modeled on our relations with others, arguing that our reactions to our own pleasures and pains can be compared to our responses to the pleasures and pains of others. Moreover, our reactions occur over a period of time. Thus, says Hume:

> The direct survey of another's pleasure naturally gives us pleasure, and therefore produces pain when compared to our own. His pain, considered in itself, is painful to us but augments the idea of our own happiness and gives us pleasure. The prospect of past pain is agreeable, when we are satisfied with our present condition; as our past pleasures on the other hand give us uneasiness, when we enjoy nothing at present equal to them. The comparison, being the same as when we reflect upon the sentiment of others, must be attended by the same effects.[10]

Ainslie contends that Freud goes further. In describing acts of choosing as reflecting a conflict between the reality and pleasure principles, Freud takes time into account. The reality principle does not eliminate but "safeguards" the pleasure principle: "A momentary pleasure, uncertain in its results, is given up, but only in order to gain along the new path, an assured pleasure at a later time."[11] Surprisingly absent from Ainslie's historical tracking of the effect of time on moral choice is attention to Heidegger's depiction of life as lived in anticipation of one's own death, thereby drawing attention to the primacy of future time. For Ainslie, these earlier thinkers failed to see the self as a population of bargaining agents, a "free for all" forum in which competing promises of reward vie for selection. More graphically, "the mind bears less resemblance to a fact-gathering or puzzle-solving apparatus than to a population of foraging organisms." [12] Also lacking in past accounts was a nuanced comprehension of the self's relation to its future or, to borrow Jon Elster's term, its "time preference," by which is meant "an expression of the relative importance that at one point of time one accords to various later times." [13]

To understand self-harming behavior, Ainslie maintains, we must grasp the self's irrational relation to time, its valuing of "future events in inverse proportion to their expected delays," so that value is discounted in relation to temporal distance. [14] Choices affecting the future that are made in the present can be expressed in two ways, as exponential and as hyperbolic discounting. In exponential discounting, it is assumed that the discounting of value for the passage of time occurs at a constant rate; whereas in hyperbolic discounting, the temporal proximity of a goal affects which goal is chosen so that choice is tilted to the poorer but earlier alternative. In order to comprehend how exponential discounting works, consider Ainslie's example: I purchase a new car for $10,000 today, and it is discounted (or loses value) at 20 percent a year. Now if we suppose that I ordered the same car a year ago to be delivered not then (a year ago) but today, it would have been worth $8000 to me; or if ordered two years ago, $6,400. On the exponential view, temporal distance diminishes the car's value at a constant rate (p. 28).

Still, it is one thing to discount time in regard to marketplace ventures, but another to discount future time in relation to self-harming activities such as excessive drinking or drug taking that may cause subsequent damage or regret. In the effort to attain satisfaction, people's preferences veer between gratifying a habit (drinking, binge eating, and the like) and giving it up, oscillations that are determined by how near in time an opportunity for indulgence may be. In such instances, "people devalue future goods not at a constant rate but proportionally to their delay, so that their discount curve will be hyperbolic" (p. 30). In effect, Ainslie's hyperbolic discounter can be envisaged as saying: "The sooner the better, even if what I get soon is actually less desirable than what I might have later on."

If, as Ainslie maintains, the self is a mélange of conflicting preferences, a population, the regularities of exponential discounting give way to the warring alternatives of hyperbolic discounting. Differing satisfactions become dominant at different points *because* of their timing. Thus for Ainslie, an option must not only promise more than competing options but also must act so that the rival options waiting in the wings do not sabotage a given choice. Not only must multiple competing rewards subvert present contenders, but they must also ward off future dangers (p. 40). That decisions can be arrived at is explained as the result of transactions resembling those that foster agreement in the larger social world (p. 41).[15]

The preference for short-range harmful satisfactions is complicated by the tendency for harmful behavior to become repetitive. Choices may be grouped into series that, when taken together, appear to constitute a personal rule, each choice setting a precedent for succeeding choices and thereby undermining other reward-getting tactics.[16] Often enough, harmful short-range satisfactions such as having a drink are interpreted as exceptions and not as intended to set precedents.[17]

Ainslie contends that these exceptions may, even unconsciously, constitute rules that (in Bateson's terms) could be experienced as paradoxical commands. Ainslie writes:

> There is an inevitable clash between two kinds of reward-getting strategies: Belief in the importance of external tasks—amassing wealth . . . discovering knowledge— leads to behaviors that rush to completion: but a tacit realization of the impor- tance of appetite motivates a search for obstacles to solution or for gambles that will intermittently undo [these behaviors]. Consciousness of the second task spoils the very belief in the first task[, a belief] that makes the first task strict enough to be an optimal pacer of reward.[18]

Might one allege, arguably to be sure, that Heidegger's view of inauthentic ex- istence can be understood as a hyperbolic discounting of death's inevitability?

We may ask: Is the evil of time-bound self-defeating behavior as described by Ainslie the inevitable outcome of every double bind? In an amendment to the older catch-22 version of his theory, Bateson considers the possibility of an indeterminate outcome when rules conflict, an indeterminacy that depends upon a widening of the context in which the rules are operative. The original double-bind theory dealt with what Bateson later calls *transforms*—we might think of them as inner content—as if transforms were actual objects driven by physical forces. He now maintains that the double bind is the result of a tangling of the rules involved in making and in acquiring the transforms. But the point of his revision is that a situation from which schizophrenia would seem to emerge necessarily might generate positive consequences, for example, the crea- tion of art or humor. A double bind can arise in an experiential nexus from which it can either enrich or impoverish, engender "gifts" or "confusions."[19] Bateson maintains that such open possibilities are "experienced breaches in the weave of contextual structures [and] are in fact double binds" that manifest an ambiguity of what he terms *transcontextuality*.[20]

Not all transcontextual situations are those whose positive outcome is mea- sured by enhanced creativity. Applying his amended double-bind theory to al- coholism, a complex alternation of sobriety and intoxication, Bateson argues that the self is in conflict with a real or fictitious intrapsychic other. When this behavior is symmetrical, the actions of two individuals are similar, the behavior of the first prompting more of the same behavior in the second. When the behaviors are complementary, each behaves differently from the other, yet the first stimulates alternative but somehow fitting behavior in the second.[21] In what Bateson designates as "alcoholic pride," an intrapsychic symmetrical relationship is established, grounded in the alcoholic's claim that she can will to overcome her addiction by asserting, "I can do it. Drink will not do me in," but ultimately giving way. This outcome of the double bind is in remarkable conformity with Ainslie's model: the long-range higher interest goal is subverted by the cumulative power of harmful short-range repeated choices.

It is argued by Alcoholics Anonymous and others, however, that a positive outcome is possible for the alcoholic if she can establish a connection with an other that is greater than the self. The symmetrical relations that issue in self-harming behavior might in that case be reversed and a new complementary relation established. Although switching to relations of complementarity may lead to behavioral changes, Bateson, however, maintains that the new configuration may not be preferable to intrapsychic relations of symmetry. Moreover, one could ask, "What if the alcoholic believed that the relation to a greater power were not itself complementary but symmetrical and emulative?"[22] Even in situations of transcontextuality, Bateson implies, there are some circumstances in which the negative side of the double bind prevails.

In/conclusions

According to Emmanuel Levinas, ethics begins with the advent of the other person who is apprehended, not as a phenomenon, an object of perception or cognition, but as an injunction to refrain from doing violence to the other. Resistance to this moral mandate is the defining characteristic of evil. Using Levinas's account of otherness as an entering wedge, I try to show that otherness can take on new ethical significations, that the term "other" can acquire a polysemy absent from his analysis.

Dominique Janicaud applies the term in the context of an all-encompassing social and linguistic framework in which otherness can be construed as an implosion of a sociocultural rationality "run wild," a techno-discourse that eventuates in the evils of a global society. Hegel's notion of history, politics, and economy ordered as a totality, as well as Heidegger's description of the relation of Being and beings, are freshly configured to take account of the logic of techno-science, not as an epistemological construct, but as a logic of power. Janicaud's innovation lies in showing that alterity works, not at the level of self and other, but within the totalizing context of techno-discourse undoing it and thereby unlocking an ethical domain of open possibility that evades the discourses of power.

What is more, Levinas provides no account of harms inflicted by the self against itself, evils that can be helpfully explained by turning to the temporal context in which self-harming moral choices are made. George Ainslie sees self-harming behaviors in the light of hyperbolic discounting, choosing temporally proximate but less desirable rewards in preference to long-term, more worthwhile goals, thus discounting value with the passing of time. Such evils arise intrapsychically, without the commanding presence of the other.

These dissimilar evils are linked by their dependence upon conflicting injunctions, the double bind invoked by Bateson to explain pathological psychic states or (rarely) acts of creative imagination. But the double bind has yet another role that has gone unnoticed, that of a necessary (if not yet sufficient) condition for the emergence of a moral field such that, in its absence, the ascription of evil could not arise.

Notes

1. Gregory Bateson, *Steps to an Ecology of Mind* (New York: Random House, 1972), p. 201.
2. The other-regarding ethic described is derived largely from Emmanuel Levinas, *Totality and Infinity: An Essay in Exteriority,* trans. Alphonso Lingis (The Hague: Martinus Nijhoff, 1969).
3. Cited in *A Derrida Reader: Between the Blinds,* ed. Peggy Kamuf (New York: Columbia University Press, 1991), pp. xxiii–xxv.
4. Emmanuel Levinas, *Outside the Subject,* trans. Michael B. Smith (Stanford, Calif.: Stanford University Press, 1993), p. 94
5. Bateson, *Steps to an Ecology of Mind,* p. 205.
6. Ibid., pp. 206–7.
7. Dominique Janicaud, *Powers of the Rational: Science, Technology and the Future of Thought,* trans. Peg Birmingham and Elizabeth Birmingham (Bloomington: Indiana University Press, 1994), p. 5. Page numbers in the text are to this work.
8. Friedrich Nietzsche, *Human, All Too Human,* trans. Marion Farber with Stephen Lehmann (Lincoln: University of Nebraska Press, 1984), section 251 as cited in Janicaud, *Powers of the Rational,* p. 251.
9. Janicaud, *Powers of the Rational,* p. 20.
10. This citation is taken from Jon Elster and George Loewenstein, "Utility from Memory and Anticipation," in *Choice over Time,* ed. George Loewenstein and Jon Elster (New York: Russell Sage Foundation, 1992), p. 218. The first paragraph is from Hume's *A Treatise of Human Nature,* Book 3, Part 3, Section 2; the second from Book 2, Part 2, Section 8.
11. George Ainslie, *Breakdown of Will: The Puzzle of Akrasia* (Cambridge: Cambridge University Press, 2001), p. 24.
12. George Ainslie, *Picoeconomics: The Strategic Interaction of Successive Motivational States within the Person* (Cambridge: Cambridge University Press, 1992), p. 362.
13. Jon Elster, *Sour Grapes: Studies of the Subversion of Rationality* (Cambridge: Cambridge University Press, 1983), p. 7. Elster had, early on, discerned the relation of rules of constraint to determining preference.
14. Ainslie, *Breakdown of Will,* p. 47. See also his *Picoeconomics,* pp. 360–61. Page numbers in the text are to *Breakdown of the Will.*

15. Cf. Ainslie, *Picoeconomics*, pp. 90–95.
16. In *Picoeconomics*, Ainslie speaks of a "private side bet" made when one stakes future behavior on precedent. An individual wagers on the basis of a series of similar choices seen as predictive of choices to come. See esp. p. 373.
17. Ainslie, *Breakdown of Will*, p. 89.
18. Ibid., p. 200.
19. Bateson, *Steps to an Ecology of Mind*, p. 272.
20. Ibid. At this point Bateson provides an example of how contextual confusion can lead to differing consequences. Suppose, he speculates, that the operant training of a porpoise to raise her head when a whistle is blown is rewarded by food, and suppose further that to show how operant conditioning works in a broader context, quite different conditioned behaviors are rewarded. The heretofore compliant porpoise is befuddled by the rewarding of new behavior, but when she still receives rewards from her loving trainer for her efforts, she responds with new tricks in creative ways. In sum, pain and confusion are produced, but they can also be subverted in a wider context that allows for creative responses.
21. Ibid., p. 323.
22. Ibid., p. 336.

Contributors

Debra B. Bergoffen is Professor of Philosophy, Women's Studies, and Cultural Studies at George Mason University. She is the author of *The Philosophy of Simone de Beauvoir: Gendered Phenomenologies, Erotic Generosities;* co-editor of three other volumes of essays on Continental Philosophy; and has published widely on issues in feminist theory, Beauvoir, Irigaray, Nietzsche, Lacan, Freud, Derrida, and Sartre.

Tina Chanter is Professor of Philosophy at DePaul University and author of *Ethics of Eros: Irigaray's Rewriting of the Philosophers* (1995) and *Time, Death and the Feminine: Levinas with Heidegger* (2001). She is also editor of *Feminist Interpretations of Emmanuel Levinas* (2001), and of the Gender Theory series for the State University of New York Press. Her book *Abjection: Film and the Constitutive Nature of Difference* is forthcoming with Indiana University Press.

William E. Connolly teaches political theory at the Johns Hopkins University, where he is Krieger-Eisenhower Professor of Political Science. His most recent books are *The Ethos of Pluralization* (1995); *Why I Am Not A Secularist* (1999); and *Neuropolitics: Thinking, Culture, Speed* (2002). His early book, *The Terms of Political Discourse,* recently won the Benjamin Lippincott award as a book in political theory "still considered significant after a time span of at least 15 years."

Peter Dews is Professor of Philosophy at the University of Essex, England. He is the author of *Logics of Disintegration: Post-Structuralist Thought and the Claims of Critical Theory* (1986) and *The Limits of Disenchantment: Essays on Contemporary European Philosophy* (1995), as well as numerous essays on nineteenth and twentieth-century European philosophy. He also edited *Habermas: Autonomy and Solidarity: Interviews* (rev. 1992) and *Habermas: A Critical Reader* (1999). He is currently researching the history of the philosophy of evil since Kant.

Martin Beck Matuštík is Professor of Philosophy at Purdue University. He is the author of *Postnational Identity: Critical Theory and Existential Philosophy in Habermas, Kierkegaard, and Havel* (1993); *Specters of Liberation: Great Refusals in the New World Order* (1998); and, most recently, *Jürgen Habermas: A Philosophical-Political Profile* (2001). He co-edits a book series, *New Critical Theory.*

William L. McBride is Arthur G. Hansen Professor of Philosophy at Purdue University. He was the co-founder of the Sartre Society of North America and is currently president of the North American Society for Social Philosophy and secretary-general of the International Federation of Philosophy Societies. He has written and edited books and articles on, among other themes, social and political theory, Sartre, Marx, existential phenomenology, and Eastern Europe. His most recent single-authored book is *From Yugoslav Praxis to Global Pathos: Anti-Hegemonic Post-post-Marxist Essays.*

Robert Meister teaches political and moral philosophy, jurisprudence, and social theory at the University of California, Santa Cruz. His previous writings include *Political Identity: Thinking Through Marx*, "Beyond Satisfaction: Democracy, Consumption and the Future of Socialism," "Is Moderation a Virtue?" "The Logic and Legacy of Dred Scott," "Sojourners and Survivors: Two Models of Constitutional Protection" and "Forgiving and Forgetting: Lincoln and the Politics of National Recovery." He is currently completing a book, *After Evil*, on the topic of transitional justice.

Adi Ophir teaches philosophy at the Cohn Institute for the History and Philosophy of Science and Ideas, Tel-Aviv University, and is a fellow at the Shalom Hartman Institute of Jewish Studies in Jerusalem. He writes on ethics, contemporary continental philosophy, and Israeli culture and politics. He is the founding editor of the Israeli journal of critical theory and cultural studies, *Theory and Criticism*. An English translation of his book *The Order of Evils: Toward an Ontology of Morals* is forthcoming.

Robert B. Pippin is the Raymond W. and Martha Hilpert Gruner Distinguished Service Professor in the Committee on Social Thought, the Department of Philosophy, and the College at the University of Chicago. He is the author of several books, including *Hegel's Idealism: The Satisfactions of Self-Consciousness; Modernism as a Philosophical Problem: On the Dissatisfactions of European High Culture;* and most recently, *Henry James and Modern Moral Life.*

Alan D. Schrift is Professor of Philosophy and Director of the Grinnell College Center for the Humanities. He is the author of *Nietzsche's French Legacy: A Genealogy of Poststructuralism* and *Nietzsche and the Question of Interpretation: Between Hermeneutics and Deconstruction,* and editor of several works, including most recently *Why Nietzsche Still? Reflections on Drama, Culture, and Politics,* and *The Logic of the Gift: Toward an Ethic of Generosity.* His book *Twentieth-Century French Philosophy: Key Themes and Thinkers* is forthcoming.

Henry Staten is Professor of English and Comparative Literature and Adjunct Professor of Philosophy, at the University of Washington. A past Guggenheim fellow and the 1998 recipient of the William Riley Parker Prize of the Modern Language Association for an outstanding essay in PMLA, he is the author of *Wittgenstein and Derrida* (1984); *Nietzsche's Voice* (1990); and *Eros in Mourning: Homer to Lacan* (1995).

Edith Wyschogrod is the J. Newton Rayzor Professor of Philosophy and Religious Thought at Rice University. Her books include *An Ethics of Remembering: History, Heterology and the Nameless Others; Saints and Postmodernism: Revisioning Moral Philosophy;* and *Spirit in Ashes: Hegel, Heidegger and Man-Made Mass Death.* She is currently working on the problem of altruism.

Index